Bruce Labruce

THE RELUCTANT PORNOGRAPHER

Gutter Press

Gutter Press gratefully acknowledges the assistance of the Canada Council and the Ontario Arts Council. Gutter Press is also grateful for the assistance of the D.A.P. folks in the printing of this book—especially Avery Lozada, Alex Galan and Sharon Gallagher.

Canadian Cataloguing in Publication Data
LaBruce, Bruce
The reluctant pornographer
ISBN 1-896356-12-5
1.LaBruce, Bruce. 2.Erotic films–Production and direction.
3.Homosexuality in motion pictures. I.Title.
PN1998.3.L32A3 1997   791.43'0233'092   C97-931934-X

Published by Gutter Press, P.O. Box 600, Station Q,
Toronto, Ontario, Canada M4T 2N4
URL:www.salzmann.com/gutter
e-mail: gutter@salzmann.com

Distributed in the U.S. and abroad by D.A.P.
Distributed Art Publishers, Inc.
155 Sixth Avenue, 2nd Floor,
New York, NY 10013-1507
(Tel 212.627 1999 Fax 212.627 9484).
To order, call 1 800 338 book
Represented in Canada by the Literary Press Group
Distributed in Canada by General Publishing,
30 Lesmill Rd, Don Mills, Ontario

Editor: Jane Flanagan
Associate Editors: Andrea Kelner, Caroline Treffler
Assistant Editors: Melissa McCormack, Dominic Stones
Design: 4dT
Cover Photo: Chris Nicholls

Manufactured in Canada

This book is largely based on columns which first appeared in
Exclaim magazine, an alternative music periodical for wayward
youth. Thanks to Hal Kelly who got me the gig as a columnist
for Exclaim in the first place; to Exclaim editor Ian Danzig, who
let me write whatever I wanted without interference, no matter
how dirty; to Dan Bazuin of This Ain't the Rosedale Library, who
brought the columns to the attention of my publisher, Sam
Hiyate; and finally to Sam, whose insane dedication to this book
has been unwavering. Thanks also to shutterbugs Richard Kern,
Mom, Marc Geller, Daniel Nicoletta and Candy Parker for donating photographs free gratis; likewise to cover photog Chris
Nicholls for his kind participation; to the anonymous cover flesh;
and to design wizards at 4dT, Sean and Michelangelo.

Introduction

By Scott Thompson

Bruce LaBruce and I go way back. In fact I've known Bruce LaBruce since he was Bruce LaBruce. We went together to Bible College in Porcupine Falls in Northern Ontario. I was a year older than Bruce, although if you ask him it was more like five. I don't mind when my friends lie about their age. I figure it brings me down in years too. We were both losers in school. Thin, effeminate, nerdy. Who would have thought that those qualities which got us beat up and ostracized in childhood would later prove to be the very qualities which would propel us both to mondo cult semi-superstardom. Although now it's a fight to stay thin, but it's still easy to remain effeminate and nerdy.

Baby LaBruce. Photo by Mom.

Bruce was a farm boy out in the bush. His parents worked a gritty little farm in soil that was more rock than dirt. They had about twenty holsteins, a few acres of cow corn and a fighting cock that was a legend in that part of the woods. I think the cock actually brought in more money than the farm. That plus his mother's Regal catalogue business kept the wolf from the door.

I never knew his parents, as they only visited once during our years at the school. When they came, I was out doing something I guess, I did a lot of that back then. Anyways, his father brought some game he'd bagged and we all ate venison for the next week, although Jojie, an exchange student from the Philippines, said it tasted like dog. All I can say is that ever since then dogs have never liked me.

We met in the Glee Club during a production of *The Cross and the Switchblade*. Bruce and I were chosen to write the stage adaptation. Neither of us actually read the book—we just based it on the lurid cover. Since this was an all-boys school, all the female parts were played in drag. So Bruce was cast as Juanita, the sexy yet troubled Puerto Rican girlfriend of the sexy minister while I was cast as Coral, the tough and also very troubled black dyke from the projects. The highlight of the show was our duet, where she cures me of my lesbianism by bringing me to Christ. We won our county drama competition and eventually we went all the way to the Sears Drama Festival in Toronto. We placed fifth overall but Bruce won for best actress. We also picked up a special jury prize for "sheer gall."

Saturday night after the awards ceremony, a group of us, five giddy teenage bible students—who were really just gay—went out on the town to celebrate. We got really drunk at the St. Charles tavern and then ran in and out of traffic on Yonge Street as suburban yokels drove up and down honking their horns and yelling out of their cars in a traditional Toronto ritual. Pierre

7

Legrand pissed his pants and Romeo Cavale and Jason Tillson kissed in an alley. We ended up at a tattoo parlour and everyone was too scared or not drunk enough to get one except Bruce who was neither. He got a tattoo of Rita Moreno on his upper left arm in honour of his role. This would be the first of many tattoos that Bruce would collect over the years. Sometime later he would fall under the spell of Jodie Foster and would have the Rita tattoo changed to Jodie's likeness, a move some of Bruce's detractors saw as racist. A few more years after that, he would tire of all tattoos and try to have

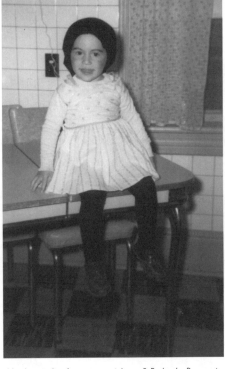

Mother, what's wrong with me? Baby LaBruce in drag, for reasons never sufficiently explained. Photo by Mom.

them removed surgically with mixed results. But back to the story.

The next night on the bus home the headmaster, Reverend Gordon Creighton, saw the tattoo and flipped. He threw Bruce out of the bus in the middle of nowhere in pitch darkness. The last I saw of him, he was standing in the middle of the road in the lights of the bus as we pulled away, his hip cocked lazily and his thumb out defiantly in the universal gesture of hitchhiking. This pose was echoed years later in one of the most famous scenes in *Super 8 1/2*. Coincidence? I think not.

I would not see Bruce for many years, and then one night in New York City I was working the spanking booth at an AIDS fair. I had just accepted a one hundred dollar pledge from someone for ten licks. On the fifth blow, I had déjà vu and looked up from my position across a motorcycle to see a familiar freckled arm raised to strike. It was Bruce! I let him finish because it was for a good cause and then I grabbed him in an embrace and demanded to know everything that had happened to him since that night on the road. He said that he was now an underground filmmaker who edited a radical gay punk zine and kept a diary largely in the pages of Exclaim magazine about his glamorous, dissolute life. I told him that I was now a famous comedian who had his own tv show. He called me a liar and slapped my face. I told him that would be ten bucks extra. He threw a crumpled Canadian ten dollar bill at my feet and said, "Would you like to be in a porno movie?" "Sure," I replied. And that's how I ended up in *Super 8 1/2*.

Since then Bruce and I have stayed in touch. We stay at each other's cottages and our children play together. When he asked me to write the introduction to his first book of non-fiction, I initially hesitated, because I hate to commodify a friendship. I think I know what that means. So he said, "Just tell a bunch of lies." So, I did. Enjoy the book.

8

The Wild, Wild World of Fanzines

notes from a reluctant pornographer

Please Note:
Some names have been changed to discourage litigious behaviour.

The filthy editors of J.D.s, the fanzine, loitering in the Tenderloin and up to no good in San Francisco circa 1988. Photo by Marc Geller.

We hate it when our friends become successful. (Morrissey) *Every fag's a jury. Twelve angry men in one.* (Buddy Cole) *It's not all autographs and sunglasses.* (Morgan Fairchild)

So I wake up one day with a hangover, as usual, and I remember that a chapter about fanzines I'm supposed to write for this book called *A Queer Romance* is due in about a week, and I hate the word "queer," and I'm just getting over a three-year relationship so I don't even want to think about the concept of romance, and I practically don't even read fanzines anymore. I'm not exactly motivated, i.e. So I drag myself out of bed and light up the first of too many cigarettes of the day and sit with my legs crossed and arms akimbo like I'm in a straightjacket or something and stare down into a cup of coffee and wonder what I can possibly say about a movement that no longer seems to be moving. I mean, isn't that why they call it a movement—because it's supposed to move?

"Queercore" is dead. I know, because I say it is. Our son is dead. I killed him. (It could be our daughter, mind you, but that's not the way Edward Albee wrote it.) *Who's Afraid of Virginia Woolf?* was on television last night and although I've seen it about a hundred times, it was the first time I really understood it—how you can create something out of a

desperate need, and make it so convincing that not only you, but others around you, start believing it too. But, well, when it becomes an international phenomenon or something, and people start referring to your imaginary creation as "legendary" and "important," it's time to deliver the telegram proclaiming that your blonde-eyed, blue-haired son is dead. It's time to move on to the next game.

Welcome to the wild, wild world of "queercore," née homocore, the cut-rate, cut-throat, cutting edge of the homosexual underworld. Enter at your own risk. I'm not going to act as some kind of authority on the subject or a goddamn tour guide (my name is not Dita), because I'm not sure I quite understand it myself—always a good sign. I'm not going to tell you how to pronounce "fanzine," or how to gain access to this exclusive little subterranean queer cartel. Some people say it's as simple as stapling together a few photocopied pages of naked boys or disembodied vaginas and dropping it in the mail, but I don't think so. You have to be a keen propagandist, a dedicated pornographer, a shameless self-promoter, and an inveterate shape-changer to exist in this ambitious little cosmology. Of course, it wasn't this way in the beginning—or maybe it was and I never noticed. Where did this desperate need to create an alternative to the extant gay community come from, and where do I go from here?

These questions burn like an STD as I prance through the aisles of my favourite bookstore, shopping for my forty-dollar weekly fix of glossy magazines. I rarely read a fanzine these days, but I feel compelled to keep in touch with what's going on in *Vanity Fair, Vogue, Spin, Sassy,* (and *Dirt,* when available), *Celebrity Sleuth, Spy,* and a host of others. Lately I've come across more controversial material in *Entertainment Weekly* than in any "queercore" fanzine I've been sent, and you can quote me wildly on that. Since its co-option by established gay literary figures and "legitimate" publications such as *Artforum, i.D., The Village Voice,* and others, "queercore" has been simultaneously demystified and glorified, diluted and trumped up into something it can't sustain. It's like when ACT UP became a big celebrity and got its picture in *Vanity Fair* – it exhausted its star potential and, in effect, the dog and pony show was over. The media will only tolerate its bad children as long as they entertain and perform within the limitations it dictates; when it is no longer amused, or gets bored, you have to be savvy enough to transform yourself into something else, or risk having your head chopped off.

Speaking of severed heads, I've recently been compared to Jayne Mansfield in the *Village Voice*, and, as the Prince of the Homosexuals, let me tell you, it's

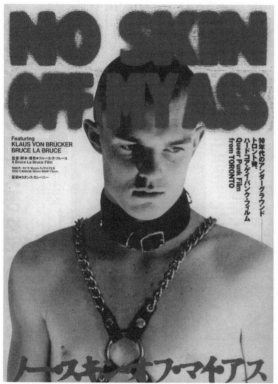

Featuring
KLAUS VON BRÜCKER
BRUCE LA BRUCE

90年代のアンダーグラウンド
トロント発、
A Bruce La Bruce Film
Queer Punk Film
1990年・脚本・撮影★ブルース・ラ・ブルース
ハードコア・ゲイ・パンク・フィルム
from TORONTO
1990 CANADA 16mm 84分 73min.
配給★スタンス・カンパニー

ノースキン・オフ・マイ・アス

Japanese poster for "No Skin Off My Ass", obviously.

not easy to keep the crown on your head when it's been wrenched from your body in a gruesome car accident. But at least Jayne did it her way, before Hollywood and the media machine did it to her. It was the ultimate career move, and an important lesson to anyone like myself who has become an international sex star: don't let the bastards fuck with your head. Do it yourself (or DIY, as they say in punk circles).

No Skin Off My Ass, my first porno, was a logical progression from *J.D.s*. I and my former partner in sexual revolution introduced homosexual pornography to the punk fanzine formula, and, like naughty kids in the basement with a chemistry set, created an explosion heard around the world, or at least halfway down the block. Not only did we unabashedly steal punk images from dirty, glossy gay magazines (which, incidentally, had already begun, at this early stage, to co-opt punk–fags are always so up on the latest trends), but we also began to exploit–gently, always very gently–our friends and various passers-by, politely requesting, after get-- ting them drunk, to remove their garments and pose for us. I was always as loaded as my camera, and spent as much time in front of it as behind.

I quickly learned a good rule of thumb for budding pornographers: never ask anyone to do anything on film you wouldn't do yourself. (Unfortunately, after a certain point in your career, this strategy doesn't always seem to work, but that's another story.) The super-8 movies that accompanied our fanzines became more and more graphic, each of us spurring the other on to go further and further, and sometimes we got a little over-enthusiastic, going just a little too far. But when you go a little too far over and over again, you wake up suddenly late one afternoon and realize that you've gone really far, and there's no turning back. It was all so romantic in the beginning, crashing through the world, not remembering how you got that latest tattoo, not caring whose bathroom door you kicked in or whose tiled floor you woke up on, not giving a damn how your wrist got slashed (as long as you got it on film), or how you got such a bruised ass–a crumpled Polaroid in your back pocket the only clue as to who accommodated you the night before. Of course, this particular style of queer romance can only go on so long before it kills you. But what the hell, I've always been a sucker for self-destructive impulses and damaged personalities, especially my own. I am not now, nor have I ever been, a likely candidate for the position of GLAAD poster child.

Years later, the exciting gay tong that once constituted Toronto homo-core is no more. Disputes over affairs personal and financial–and credit, always credit with fags and dykes: who thought of which idea first, who contributed more, who deserved to become more famous–has torn asunder the terrible triumvirate that started it all. New alliances and allegiances have been formed, different strategies developed, but the bitterness remains like the bad aftertaste of an imprudent blowjob that is momentarily savoured but immediately regretted.

After the "modest" international cult success of *No Skin Off My Ass* (believe me, modesty had nothing to do with it, to paraphrase Mae West, another one of my role models), I became the pariah, the sell-out, the Judas, the Amy Fisher of "queercore". (No, wait a minute–I guess Amy deserved what she got.) No one is particularly interested in hearing that I've yet to make any monetary profit from my little movie–unfortunately, it's a lot easier to get famous than rich in this world. No one cares to hear that despite all outward appearances, I'm really not that much different than I was before I became a household–or, rather, bathroom–name. I'm comforted by my favourite Madonna quote: "Everyone always talks about how fame changes you, but no one ever mentions how it changes the people around you." Although I remain the lowest form of celebrity, my fellow "queercore" alumni choose to believe that I have sold my soul to the devil. Well, after all, Jayne Mansfield was a devout disciple of Anton LaVey, as was Tuesday Weld, whom I play in *Super 8 1/2*, a loose remake of *Play It As It Lays*. Perhaps now you can begin to see how it all connects.

After poring over my new stash of magazines, I mince over to the local repair shop to pick up my busted VCR. The East Indian man who owns the place is obviously quite taken with me; after studying several of my fashion flourishes, he comments conspiratorially, "Oh, I like your outfit. It's very fancy. Very fancy," significantly raising his bushy eyebrows. Of course he's trying to tell me that he understands I'm a fag and would be interested in getting to know me a little better, perhaps in the back room. But being the shy, self-conscious pornographer that I am, I merely blush, mumble "thank you," grab the VCR, and swish out of the store. On the way home I think of how I sometimes wish the homosexual world were still like this–the furtive signals, the hidden signs, the unanalyzed affectations that suggest, rather than proclaim, deviation.

I suppose I'm an anachronism, a throwback, but at times I imagine myself more at home in the thirties or forties-surreptitiously, or perhaps brazenly, entering a movie theatre with my special friend to watch a Cocteau movie, our flamboyant style alone causing people on the street outside to speak in hushed tones. Or sitting around languidly in cafes with companions drawn together only by an aesthetic, arguing feverishly about the importance of sexual revolution without actually revealing the exact nature of our own sordid sex lives. I picture myself in the sixties, when even our parents were swingers, and everyone had to work harder to distinguish homosexual style from the general frenzy of mod fashion. There was no need to identify yourself as gay then, because everyone was having an identity crisis anyway, and sexual experimentation was hip. All the girls looked like Jean Shrimpton, the boys like Christopher Jones, and Max Frost didn't care if his male followers liked other boys-in fact, he flirted with the idea himself. If you look at seventies homosexual pornography today, none of the actors look particularly gay-they could be any man on the street who happened to stumble into a dirty movie career. Something about that excites me.

Later in the evening, I have dinner with a friend who is just as alienated from the gay community as I am, if that's possible. There is nothing about his style or mannerisms or the subjects he chooses to talk about that might indicate that he is a homosexual; in fact, whenever I talk to him I always forget he's one of us. He says he envies me because although my arms are covered with gnarly sailor and punk tattoos and I'm wearing a huge bondage dog collar and tight butch black clothes and knee-high motorcycle boots, I can still sit with my legs demurely crossed at the knee and smoke a cigarette in a holder and be a total fag. I guess it is a talent of mine. He tells me I should direct the marketing for my new movie towards a "regular" audience, and steer clear of the ghettoization of the gay and lesbian film festival circuit. I'm at a bit of a loss to think how an explicit movie about a washed-up gay porno star who is shown sucking a lot of cocks and getting fucked up the ass could appeal to a heterosexual crowd, but I guess you can market anything these days. And, you know, somehow I think he's right.

Here, then, is my dilemma. I, Bruce LaBruce, the Prince of the Homosexuals, one of the most famous fags in the world, do not now feel, nor have I ever felt, part of any gay community. Don't get me wrong-I enjoy being gay, and if I had a choice, which I don't, I suppose I wouldn't be any other way. But there's something about gay society as it exists today that really goads me. When I first came to the big city as a naïve, virgin farm boy, desperate to lose my cherry, the gay community offered me no solace. Yes, I cruised the bars then-unsuccessfully, ineptly-but I always found it a cruel, impenetrable world; as impenetrable, it seemed, as I was, though not for lack of trying. I never quite understood why everyone tried to look like everyone else, and why if you didn't conform to the precise uniform and the Pavlovian behavioural patterns and the doctrinaire politics, you were treated with a contempt that you might expect to

13

you were treated with a contempt that you might expect to be reserved for some kind of enemy. To me, it was as cold and uninviting a country as the straight world that loathed me. I began to work the streets, not because I needed the money, but because it felt like a warm exile by comparison. I hung out in front of the French Embassy with the hustlers (though I never really felt like a member of their community, either), getting picked up by lonely, married men in family cars with photos of their wives and kids taped to the speedometer, and listening to their problems after blowjobs in seedy lake-front motels. It was oddly comforting for a while, but then it started to get sad, so I stopped.

Eventually, I fell in with a bunch of punks. The gay underworld used to be the refuge for misfits and malcontents, a meeting place not only for the sexually adventurous but for anyone who didn't fit in, or resisted being programmed, or was rejected or ostracized by the heterosexual system. But now punk had become the repository of lost souls, and all the excesses and conceits of style and political radicalism and the pure anarchic melodrama that had once been the crowning glory of homosexual disenfranchisement suddenly belonged to a mob of snot-nosed, fucked-up kids. The gay scene must have been kind of like this once: rebellious and wild and impulsive, full of individuals who knew how to become

I and Kathleen Maitland-Carter, who started calling me LaBruce because I was always acting so grand. Photo by Unknown.

part of a movement without sacrificing their own style and temperament and ideas. That's what punk was, for a while. But today, political correctness has brought even punk to its knees, everyone adhering to the party line. It almost makes me long for the days when my girlfriends had to protect me from getting beaten up at the hardcore shows.

I'm not going to be a fucking sentimentalist now and I'm not going to write about punk, because whenever anybody tries to, they come off sounding really stupid. Punk isn't supposed to be written about, just like "queercore" fanzines aren't supposed to be catalogued and canonized and analyzed to death, for Chrissake. They're supposed to be disposable. That's the whole point. Throw your fanzines away right now. Go ahead. Photocopied material doesn't last forever, you know. It fades.

I'm not going to write about punk, because sometimes to explain is to weaken. All I can say is that once again, I had become disillusioned. Oh, it was a dangerous, edgy, intense milieu, and I lived in a dilapidated household of militant women who taught me everything I know, but the scene itself didn't exactly put out the welcome mat for a raving queen like myself. In fact, I was beaten up on more than one occasion, simply for being me: for showing super-8 movies with brash homosexual content, or appearing in bands with a decidedly fruity demeanour. I even fell in love with a skinhead hustler who hated fags and, during our tempestuous relationship, had the shit beaten out of me on more than one occasion. It was entertaining at the time (sort of), but I longed for something better. That's how I came up with the idea of homocore: the bastard child of two, once-exciting, volatile underground movements, gay and punk (now failed and spent), the little bugger who knew how to boost the best from both worlds.

Homocore had its moment, I suppose, but utopian ideologies hatched in cold basement apartments on long, lonely nights never really stand up to the light of day. You have to understand that fanzine editors live in an imaginary world of ideas, protected by the anonymity of the mail. We invent ourselves on paper however we choose, create an ideal version of ourselves (or a monstrous one), give it a name and an identity, and drop it off at the post office, waiting patiently for it to take on a life of its own.

At least that's what I did. Bruce LaBruce was, originally, a fiction: a character I longed to be. At first I tried to maintain a certain distance between myself and my pseudonym—I even interviewed myself in more than one periodical—but the day came when I had to venture out into the real world and live the part. You don't know how terrifying that was. For years I felt like I could never live up to the image I had created, but not so long ago I realized that reality and fiction had become indistinguishable and, as in a bad ventriloquist dummy movie, the puppet had finally taken over the act.

Things are different now, and the world can never be the same after Kim Gordon's Gap ad. (I'm sure I meant that as a compliment, considering how amazing she looks in it.) Apparently I have become some sort of spokesmodel for a movement called "queercore," a word that I cannot even write without putting quotation marks around it, as you may have noticed. I have also been lumped in with something called "The New Queer Cinema," which to me is equally meaningless. You see, I don't feel I have a lot in common with a bunch of rich kids who have degrees in semiotic theory, who make dry, academic films with overdetermined AIDS metaphors and Advocate men in them. I've never felt comfortable with the new "queer" movement, never attended a Queer Nation meeting or participated in any marches or protests or actions. Some people may think that's irresponsible, but what can I say? I've never been able to surrender my mind to prefabricated dogma, or reduce my politics to a slogan, or even situate myself in a fixed position on the political spectrum. No, I'm not "queer", and I don't know why they had to go and ruin a perfectly good word, either. They are so gay.

What I am, I think, is the reluctant pornographer. I've had to ask myself lately how it is that an innocent farm boy who didn't lose his virginity until he was twenty-three, who had a perfectly healthy, wholesome "Waltons" child-

15

hood, has come to the point of disseminating pornography on a global scale. There is no pornography industry in Canada—I mean, essentially, I'm it. So why do I put myself in the position of having film labs call the cops on me, of having people pull morality trips on me, of driving directors of photography into the nut house with me not far behind? I don't really have an answer to that question, except to say that I seem to be at my happiest flat on my back with my legs in the air in front of a whirring camera. I guess that's my way of asking the world to love me.

Die, Bruce-Bashers, Die!

Bruce LaBruce is back and better than ever after a week in Los Angeles. This time, the excuse I used for going to my favourite city in the world was *Spew Two*, the second international fanzine and spin-off product merchandising convention. I also attended the first *Spew* in Chicago last May as part of the jaded entourage accompanying fanzine editrix, blacktress and spokesmodel Vaginal Creme Davis, the Halston of the underground publication set. (If that makes me Liza Minnelli, may Skylab fall on my head.) For those of us who have been doing fanzines for more years than we care to count (we always lie anyway), the *Spew* phenomenon is a curious one: what started out as the cheapest (by necessity) and crudest (by choice) means of expressing oneself outside of the conventional publishing world has transmogrified into a mini-literary establishment, as unfocused yet elitist and exclusive as the Bloomsbury Group. (Who's afraid of Virginia Woolf? I am, George, I am.)

Now I don't want to be a stick in the mud, but *Band Wagon* isn't just the name of a 1953 Vincente Minnelli musical. (Can you tell by my literary and cinematic references that I'm a fag?) When what have been dubbed "queer fanzines" started out in the mid-eighties, the target market (it was faux-capitalism in those days) consisted of isolated, confused hardcore kids from small towns and cities across North America who might have just as soon hung themselves in their parents' double garage with an old skipping rope than come out with no support. The homosexual community wasn't offering much of an alternative, unless you were willing to conform to the rules of being gay, which included a surprisingly strict dress code, a complete surrender of political and intellectual individuality, and the rejection of fairies, bull-daggers, and various other non-conformist types who were once more than welcome in the twilight world of sexual deviancy.

The most exciting mail I ever got as a fanzine editor, besides various detailed correspondence with several sexy death row prisoners and a recent mash note from *Sassy* magazine, contained zines in which teen punks declared their homosexuality in daring and oh-so-sincere editorials, baring their souls to the world, or at least to a few like-minded individuals out there at anonymous post-office boxes, who wouldn't hate, reject, or judge them for expressing their innermost secrets.

Half of the worst of the new "queer" fanzines jumping on the band wagon aren't done out of any sense of urgency or necessity or because it's the only means available to them to publish their work, thoughts, and opinions. No, they're produced by privileged T.F.K.'s (Trust Fund Kids, baby) with literary aspirations, slumming it until opportunity knocks. The other half of the worst are hateful and elitist; ironically, in attempting to dictate what the alternative to "gay and lesbian culture" should be (a moronic oxymoron if ever there was one), and precisely who should be ensconced as the roy-

The Prince of the Homosexuals. Photo by Candy Parker.

alty of the new movement, they are behaving exactly like those queens on the rag they so desperately seek to disassociate themselves from. Heady with power, these queer top-ten-percenters are so enamoured of their own world view that everything they write comes across as pompous and self-congratulatory propaganda.

How, exactly, did the whole queer zine phenomenon become the tired mess it is today? What follows is an excerpt from an editorial for the upcoming *J.D.s* spin-off fanzine *Monstar: the Sincere issue*, dedicated to the memory of Kenneth Halliwell. It's a cautionary tale—some will be offended, others shocked, but the story must be told.

The Valley of the Zines: A Fable

You've got to climb Mount Everest to reach the Valley of the Zines. It's a brutal climb to reach that peak. You stand there, waiting for the rush of exhilaration, but it doesn't come. You're alone, and the feeling of loneliness is over-powering. I never meant to start that climb. I took the first step the day I left that ramshackle slum-house at Queen and Parliament....

A lot has happened to me since I and my former partner first began *J.D.s*, the original homocore fanzine that has precipitated a deluge of "queer zines". (It originally stood, of course, for Juvenile Delinquents, but also encompassed such youth cult icons as James Dean, Joe Dallesandro, J.D. Salinger, and, later, even Jeffrey Dahmer, to name but a few.)

Yes, homocore was our term then, and we lent it out with

17

abandon, unconcerned with credit and copyright or the prospect of others co-opting or copying our ideas, our style, our format of expression, our very lives. We had parties then, parties that had a reputation, attracting the self-proclaimed coolest of the cool—the artists and the art school crowd, the hangers-on, the wannabees, the thrill seekers, the poseurs, the curious. I was always too wild, too drunk, and having too much fun to notice that secretly, furtively, certain Eve Harringtons, certain Iagos were creepily watching my every move, biding their time, coveting the throne, waiting to attempt to overthrow the Prince of the Homosexuals. In particular, the dubious duo were slumming around then. Trapped in their own stifling world of professional responsibilities and hateful monogamy (doomed to

sleep with each other for the rest of their lives—what an appropriately miserable life sentence for them), pathetically searching for someone else's life to emulate, living vicariously through—of all people—me. For years they were even afraid to introduce themselves, such was the shiny appeal of the evil apple of my success. In time they would vainly essay to steal my life outright, but that's another ugly story.

Now it was around this time that my former partner made the age old mistake of falling in love with her creation, her Frankenstein's "monstar." Well, that's what I was, in part—I freely admit it. I allowed myself to be exploited by her without limitations. I performed for her, took my clothes off on command, drunkenly posed for naked photos, became the subject of her movies, danced as a pure sexual object for her band, and sat with her night after night as she perched on her tarnished throne, the two of us hatching schemes, mapping out revolutions and planning to overthrow the world as it stood. Yes, we were in love— a strange love, a forbidden love.

Alas, her attachment was more of a romantic nature than mine (although mine was no less profound), and what had been a partnership as strong as any I had known, as indelible as any tattoo I had received, took on an uncomfortable sexual twist: despite having participated in building me up as a homosexual icon for the world to stare at, be shocked by, mock, ridicule, adore...she fell tragically in love with her creation, hoping that somehow, miraculously, regardless of all indications to the contrary, that he could be reformed.

I have no regrets. Unlike some others—some back-stabbing usurpers whose sole function in life, it seems, is to hoist me upon a cross and watch me slowly bleed my way to infamy—I do not intend to rewrite history. I do not take away from my partner's genius, nor her beauty. I had to grit my teeth through too many years of insults and hostility directed toward her, my idol, from horrible people who failed to recognize how beautiful she really was, to stoop now to the level of diminishing the memory of our relationship. We sat together for too many years, smoking too many cigarettes, and drinking too much take-out coffee, sitting late into the night devising a better fag, a better dyke, to let go of that memory now, as, apparently, she has. It is too, too important to me for that.

The world we envisioned did not exactly turn out as planned. Unsure of her own sexuality in the beginning, and unwilling (then) to exploit herself or allow herself to be exploited like I was, she lost control of her creation, her "monstar." She had failed to notice that he was, and always had been, very much his own creation—there had been antecedents equally if not more influential than she—and that, indeed, he had a particular way of looking at things that captured the imagination of a generation of lost homosexuals and others. I, a monstar, had actually invented myself. I was no Eliza-fucking-Doolittle. In fact, she had also begun to model herself after me.

Eventually, my Halliwell could not, unfortunately, deal with these realities. Enlisting others to do her dirty work (those nameless others who appear to be her pawns, but who are now subtly taking credit for all of her work—will Childy never stand on her own?) aligning herself with rank liars and vicious bullies, she sits and obsesses about her own private Orton, her metaphorical hammer perpetually in hand, scribbling away at mean little collages of her former paramour.

Her new protégée, from Stepford, a star in nobody's mind but her own, blandly defends her Sugar Queen, the only possible ticket to the fame she would do anything to achieve, lashing out like a sniping crone at anyone who dares not supplicate to her Mistress. The lowest form of celebrity, this tag-along girlfriend who once brayed "king" in my face, now gleefully participates in Bruce-bashing—the favourite sport of the jealous—loudly protesting too much that no one is paying attention to her. Sadly, no one is. She is joined in her assault by that stylistically-challenged bougie gay couple posing as "the new queer radicals"—the man who would be boy, and his house-boy who would be demented chicken—the trio of flops clumsily defending their Earth Mother, their Martha.

So while the Three Men and a Baby rant and rave and choke on their own bile, marinating behind the single rag they share, I blithely forge ahead ignoring their one note tirade, refusing to allow them to drag me down to their level, their utter reinforcement of stereotypical behaviour of homosexuals. Never do I mention their names, because I, and apparently I alone, understand the value of negative publicity.

There are others—and they know who they are—who have taken up the mantle of a movement which they will never understand: dilettantes and librarians who collect and copy and catalogue, and ultimately take credit for, ideas which should be left to those who live them. These bookshop radicals may be bullied into acquiescence by the likes of Bob and Carol and Ted and Malice (I apologize for the reference—it disgraces the memory of Natalie Wood), but their misguided allegiance only attests to the weakness of their wills and minds. I am sorry, but it is my curse to tell the absolute truth, and like Blackie in *Boom*, I will always dare to say what I know to be true.

To those Bruce-bashers out there, who have, incidentally, unwittingly acted as the best publicists a Linda Blair could ask for, I offer no apologies. They can throw my reputation in the toilet like Susan

19

Hayward's wig, but Helen Lawson does not skulk out the kitchen exit. She goes out the way she came in, with dignity. And while the Neely O'Haras of the world scream and rave alone in a back alley, a crane shot their only friend, before fading out of the picture, I shall walk in the New England snow with Barbara Parkins, humming the love theme from *Valley of the Dolls*.

The moral of this fiction is, to pull a quote from the movie *JFK* (and I'm paraphrasing here): "In the homosexual underworld, people like to make themselves out to be more important than they are in reality."

Newsflash: It's not surprising that the co-ed foursome is upset by my fable—mirrors can often be cruel and ugly. But after a year of being slagged behind my back, slandered while I was not around to defend myself, of putting up with rampant Bruce-bashing rivalling the

20

Rodney King incident in its brutality (not to downplay the importance of that event), I could no longer keep silent.

I wrote the piece in direct response to a retrospective of my former partner's work in which she and her cohorts challenged my contribution to *J.D.s*, the fanzine that, for better or for worse, launched the homocore movement. Said retrospective, which I picked up by chance while at a conference in Boston (it doesn't seem to be too readily available in Toronto—maybe they didn't want to reveal the extent of their savagery so close to home), also includes one of a number of her drawings depicting me as fat (I guess she's sizist), old (ageist), and ugly (well, she did once tell me I looked like Don Knotts, and meant it as a compliment).

Her two rich fag henchmen have spread rumours that I have AIDS and, worse, that I come from a wealthy family. Considering the fact that I was raised below the poverty line while my detractors all come

LaBruce: a homosexual icon for the world to stare at, be shocked by, mock, ridicule, adore. Photo by Daniel Nicoletta.

from middle- to upper-middle-class backgrounds, it is significant that they accuse me of economic advantageism on the basis of gender, i.e., that simply because I am of the male persuasion I must somehow automatically have access to vast amounts of cash—such is the loopy logic of their feminist falderal.

Our relationship was not physical, and I've never said that it was. I merely stated that we ended up being in love in a strange way, which might explain the ensuing bitterness. It has been a messy divorce, but I am willing to bury the hatchet somewhere besides the middle of my back, where it is still firmly lodged. I will continue, however, to speak out until the lying stops. Anyway, it'll all be in the book. Rumours, p.s., have been circulating that the entire Toronto zine war is a carefully orchestrated publicity stunt. If only it were that simple. But if it is true, it was my idea.

Forget "Star Trek," old or new. CKVR, a local television station with some very creative re-run programming, has been showing the vastly superior "Lost in Space" for over a month now, its albeit erratic broadcasts having become the highlight of an otherwise dreary summer. In fact, when one episode of this landmark sixties series was pre-empted by "Land of the Giants," an embarrassingly inferior sci-fi show from the same era, the station received a very irate phone call in the middle of the night from a certain queen who was not at all amused. You see, we needed our hit of Dr. Smith.

There's a Little Dr. Smith In Everyone

You don't find characters like Dr. Smith—the stowaway scientist who finds himself lost in space with the American Family Robinson—on television anymore, probably because GLAAD (the Gay and Lesbian Alliance Against Defamation) wouldn't allow it; they would no doubt protest out of existence what might be perceived as a negative gay stereotype. Although not an overtly homosexual character, Dr. Smith is so heavily coded as gay that today it's almost shocking to realize just how far he was allowed to go. Power-hungry, greedy, conniving, and vain; a frustrated actor, dancer, and singer totally unaware of how singularly untalented he is; gullible, highly susceptible to suggestion and hypnotism; and hypochondriacal to the point of absurdity (his "delicate back" is mentioned in virtually every episode: "Oh, the pain, the pain"), Dr. Smith is the embodiment of every widely perceived cliché and fear of the homosexual that persists even today.

Smith sells out the resolutely heterosexual nuclear family he is stranded in space with at the drop of a chapeau to become the leader of an alien race, a royal with a crown and sceptre (once even acquiring the King Midas touch), or to become a weak-willed slave, stooge, or court jester to a superior being. In one episode he even eagerly betrays his own sex, to become the consort of an Amazonian space traveller who believes women are vastly superior to men and destined to rule the universe. While the other male members of Jupiter 2 complain about their temporary enslavement to the female warrior, Smith opines, "I prefer not to participate in this dreary masculine protest."

As a result of his treachery, Smith is often ostracized by the Robinson family or forced into self-imposed exile. Much to the chagrin of his male shipmates, he is mechanically inept and abhors manual labour, but is proud that, as he puts it, "all Smiths (read: homosexuals) have very definite artistic flair." As if to amplify Smith's repugnance to the audience, he is seen almost exclusively in the company of Will Robinson, a pre-pubescent boy, whom he often takes on suspiciously long hikes and overnight camp-outs. Their only chaperone is the male Robot, another heavily coded gay character who is also prone to vaudevillian turns, overly sensitive, often alone, ostracized or exiled, easily hypnotized or disempowered (by removing his power pack), and always willing to don a crown and sceptre when the opportunity presents itself—which, apparently, is more often than you might expect in outer space.

Like many other classic homosexual characters, both Smith and the Robot are often doubled, each starring in separate episodes, for example, in which hundreds of their clones roam the planet. (You know how quickly the number of homosexuals multiplies—not by breeding, of course, but through recruiting.) To add insult to injury, Dr. Smith is terrified to the point of hysteria of any romantic attachment a female may develop toward him. One particular episode, in which a green siren who falls in love with the bad doctor beckons him to leave the ship and join her in space, makes the Smith tendency particularly clear; it was, in fact, this very episode, my mother later informed me, that, as a child, gave me nightmares so severe that I had to sleep with the lights on for six months.

I guess that's why I'm a fag.

Yes, Dr. Smith was a model fairy. That's why "Lost in Space," in all its perverseness, made him such a complex, evil, and sinful character (as opposed to the other non-family member of the show, the dependable, strong, and hopelessly heterosexual Don, who despised Smith most of all)—so much so that the show remains chilling to this day. It's good to have everyone's hatred and terror of homosexuality projected onto one of the most fascinating and entertaining characters ever created for television. It's also good to have homosexual characters who are universally loathed and feared—it keeps straight people on their toes. But somehow the beauty of Dr. Smith (to me, anyway) is that he remains a sympathetic and, yes, even lovable character.

To the members of GLAAD who, if they had their way, would make characters like Smith extinct, or to any group of gays, lesbians, or queers who try to dictate how we are supposed to behave or be represented, I suggest you take a look at "Lost in Space". There's a little Dr. Smith in everybody. He's a philosophy, a point of view, transcending his camp appeal. As Will Robinson once said in defence of his fey, middle-aged friend and mentor, after some terrible Smithian blunder, "I know he did something wrong, but that's Dr. Smith. You just expect him to do things differently from everybody else."

By the way, eighty-three episodes of "Lost in Space" were aired between 1965 and 1968. That's a lot of episodes to watch for. And remember, be good to your television and it will be good to you.

I wake up at eight o'clock in the morning, damn it—unfathomably early for me. It's that fucking printing press downstairs, endlessly pumping, pumping, pumping. I can't seem to get used to it like I do traffic noises. There's a number stuck in my head. Seven digits. It's my ex-boyfriend's telephone number. It reminds me of the dream I just had. So that's why I'm so full of anxiety already. I dreamed he came into the apartment in the middle of the night and crawled into bed with me and put his arms around me and forgave me for treating him so badly.

A Day in the Life of a Fag

That never happens in my movie. It's black in this goddamn room. No windows. Stepping out of bed, I slip on the latest issue of *Sassy* and twist my ankle. Limping, I grope my way to the door and head for the kitchen, make some coffee, and have my first smoke of the day. I just started again after a year. I didn't realize how much I had missed it. I flip on the kitchen tv. Anthony Perkins, it seems, has died of AIDS. Oh no. I was just getting over Peter Allen, and I wasn't even a fan of his. But Anthony Perkins. I loved him. I mean, *Fear Strikes Out, Psycho, Pretty Poison, Play it as it Lays, Mahogany*. Fuck. It won't, however, be as bad for me as when Natalie Wood died: I overheard that choice piece of news on a crowded bus on my way to school, and had to get off and cry and catch the next bus home. Which reminds me of the last time I saw my ex-boyfriend. I said maybe we'd get back together someday, like Natalie and R.J. He said we'd just end up arguing over who gets to fall off the boat. I miss him. And her.

I'm supposed to meet an even older, New York boyfriend for breakfast today. I haven't seen him in years. He called last night from his hotel room: he's in town on business, works for *Details* now, can we have breakfast? Sure, why not? After all, we did lose our virginity to each other in a tacky hotel room in Provincetown—just like Tennessee Williams—another hopeless gay cliché to live down. I go to the foyer to get my bike. It's gone. Does that make three or four this year? I start walking to the hotel. It begins to rain. I go into seven different stores before I find an umbrella, because of course it has to be a black one. I'm soaked.

I'm sitting across from this old boyfriend of mine at breakfast, Bloody Mary in hand. I barely recognize him. His chin has gone away, and his hair is in retreat. I can tell by his eyes he's been broken a few times. We chat uncomfortably. He stares nervously at my tattoos. *Look me up the next time you're in New York.*

Sure.

I'm on the street. I sit on a park bench for an hour in the rain, thinking about my latest ex-boyfriend, who recently dumped me. I'm still in love with him. I must have listened to "Hanging on the Telephone" twenty times yesterday. How maudlin of me. I rush home and change into some dry clothes. I'm meeting another old friend for lunch.

I sit across from her in the restaurant, Bloody Mary in hand. She's still beautiful. We commiserate about men and breakups and humiliating yourself and taking a year to get over it and all. We jointly decide I won't see him anymore. We pay the bill and walk out into the now bright, sunshine-y day and run straight into him. Of course. The genius of it.

In a moment of weakness, I decide to go to an outdoor pub with him and we spend the afternoon drinking seventy-five dollars' worth of Bloody Marys. Grocery money. I say everything I told myself I wasn't going to say. I'm so normal, I can't stand it. He says he misses me. Sometimes. I discover his new "friend" is someone who was staying at the same house as me the last time I was in San Francisco—you know, the time I got rolled by a trick and had a nervous breakdown and made a drunken spectacle of myself for two solid weeks? The genius of it. I wonder if my ex-boyfriend knows that losing my cameras, film, all my money, ID and passport, all

24

my favourite clothes, watch, Walkman, et cetera, wasn't the real reason for my hysterics that day. It was because I missed him so much.

I'm on the street again. I can't stop thinking about Woody and Mia. I'm feeling very Mia these days. What did she call it? The meltdown of her soul. I'm writing a song about it for my movie. I call up my friend Honey Velour from a phone booth to see if she wants to go to *Fire Walk With Me* with me. She meets me at the Eaton Centre. The screening is in the basement. It's cold and damp and the air conditioning is on full blast and I'm wearing next to no clothing. Half-naked man. I sit shivering and drunk in my broken seat, mesmerized by Sheryl Lee. Not since Theresa Russell in *Bad Timing: A Sensual Obsession* have I seen such a tortured performance. I'm identifying like crazy. Just like Edward Furlong in *Pet Cemetery II*. Those beautiful dark circles under those damaged young eyes. The face of the nineties.

As we leave the theatre, a pigeon shits on my head. Honey laughs, but I start to cry. She says she's sorry she laughed, that it's supposed to mean good luck. I stop. I tell her about Anthony Perkins. She tells me I'm the character Mart Crowley forgot to write. "Somewhere between Michael and Emory". I laugh. We go to her house and play Nintendo. And Tetris. I'm really really bad at it. What would Camille Paglia have to say about that? Aren't men supposed to be good at this sort of thing? I can't stop thinking about Camille. She's so scathing. Cramming for Camille. I keep fucking up at Tetris, and especially Dr. Mario, and in frustration Honey calls me a "clump", a la Dr. Smith; I start to cry. After a while we both laugh about how pathetic I am. It's late.

On the way home some insane man starts yelling at me on the street that I will be dead in forty-seven hours. Forty-seven, mind you. They can always tell when you're vulnerable. At the all-night convenience store a prostitute asks me if I want a blowjob. She notices the way I sashay away from her. She yells, "Oh, you're gay!" and then, to the guy behind the counter, "You see? I can't even sell a blowjob to a faggot tonight." She isn't being mean, though. Just honest. I buy some tofu weenies, an absurdly minimalist concession to health, and some smokes. I go home to crawl into bed, have a smoke, and another, and another, and drift off into sleep, thinking about my ex-boyfriend. When I wake up the next morning—pumping, pumping, pumping—I notice a burn between my fingers.

Get to Know Your Bisexual Potential

My stripper girlfriend's electrolysis technician, who frequents the place, gave me the idea to write a shocking expose of the Bovine Sex Club—that low-hangin', cock-rockin', long-haired galoot saloon on Toronto's trendy Queen Street strip. Not since the heyday of the Cameron House those many years ago has a local bar captivated the crowd-du-moment and the attendant suburban flotsam which doggedly follows it like remoras after sharks. The Survival Research Labs decor spills over onto the club's edifice—an Iron Man marquee—drawing in bleary-eyed rock pigs, tortured artistes, semi-hip journalists, "film people," and some of the most impressive sluts I've seen since high school. (I say this with admiration—at my high school, the sluts were the coolest and most stylish kids of all, and very protective of a little faggot like me.)

Legend has it the Sherilyn Fenn-like bartenders at "the Bove" (as certain hipsters affectionately call it) used to hold church keys between their ample bosoms to pop the caps of beers and leering customers alike. Indeed, its dank combination of stale smoke and lost souls is not unlike the subtitled bar in *Fire Walk With Me*, with its low tracking shot of deep-dish cigarette butts. But let's not get too romantic. Don't forget those early rumours of an unspoken country-club-like-no-blacks door policy that were quickly swept under the filthy carpet. Remember, every ugly underside of life has its ugly underside.

If you think about it—and I know that you do—the atmosphere of the BSC is alarmingly gay in a way, a basket-bar replete with relentless cruising for anonymous sex which reaches a fever pitch come last call. Not that homosexuals have a corner on this meat market, mind you, but we have taught the competition a thing or two in the field over the years. And neither is the Bove an exclusively heterosexual domain, despite outward appearances. My Deep Throat connection for this piece (double entendre intended, I'm sure)—an extremely handsome gay male acquaintance and former trick of mine—has told me several stories of picking up lots of rock 'n' rollers at this dour dive, albeit with mixed results.

The usual scenario involves the drunken, disgruntled rocker being dragged home and passing out after heavy sex, only to awaken a few hours later to disavow any memory of the incident. He generally thanks the "dude" for letting him crash for a few hours and falls over himself making his getaway with his pants practically down around his ankles. If the victim happens to sleep through until morning, he usually comes down with a case of the "Christ was I drunk last night" syndrome—an expression popularized by William Friedkin's production of *The Boys In The Band* (no, silly, it's not a musical)—proclaiming alcoholic amnesia to excuse his foray into the gay lifestyle. And breakfast is absolutely out of the question.

Lord knows there are plenty of gay men who find this kind of experience ultimately satisfying, and I guess even a fucking sentimentalist like me can get into sucking a dude's cock without the possibility of reciprocation from time to time. But somehow, I don't think bisexuality should entail this much effort. The alter-

native, of course—trying to convert these reluctant swingers, these cautious convertibles, to the gay lifestyle—is worse. Recently I had sex with an actual gay-identified rocker, who insisted upon repeating for the duration of the sexual experience, "Hey, little brother; rock on, little brother." Obviously, this is no solution. But is it the only option? Must we be embarrassed about exploring our "bisexual potential"?

On a recent drunken excursion to the BSC, I ended up necking with a couple of female doll-popping stripper friends of mine and, inspired by a recent experience I had at an adult spanking club in New York called Paddles, where you could exchange your keys at the bar for one of a selection of spanking devices, had my ass whipped by both women in public. Apathetic onlookers tried to pretend they were too jaded to be interested in our little show but, when I started bumping pussy with one of my medicated demimondaines, my legs in the air, a few people did take notice. Was I embarrassed? Contrary. In fact it was so inspirational that a couple of nights later I had a hot-buttered bisexual threegie with a woman and a mulatto male stripper. And believe me, if I, Bruce LaBruce, the Prince of the Homosexuals, can explore his bisexuality, anyone can. So dudes, the next time you find yourself at the Bovine Sex Club and you get really polluted and wake up in the ghetto without the slightest recollection of how you got there, don't be ashamed. Take the limp-wristed wastrel to breakfast, and get to know your bisexual potential.

The Diary of a Mad Movie-Maker

Movies are fun to watch, but hell to make. When you watch a movie unfold artlessly before your eyes, rarely do you think of the near impossibility of it all—the endless hours of setting up cameras and lights and equipment, dealing with temperamental actors and high-strung d.o.p.'s, not to mention the uncooperative and fickle nature of the elements, lady luck, and cultural restraints like, oh, the police, for example. When, on top of these obstacles, you are trying to make a pornographic movie—i.e., cope with all of the above plus get it up at the precise moment that all the technical details come together—you are entering nervous breakdown territory, to be sure. Believe me, it's not as easy as it looks.

Now, I'm not complaining, you must understand. The pornographic experience can be a rewarding one, but allow me to share with you a few cautionary tales that may help you the next time you decide to make a porno.

Shooting pornography outdoors is a complex endeavour under the best of circumstances, but terribly difficult when you're not, oh, say, Madonna, hitchhiking nude in the warm Florida sunshine with a limo waiting to whisk you away and enough money and clout to buy off divisions of police. My first experience with pornographic exteriors took place one spring, somewhere north of Toronto, on one of the initial shoots for my movie, *Super 8 1/2*. With a borrowed truck, a skeletal crew, and a few hundred bucks in my pocket, I set out one sunny day to find a deserted stretch of highway to film a little fisting scene. Nothing too elaborate, just a soupçon of anal penetration to approximate the mood of an R. Kern film.

We pull off to the side of the road to shoot the victim—a hitchhiker on crutches—being picked up by a couple of high-heeled and black-gartered dyke serial-killer sisters who would soon rape his ass and discard him, in adult diapers, by the side of the road. Not realizing that the shoulder is a bit too soft to support a half-ton truck and eight people, we soon find ourselves up to our axles in mud, with no tow-truck in sight. Fortunately, every single car that passes by on this busy stretch of deserted highway seems to have a cellular phone, and one good Samaritan—a business-like lady with two kids strapped in the back seat—calls a nearby garage, making us promise not to get taken for more than fifty bucks by these highway bandits. When the tow truck arrives, I get the scathingly brilliant idea of having my two black-bra-ed actresses hold the very real-looking fake gun we have with us to the head of the overly cooperative mechanic to make it look like he is being coerced into towing the vehicle—an exciting additional impromptu scene for my movie.

Unfortunately, the scene looks a bit too real, and within a matter of minutes, five or six squad cars squeal to a halt nearby, the emerging cops surrounding us as they pack their pistols in a very television-inspired operation worthy of "Cagney and Lacey". In fact, one female cop in particular has obviously been heavily influenced by that show: she tells us in no uncertain terms that her gun is loaded, and that at the police academy they were taught to shoot first, ask questions later. I immediately employ the always reliable strategy of telling the cops that we are students from the Ryerson film school, which would explain our ignorance in such matters as getting permission to shoot in public and the use of phony firearms. It takes me about an hour to talk our way completely out of it, but finally success is mine, and I promise that we'll drive straight home and not look back.

Having shot only one scene, however, and with daylight to spare, we proceed directly to a slightly more isolated location not far away, for the big "sex" scene. Our hitchhiker is thrown up against the truck, his pants pulled down and his legs spread, the gloved and lubricated hand ready, but each time we try to shoot, a

27

gravel truck or some local farmer drives by, forcing us to throw a blanket over the poor naked actor as everyone stands around him pretending to pose for a family picture. The actor in question also turns out to be an anal virgin, so the director (i.e., yours truly) is forced to stand in as a butt double. After several more interruptions, my ass is hot, the scene is shot, and we get the hell out of there before the police show up again.

By the time I get around to filming more exteriors it is autumn and bitterly cold. Inspired by Madonna, I have incorporated the nude hitchhiking scene into the movie. Once again it's almost impossible to find a deserted location in this suddenly overpopulated world and, having forgotten the blankets, my

co-star and I are wearing nothing but boots and a smile, jumping up and down trying to keep warm. It's liberating to run around outdoors with no clothes on, but the extremes I'm going to seem to be taking their toll on my d.o.p., who will soon crack under the pressure and have to be replaced. A week later, on an even colder day, and with a new d.o.p. in tow, we shoot the blowjob-on-the-road scene. I have a slight case of hepatitis A, which gives my eyes and skin a gorgeous yellow cast (happily, we're filming in black and white), and which—fortunately for my co-star—is no longer contagious, my doctor has informed me. The pavement is like ice against my bare ass, which is not helping my condition, I'm sure. For the first time I'm beginning to wonder if it's all worth it.

A few days later we actually get to shoot a sex scene indoors at my spacious if run-down studio. Due to circumstances beyond my control, a four-day shoot has had to be condensed into two, so we are filming at whiplash-inducing speed. At one point, one of the production assistants trips and inadvertently busts open a closed-off water pipe, which causes much water to begin to cascade across the floor and leak down onto the expensive printing presses of the business on the floor below us, which just happens to be owned by my landlords.

As it is past six and we thereby have no access to the water controls in the building, the city utilities people must be called. They saunter onto the porn set in their coveralls, eyeing us suspiciously, especially the one who looks like the late, rotund character actor Kenneth McMillan. By the time they fix the leak and we get to the explicit scene, it is 8:30 p.m., and I'm expecting twelve extras at nine o'clock, half of whom are actual journalists in real life, for a press conference sequence. My co-star and I are naked and camera-ready but, suddenly, after two smooth days of shooting, the camera mysteriously stops working. I'm running around half-clad with a phone in my hand, trying to dig up another camera somewhere, when the first of the extras arrives. It doesn't get any better than this. Somehow, we manage to find a camera, and the day's shooting is miraculously completed.

I have only included a few of the spectacular events that took place during my little shoot, conveniently leaving out the more emotionally devastating parts. I don't want to break your heart. The movie business is a brutal one; the porno industry, a nightmare. So the next time you rent a pornographic movie, consider what those poor souls have gone through just to entertain you. Hug a pornographer today.

Hug A Pornographer Today: The Making of Super 8 1/2

(Previously Suppressed Excerpts From the Diary of a Mad Movie-Maker)

It's ludicrous to even begin to attempt to sort out everything that's happened during the mess that we'll call the already infamous shoot of *Super 8 1/2*, chapter two, the I-wonder-why-I-even-bother years. I guess it all begins with Bjorn, as everything seems to have for the past couple of months. After vacillating between having him participate in the movie or not for weeks and weeks, considering we just broke up rather murderously only a matter of weeks ago, I finally come to the wrong decision that of course he will. It will be sheer emotional hell, naturally, but after all, that's what the movie is partly about, and I want a document of it, perverse soul that I am.

So we have a meeting before I escape to New York, and by the time I get back he has pretty much taken the project in hand as production manager and accountant, having prepared scene breakdowns, shot lists, a shooting schedule, and a full budget. I am somewhat

I and Dirty Pillows during the ponderous production of Super 8 1/2. Photo by Candy Parker.

29

taken aback, somewhat suspicious, somewhat relieved, and suddenly dependent on him once more. It takes me only a little while to realize his motives are probably more selfish than coming out of any real sense of belief in me or the project, or any wish to help me through it emotionally and be supportive. He turned his heart off toward me the moment we

I, LaBruce, in the nude hitch-hiking scene. Kindly note the snow on the ground. Photos by Candy Parker.

broke up, and has been insensitive above and beyond the call of duty ever since. But let's flashback to the beginning, shall we?

Bjorn and I had an initial meeting and everything was fine. We drank too much wine, and made the mistake of going to a fag bar together. I got him drunker and drunker and he ended up crying, something he rarely ever did in front of me. I gave him all this bullshit (at the time, sincere bullshit) about how we would still be close friends, but of course I was just fooling myself, which, it seems, is my avocation: I was still totally in love with him, and merely begging for a bone. I guess the press conference for the cult film festival came after that. I got way drunk on the free booze, as did he, and I ended up coming on to him in the bathroom back at my studio. We argued for a long time, none of which, mercifully, I can remember, except for him calling me pathetic. Then I did the worst thing I could possibly have done: I ended up going with him and Laszlo, my d.o.p., to a fruit bar to meet his new "friend," with whom, unbeknownst to me, he had been having a rather high profile affair before and after we broke up.

As I blithely slurred on about how so very adult we were all being, how very *Bob and Carol and Ted and Alice* of us, his "friend" sat terrified, as if I were about to smack him or devour him whole at any moment. Before I had a chance to go postal, the twosome left me alone with unsupportive, selfish Laszlo; as I cried and cried, he tried to pick up someone at the bar. The next day he said he hadn't even noticed me crying, even though I had been publicly blubbering like a fool.

Moving swiftly along, let's jump to the Friday before we are supposed to begin shooting. Suddenly, out of the blue, Laszlo decides he can't shoot the pic-

ture. He doesn't feel prepared, and he doesn't like the "prevailing attitude" of the pre-shoot. I'll give you prevailing attitude. Meanwhile, he and Anouk, one of my stars, both of whom I also happen to be sharing a studio with, are at each other's throats, and I am vainly trying to keep the peace. At this point, Bjorn and Laszlo start up their little conspiratorial trip, their little complicity. Laszlo, ever the nimble

LaBruce straddles Bjorn: Nudies, that's all they are! Nudies! Photo by Candy Parker.

whole wide world, he is definitely on my shit-list, which is beginning to rival *Atlas Shrugged* in sheer volume. Anouk has to dress up as a guy to take his place, and she's pissed off. Of course, none of this footage will end up turning out anyway, but that's another story.

manipulator and attempted seducer of my friends, begins to pit Bjorn against Anouk, and ultimately against me as well. Laszlo finally agrees at the last minute to shoot the fucking thing.

So the first day of shooting, Monday, is the graveyard scene with Anouk as Googie. Of course we can't afford permits, so we're sneaking around like grave-robbers. We've borrowed my boss' half-ton truck again, which is a tad conspicuous, but we have an okay time of it, except that it's now October, all the leaves are brown, and we're supposed to be matching reverse-angle shots with the ones that were taken when everything was lush and green last spring. But that's okay, because "I don't give a damn about continuity anyway" has become my mantra. Later, after Anouk kindly makes spaghetti for everyone, we are set to shoot a night exterior.

One actor, Pierre, not only doesn't show up or call, he hasn't even called since to beg my forgiveness. I don't care if he is the most beautiful boy in the

After the shoot, Bjorn comes into my room, after an intense chat with Anouk, to inform me that he's not going to do any of the sex scenes he told me he would do. I assume he means he doesn't want to perform unsimulated sex, so I agree, considering we're no longer fucking off-camera, but I can't stop myself from commenting on his poor timing. We get into a messy discussion about our former relationship, which I initiate, naturally, and I commit the cardinal sin of telling him I'm still in love with him,

31

seems to have been disconnected—so he always sends it in smaller amounts, and it's always less than it's supposed to be. It's almost worth it, though, because I feel like a spy, sneaking into the American Express office asking for money from Berlin, whispering the secret code word.

Tuesday is a day of rest. I can't remember what I do, no doubt go out and get plastered somewhere. Wednesday is the nude hitchhiking scene. Bad Craig is driving us in his VW van, and he takes us north of Toronto to search for a deserted road, which takes longer than you might expect. It's freezing and there is snow on the ground, which does not bode well for running around in our birthday suits. Laszlo is acting as usual like a professional cinematographer, "acting" being the operative word: he has on his stupid sunglasses and walks around with the camera on his shoulder in a smugly superior way. I would love to inform him that he is no James Wong Howe, but I can't say anything to him, not even about his constant tardiness or his complaints and whining, because he owns both the cameras we're using and my budget doesn't allow for rentals.

which I am, for some unfathomable reason (i.e., I make a fool of myself, again).

I try to get some sleep because we have another shoot scheduled at dawn, but I am kept awake by the inscrutable whisperings of Laszlo and Bjorn, who stay up all night in a huddle, strengthening their creepy little alliance. When I get up to jump-start the shoot, I pass by the front window, only to discover my boss' truck has been towed, or stolen. Retrieving the truck ends up costing a hundred and fifty dollars, putting a serious dent in the budget for the rest of the week. Originally, I was supposed to get the money for shooting all at once, but Dieter, my producer, has been running into financial difficulties—in fact, when I call Berlin, his phone

LaBruce, left, and Mikey[2], right, in the author's favourite production still from Super 8 and a Half. Puerile, I know. Photo by Candy Parker.

So I'm running around naked save for sunglasses and boots, and then Bjorn takes off his clothes and we're doing a nude scene in the van. Spontaneously, I straddle him behind the wheel and start to pretend to fuck him in a very over the top, comical way, in my opinion. Bjorn seems okay with it, and goes ahead and does the pee scene, too. That night at 2 a.m. I get a call from Bjorn: "I just want to tell you what scenes we shot today that aren't going to be in the movie," he says menacingly. I can't even begin to deal with this right now. Anyway, soon it will be the least of my problems, because Laszlo will start claiming to be uncomfortable shooting any of the sex scenes, something I heard nothing about from him before this little incident.

Kitty and Anouk and I go out drinking, not deigning to invite Laszlo or Bjorn. We need to talk, girls only. We get really drunk really fast and talk non-stop about all the bullshit that's been going on. Kitty and Anouk start making out on the pool table as per ushe until a girl comes over and punches Kitty in the nose for spilling her drink on the green velvet. As the girl's boyfriend shoves her twenty feet across the bar (shoves his girlfriend, not Kitty) the three of us tip-toe out the back door. The next day Bjorn bitches about us going out and getting bombed in the middle of a shoot and excluding Laszlo. The girls, I inform him, took me out because they thought I needed to let off some steam. In a way I really did, except that at this point I'm smoking at least two packs a day and have been drinking to excess for the past two-and-a-half months.

The next day I have to get up early to go all the way across town on my bicycle to pick up the straightjacket and more film. When I return, Laszlo is waiting for me (up on time, for a change) to tell me that he refuses to shoot either of the scenes that are scheduled for the day (the mental institution and the schoolyard locations) because he doesn't agree with them on moral grounds and he doesn't want to risk his camera being confiscated. He says it just isn't right for insane people and children to be used in a porno movie, laying this whole morality trip on me.

I'm enraged, but don't give him the satisfaction of displaying it publicly, merely telling him, as I've told Bjorn a million times, that you can't make good art without taking risks. He's obviously a major pussy of this or any other season. He also happens to think that the RCMP is monitoring us, no doubt encouraged in his paranoia by the always helpful Bjorn. I am toiling on a shoot for which I have to bend over backwards to appease the d.o.p. who is threatening to drop out at any moment; I am having the same problem with the production manager and co-star; Bjorn has been routinely late without apology; I've had to drag Anouk out of bed more than once; and even Honey is quite often tardy, claiming that she is late because she figured everybody else would be anyway. Why am I even bothering? To be fair, Anouk and Honey have been supportive and together for the most part, I have to say.

I have enlisted Alphonso, the dishwasher at work, to shoot the second "Ride, Queer, Ride" sequence. Laszlo is already starting to talk about wanting his name disassociated from the picture, and wants the negatives for any production stills in which he appears destroyed. He's really starting to crack up. The next day he doesn't show up for a shoot, which isn't the first time. He's officially fired. Anouk and Honey and Bjorn and I rent a Bolex for twenty-three dollars and shoot the damn scene ourselves. The next day I meet with a couple of Laszlo's friends, who inform me he's been institutionalized. Who knew that he had a history of mental illness? He believes that I am affiliated with the Chinese Mafia and that I am an exploitative pornographer who will go to any lengths to complete his filthy picture. Apparently he has gone over the script at great length inventing imagined references to himself, concluding that it has been my intention all along to draw him into my pornographic web of deceit, to disorient him by blurring the line between movies and reality.

34

Don't worry—for me, the distinction also becomes increasingly academic. When I yell, "You're exploiting me, you're exploiting me" to the camera, I'm referring, of course, to Laszlo. He really is nuts. He is also threatening to send a letter to every film-house, lab, and movie company in the city disavowing any association with me and, essentially, warning them about me. I decide to remove my negatives from the lab in case he tries to destroy them. I stash them at various friends' places because Laszlo, whom I've kicked out of the studio, still has a key. I'm relieved he's off the shoot, though. At least I don't have to continue negotiating credit width, height, and duration with him.

As for Bjorn, I still can't figure out why he is putting so much time and effort into this goddamn movie. He's still being an arrogant little son of a bitch, although he's more tolerable now that Laszlo is out of the picture. This week we manage three shoots, including the conclusion of the "Ride, Queer, Ride" highway sex sequence, which I had to do in subzero weather with a slight case of hepatitis A and my naked butt on the frozen asphalt. My ulcers have flared up and my eyes and skin are a gorgeous shade of yellow. But I have managed not to have a cigarette or a cocktail in five days. My body has accomplished what my mind could not—stopped me from killing myself.

The two day hell-shoot that was scheduled for four but had to be crammed because Radclyffe, my new dyke d.o.p. had other commitments—is over. It went relatively well, all things being relative to hell. It was almost fun, on the verge of being fun. It was great to finally be working with someone who really knows what she's doing, Radclyffe having done assistant camera on Cronenberg's *The Brood* and *Videodrome*. Thursday was pretty brutal, though. Some of the lines that were being bandied about cut me to the quick and left me dazed; Bjorn helpfully changed some of his lines slightly to make them even more hurtful. Scott Thompson of Kids in the Hall fame dropped in for a cameo, which was great, although we did have to write his lines in huge letters on the floor because he didn't have them memorized even though he wrote them himself, but it actually fit right into the whole Warhol angle I have going.

So we're shooting, bang, bang, bang, and when it comes time to film the sex scene between me and Marcel, the camera stops working, naturally. It's Friday the 13th, p.s. So I'm running around, with the phone, naked, trying to dig up another camera. I've also run out of film and have to use very outdated colour stock for the following scene even though the rest of the movie is in black and white. Oh well. It'll be artistic. Who knows if it will even turn out. I guess the movie is about ninety per cent shot now. I've been having severe post-shoot depression. I don't even know why I'm making this fucking movie, and I don't have a boyfriend anymore to explain to me exactly what the hell existentialism is, anyway.

Oh well. I guess that's my responsibility.

Mother, What's Wrong With Me?

So I'm feeling kind of depressed and lonely and, well, fucking disconsolate if you want to know the truth, and there isn't a drop of liquor in the house. So I decide to go out for a drink, or eleven tequilas. Lately I haven't been able to set foot in the gay ghetto. Literally. Like, I can't even walk down the east side of Yonge Street for Chrissake. But tonight I feel that inexorable pull, that attraction to a gathering of my own kind, which can be the unkindest kind of all. I find myself somnambulistically hailing a cab and blurting out the name of the only gay bar that I feel mildly comfortable in, owing to the strippers, je suppose, with whom I think I have a certain affinity, as a pornographer and all.

As we rush headlong through the ghetto, I can't help but feel like a prince returning from his self-imposed exile in a country as far away as Health, moving unrecognized (disguised in an Andy Warhol wig) amongst his former subjects. I have recently lost a brother to the ghetto, the Forbidden Zone which, if you allow it to, will swallow your identity and turn you into a pod fag, so I feel particularly wary tonight. If you stay too long in this zone, you may find your jeans becoming too tight and riding a bit too high, or your politics, perhaps, becoming doctrinaire, or you may even find yourself uncontrollably drawn to bad drag, gay theatre and anachronistically meaningless modern primitive tattoos. Is the gay ghetto a fortress to keep out the evil invaders, the bashers, and the breeders, or is it a prison of style rendering its inmates uniform, sedated and well-behaved? Maybe a drink will make me stop this gay medieval metaphor that has become far too extended.

After over-tipping the cabbie, as usual, I sweep into the bar, though no one seems to notice my entrance or even glance at me sideways. Planting myself on a barstool, I order a Bitch—scotch and orange juice, a good, solid Provincetown dyke drink. As I look around for a stripper acquaintance of mine, I notice that my style is at odds with everyone else's in the joint, that I bear none of the signifiers to facilitate a pick-up. My pants are too wide and my body too thin;

35

my tattoos aren't modern prim; and my hair is not short enough, it's long in the wrong way and completely artificial in colour—not something that a self-respecting fag should resort to anymore. I'm wearing too much make-up, too many rings, I don't have a tan (artificial or otherwise) and I'm not wearing Doc Martens. Mother, what's wrong with me?

Feeling uneasy and just a little self-consciously flamboyant, I pick up a copy of the *Advocate* that someone has kindly left at the bar for such awkward occasions, and flip to an interview with Sandra Bernhard. "I might be more inclined to join the group," she says, "If the gay community got back to being a bit like it was in the twenties and thirties, when it was more varied and more about being intellectual and sophisticated and about doing great things like playing bridge or going on fabulous trips to Paris and sitting around cafes being brilliant." Thank you, Sandra. I couldn't have said it better myself. What ever happened to the Quentin Crisps, the Truman Capotes, the Warhols, the Halstons, or the Great Kenneths (Williams, Halliwell, and Anger)? The Oscar Wildes, the Joe Ortons, the Paul Lyndes, the Charles Nelson Reillys? The Jonathan Harrises, the Edward Everett Hortons, the Billy de Wolfes? The Emorys, Michaels, and Harolds?

The names of great fags swirl in the cocktail I stir in front of me. My mind flashes to something else I heard Sandra say recently on some damn infotainment show or other. Referring to her "split" with Madonna, she wondered, in a rare and utterly vulnerable moment, how people can stop themselves from loving, how they can stop loving a lover or a friend. How can people just turn their hearts to stone? Sandra doesn't know and neither do I, although there is someone I'd like to pose that question to right now. And then I would say, Gena Rowlands-style, "Let me tell you something about love. Love is a constant stream. It never stops."

An effeminate man with a moustache and blotchy skin, who looks to be about forty, spies a temporarily empty barstool beside me and parks on it. I turn my head to meet his eyes and smile politely as fellow barflies often do; unexpectedly, he bursts into tears. "My Mum died yesterday," he confides in an unmistakably Maritime Fag accent. Then: "Can I hold your hand?" As deposed royalty, I feel I can hardly refuse—Noblesse Oblige, and all that. I listen as he describes the circumstances: how she dropped dead of a heart attack in front of him in the house they shared, how she didn't know he was gay, how she used to wear fur coats and rhinestone jewelry and pancake make-up and he used to tell her to fuck off all the time but now regrets it. "Everybody tells everybody to fuck off all the time,"

36

I try to console him. "Don't worry about it. Don't be depressed about that." He keeps assuring me that he's not depressed, then bursts into racking sobs, squeezing my hand as I look around nervously, and in a little pain, to see if we've reached spectacle status yet. I find it a bit odd and a bit sad that this fortyish-seeming man—who, as it turns out, is significantly younger—is alone in a depressing gay strip bar named Colby's the day after the death of his mother. "Don't you have any friends you could be with tonight?" I ask naively. "Yeah," he replies. "They're all at Trax."

My stripper friend eventually rescues me from the situation and I go to another bar to play pool with him and his girlfriend. On the way, we pass a couple of cops and in my drunken state I involuntarily snort, pig-like, at them, somewhat malevolently, if one can be involuntarily malevolent. "Do you have a fucking problem?" they inquire, ready to grab me by the lapels, drag me into their squad car, and take me to Cherry Beach for a good, old-fashioned fag-bashing party. My friend coolly talks them out of it. He's straight and very masterful. I've already had sex with him, and although I guess I have a crush on him, I don't really feel like spending all that energy trying to get him into bed again. He's a martial arts guy and he says that if I want him to, he'll beat up, to within an inch of his life, somebody I've been complaining about non-stop, which somehow makes me feel good, although I demur demurely. At the next bar I end up picking up a captain of the Armed Forces who got booted out for being a fag. He's fighting the dismissal but no longer wants to be in the service. As he fucks me he says he'll make me remember his name, but I forget it before I come.

The Celebrity Cameo

Lately, I've been feeling very Federico Fellini's production of *8 1/2*, especially the press conference scene at the end, when the reporters are barking questions at Marcello such as, "Don't you take yourself a little too seriously?" and, "You has-been! How could the story of your own life interest the public?" Then, in extreme close-up, the face of a strident woman wearing severe glasses turns toward the camera and she brays defiantly, "Ha Ha! He's lost! He has nothing to say! Ha Ha!" Of course, I identify as much with Guido slash Marcello—the philandering, creatively blocked movie-maker—as with Luisa, the long suffering wife he cheats on. Yes, I've been feeling very Anouk Aimée these days, if you want to know the truth.

I saw *8 1/2* recently, for about the ninth time. It never really had that big an effect on me before, but suddenly I realize almost everything in it applies to my life, albeit on a slightly less grandiose scale. My producer is German, not Italian, but he could definitely be a character straight out of *8 1/2*. Guido's producer says things that mine might say, like "Everybody's just waiting to pan this film. You don't have many friends left." My producer did say recently, in his Sprockets accent, "Broose, I sink your rushes are very bo-o-rring." Or words to that effect. Actually, I guess you'd be more likely to find his counterpart in Fassbinder's *Beware of a Holy Whore*, now that I think about it.

Anyway, when I was in New York to film the cameo

Richard Kern promised to do for my movie *Super 8 1/2,* my producer was over from Berlin on business, so we hooked up at Richard's apartment just before the shoot. R. Kern, I might hasten to add, since a lot of people, fags in particular, don't seem to know who the hell he is when I drop his name, is the guy who does all those naughty Lydia-Fuck-Me-You-Pig-Fucker-Lunch movies like *Submit To Me* and *The Manhattan Love Suicides* and *The Right Side of My Brain* and *Fingered.*

Ben Weasel goes the distance for the sake of art. Photo by Unknown.

My producer distributes Kern's films in Europe, so a couple of years ago he invited Mr. New York Underground Film Auteur to a post screening party he was throwing for me at a Eurotrash bar on the Lower East Side. Judging from his work (never a good idea), I was expecting a mean, malevolent, sinister kind of character, but Richard turned out to be very sweet and unassuming–a pussycat, like me. I think he was driving a cab for a living at the time and either was, or had recently gotten over being, a junkie. (Who hasn't?) He was very tall and kind of handsome and he wore those cheap, nerdy, black-framed glasses that you can buy off a spinning display case at your local apothecary. Of course his reputation as a misogynist preceded him, so we did have a certain amount in common. (Bad reputations, I mean).

Months later, when it came time to write my next script, I decided to include a little homage to Mr. Kern's oeuvre: the underground dyke cineaste in *Super 8 1/2* would make a movie-within-the-movie called "Submit To My Finger" in which a couple of Aileen Wuornos-inspired lesbian terrorists pick up unsuspecting male hitch-hikers and introduce them to various humiliating sexual acts. When R. Kern got wind of this little tribute and wondered why I hadn't asked him to appear in it, I got on the blower immediately and set something up. He would appear as himself in a fantasy sequence within the movie-within-the-movie, as the wet dream of one of the disputatious dykes.

So here we are at Richard's surprisingly upscale Manhattan apartment, me and Jürgen, and Glory–an actress slash sex worker friend of mine–and our host announces that he may have found a crab this morning. One, mind you. Glory and I don't know if he's telling the truth or what, because a couple of nights earlier we'd almost scared him off by getting a little over-enthusiastic and telling him all the nasty things we were going to do to him in front of the camera, so we think he might be getting cold feet. A true professional, Glory

The Author. Photo by Richard Kern.

takes the matter in hand and insists that somebody go to the nearest drug store for some crab medicine. My producer, who is well versed in the occupational hazards of porno shoots, and always very accommodating, readily volunteers. Meanwhile, the very straight-laced camera man I've dug up for the occasion is trying to act cool, but I think he might be getting a little nervous around the edges. I only have him for a couple of hours, so I'm watching the clock and hoping he doesn't skip out.

After the crab has been shown the door, my producer discreetly takes his leave and we get down to business. Richard and Glory get very creative with a wig and a good sized strap-on dildo, while I convey my direction to the d.o.p. with my usual precision: "Um, zoom in and out a lot, and, uh, make sure you get everything, okay?" We put a stocking or something over the lens to give it a kind of Penthouse-y feel, and although Richard's having a little trouble getting it up for the camera (don't we all, at times), I most-ly get what I want. We don't get his cherry, but hey, you can't have everything.

I'm not going to provide all the gory details; let's just say that when I recently got the footage back, even I was kind of shocked. I mean, I guess it's not so extreme by porno standards–certain people are always telling me I don't go far enough to be able to call myself a true pornographer–but I guess it's a good thing that I still blush at my own work. And by the way, just because I don't make sex look like a collection of gaping wounds and disembodied organs slobbering all over each other doesn't mean I'm not a pornographer. Why shouldn't it look pretty?

The next celebrity cameo that I worked into the script just so I could name drop some more was by none other than Buddy Cole, a.k.a. Scott Thompson. I hesitate to write about it because I haven't got the footage back yet so I don't even know if it turned out. Let

39

me say that Mr. Thompson arrived with his lines—which he wrote himself—unmemorized, but had the reading cold in two takes. Anyone who caught his Martin and Lewis routine with Don Cherry on the "Ralph Benmurgay Show" knows what a comic genius he is, but to capture a little of it myself on film felt almost as good as accomplishing a competent come-shot. Of course I didn't want it to go to his head: when Scott asked mischievously if he was the most famous person in the movie, I shot back "Next to me, yes." Fags are so competitive.

The only other celebrity cameo in my movie that you might want to know about is by Vaginal Creme Davis, the six-foot-six-*Ebony*-reading-blacktress-spokesmodel who resides in West Hollywood.

40

Ms. Davis gave it all up for the camera when I was there last year, performing her very first celluloid sexual act with, of all people, me. It was shot, incidentally, in glorious super 8 by glamourpuss fag photog Rick Castro. But now I'm giving too much away. Go see the movie, if it ever comes out—which at this point doesn't exactly seem like an historical inevitability. Maybe I should go straight ahead to the novelization.

If there are any rich fags out there, p.s., who want to see my movies come out faster, feel free to send me lots of cash, preferably small unmarked bills. Thank you too much.

Everything Old School Is New Again

"I'm not embarrassed by the word "gay", but it's not in the least bit relevant. I'm beyond that, frankly." Morrissey

What have I been reading lately, you ask? The latest Smiths biography, obviously. *Morrissey and Marr: The Severed Alliance.* It's my favourite type of book–chronicles of messy, malevolent smash-ups as told by those who once worked closely with a cherished colleague but find themselves suddenly, impossibly estranged, with no hope of reconciliation. You know, back full 'o' knives, throat casually slit from ear to ear, faith in humanity severely retarded type of thing. Hopeless. Oh well, as Ethan Hawke says in *Alive*, "What's so great about hope anyway?"

Although I've never been a big fan of Morrissey's music per se, his pop persona has always enervated me, in a good way (and no, it's not a malapropism–I'm perfectly well aware of the meaning of the word "enervated", thanks to Barbra Streisand in The *Owl and the Pussycat*); the spoilt, lonely, pouting ponce who blatantly refuses to play in the heretofore presumably exciting sandbox of boy-on-boy love; the morose Mancunian who perpetually resists any simplistic homosexual identification as a homosexual (assuming, of course, that he is one–and if he isn't, he might as well be).

Morrissey should be considered very new school. The latest movement is, in fact, the one that leads straight back to the closet. It's okay to go back in now. Really. It might give you a chance to recharge your batteries, regroup you troops, rethink your style. Think about it. Do you really want everybody to know all of those dire details about you, or to be able to sum you up and dismiss you with a single epithet? Wouldn't it be kind of fun for a change to be a little more ambiguous or mysterious, to keep people guessing? Isn't that a powerful position to be in? Of course, it's too late for the likes of me. I have no closet space left. But for those of you who are about to make your first tentative step out onto the stage, consider your options. Are you really cut out for a life in the theatre?

I know, I know, I'm being politically incorrect. How dare I command some poor, tortured soul who has just worked up the courage to come out to his or her parents and friends to turn right around and march back to that closet. Well, I could encourage kids to become "queer" activists, I suppose, but somehow fighting for the right to be perceived and represented as just as normal, unimaginative and mundane as the straight world seems tautological at best, suicide-making at worst. I mean, why put up with all that grief, struggling for years to become a respectable replica of the heterosexual paradigm, when you could stay in your cozy, walk-in closet and achieve the same results? I'm just being practical.

New school means new strategy and, ironically, a nostalgia for certain old school values. What, after all, is Morrissey or Michael Stipe or Sandra Bernhard, if not a return to the James Dean, the Johnny Mathis, the Rip Taylor, respectively, of yesteryear? I recently had the opportunity to meet Mr. Taylor when Scott Thompson invited the seasoned, sexually inscrutable, confetti-tossing comic veteran to Toronto for a cameo appearance on the "Kids in the Hall" show. It was a remarkable moment in gay history—the old school, closeted show business queen of comedy meeting his nineties counterpart—the in-your-face, aggressively open gay comic star (I mean Scott, not me).

Although we, the entourage, sat in one of the tackier, obviously gay bars in Toronto, to Mr. Taylor—whose career has been cushioned by euphemisms—we were merely in another "piano lounge". Every fag in the joint over thirty recognized the flamboyant entertainer in the corner, but to Mr. Taylor, they were nothing more than your ordinary, run-of-the-mill adoring fans. There's something exciting about this style of complete denial that has as a survivalist technique been fostered over decades. And although I completely applaud Scott's quest to become the world's first openly gay superstar—kudos, even—I also still appreciate your Rip Taylors and Morrisseys, who carry on the tradition of the unspeakable. As Pee Wee Herman so poignantly stated in his *Big Adventure*, "There are things about me that you wouldn't understand. Things you couldn't understand. Things you shouldn't understand."

"Despite his feminist leanings, Morrissey was always willing to explore the dramatic possibilities offered by displaying women as money-grabbing or voracious...."

Somewhere between the old and new schools of faggotry exists a generation of homosexuals who forgot about women. Old schooler Rip Taylor hangs out with the likes of Debbie Reynolds (we all know about her longtime companionship with

Agnes Moorehead, don't we?) and Ann Miller (I wouldn't care to speculate); new schooler Morrissey has always had unusually close relationships with women. In the new school, boys and girls play together, but sometimes, understandably, it gets a little rough. Like Morrissey, I've been accused by my enemies (yes, they do exist, believe it or not) of using female type people for exploitative purposes. Well, maybe that's because I'm not interested in representing women in a politically correct fashion any more than I am interested in representing fags in that way. I call them as I see them. Everyone knows I've always been female-identified, even more so than certain women I know. That's one reason I'm currently exploring my drag potential, although I know I'll live to regret it.

On a recent trip to New York I guest-hosted "Glennda and Friends," the Manhattan

Cable tv drag interview show produced by my good friend Glennda Orgasm. It was my third time in serious drag, my first in public (i.e., prancing down the street in broad daylight). You can tell a lot about a boy by the way he acts as a girl (and vice versa); I am, as you might expect, very feminine, but ballsy, like Stella Stevens in *The Nutty Professor*. Glennda and I conducted this little show at the Riot Grrrl conference, interviewing angry young women about a variety of pressing issues. Riot Grrrl has a reputation for being a distinctly middle class movement (even *Sassy* says so), so maybe I shouldn't have been so surprised by how sedate the atmosphere was, or how P.C. it was, or by the old school feminist politics being tossed around like a lead beachball. Style-wise, however, it was an exciting show, and for the most part the Grrrls reacted favourably to this pair of ancient drag queens posing as Uptown middle class women who read about the event in *Cosmo*.

But you know, I have to say, it all made me long for the days of old school punk, when it was the duty of the girls and fags alike to infiltrate and navigate through the occasionally dangerous, sometimes violent, predominantly straight male punk scene, alternately indulging in it and taking the piss out of it. Impatiently waiting for a riot that never materialized that day, I found myself almost waxing nostalgic about getting beat up for being a fag in the good old days. At least you knew where you stood then and who your enemies were.

Well, things have changed and the world will never be the same after Kim and Kelly Deal went their separate ways. I no longer have any illusions about a movement that is exclusively gay or all-girl, particularly since discovering that in the asshole department, women and fags can compete any day with straight men.

We hate it when our friends become successful
And if we can destroy them,
You bet your life we will destroy them
And if we can hurt them, well, we may well
That's really laughable
You see, it should have been me
Everybody knows, everybody says so

Yes, if Morrissey isn't a fag, he certainly does a good imitation of one, that's all I have to say.

Man Bites Dog

Oh man, how much more revealing can I get about my life in this sordid little diary? Well, as Elizabeth Taylor brays in *Who's Afraid of Virginia Woolf?*: "I'm just beginning!" My new dog, Cookie, the pit bull, and I have both recently enrolled in obedience school. Mine is called '"therapy". I have to go to hers; she doesn't have to go to mine. Hers is working. To be fair, she has been to more sessions than I have. So far I've learned that I'm a control freak and that I have a massive inferiority complex. Can you believe it? Me, of all people. Ironically, I've always thought of myself as above therapy, or beyond it, but now I realize I'm a therapist's wet dream: intelligent; over-educated; sensitive, prone to depression (it even runs in my family); a sexual deviant; a drunk long since over his drug days except for coffee, and lots of it; an avid smoker who actually laughs at *New Yorker* cartoons; a tortured artiste, disappointed in love, who only likes Woody Allen's dramatic pictures (especially *Interiors*), has the general disposition of Mia Farrow, and the emotional maturity of Sun-Yi.

Now don't get me wrong—therapy is serious business, especially when you finally acknowledge you might actually really need it. I also wonder about the appropriateness of someone who has as many tattoos as I do and who directs and stars in X-rated movies having a therapist. I mean, what did I expect? What could I have been thinking? And then there's the bothersome concept that "great art" is born out of conflict, or even madness, so why take a chance at becoming well-adjusted and normal when it might turn you into a bad film-maker? Look at Mike Nichols. In 1966, after a turbulent relationship and subsequent break-up with the exciting Elaine May, his comedic collaborator, he was making *Who's Afraid of Virginia Woolf?* and now, after probably twenty years or so of therapy, and a happy marriage to the boring Diane Sawyer, he's making movies like *Heartburn* and *Regarding Henry*. Ouch.

Anyway, the thing that disconcerted me the most on the first visit to "my therapist" (it has a great ring to it doesn't it? Like "my hustler") was that he wasn't wearing any shoes. I was expecting someone with polished black oxfords and a tie, but then I realized I was dealing with an Adlerian, the most humanistic of post-Freudian splinter groups. I quickly got over it, though, because transference set in almost immediately: this gentle, soft-spoken, even-tempered man started to remind me of my father and a couple of my ex-boyfriends. I can hardly wait for counter-transference to kick in.

Until you go to therapy yourself—and you will—you never realize how many people are in it. Which brings me to my topic of the month—Ben Weasel, the *Maximum RocknRoll* columnist, whose band Screeching Weasel recently blew through town on tour. I got to know Ben years ago when he sent me a letter asking if I would put an ad in my fanzine for Sloppy Seconds, a band that he was promoting. The title of their single: "I Don't Want to be a Homosexual". With a heavy sigh I crumpled the letter into a ball and shot it for two into the corner of my room with the rest of my fan mail.

Six months later I went over and uncrumpled the letter and fired off an angry missive to the Weasel, chastizing him for being homophobic (in the wrong way), and challenging him to write a song for his own band called "I Want To Be A Homosexual," for which I even suggested some lyrics. Being the model punk rocker that he is, Ben not only wrote the ditty, but also invited me to a recording studio in San Francisco to provide a spoken word intro and to pose with him giving me a faux blow-job for the cover of the single. It's nice to know that some heterosexual men don't care how sick and perverted they

make themselves look. Anyway, as it turns out, Ben is a veteran of therapy, having been confined to a camp for juvenile delinquents for several years during his adolescence (I won't go into details as he is writing his great American novel about it) and subsequently having suffered bouts of severe anxiety and agoraphobia. Being such a masterful, assertive, together-seeming kind of guy, you would never expect that he is actually on medication to regulate his various neuroses. I asked Ben if he thought some form of medication might be appropriate for me, and he suggested Prozac, even though this wonder drug has been blamed for sending more than one patient in the U.S. on a killing spree. At this point, I can think of nothing more therapeutic.

Despite several promotional glitches, the Screeching Weasel show at the Silver Shack was mighty, and I had fun yelling at Ben to take his clothes off—something I never seem to get tired of. Afterwards, we retreated to my studio to shoot Ben's celebrity cameo for my movie, *Super 8 1/2*. I don't know what it was, maybe it was his new gays-in-the-military style buzz-cut, or maybe it was my new pit bull obedience training, but I was inspired to have Mr. Punk Rock put a dog collar and leash on me and slap me around for this particular scene. Ultimate good sport that he is, Ben disrobed without too much provocation and willingly whacked me a couple of times across the face, but I had to coax him to slap me harder and more realistically—for the good of the movie, of course. When he finally drew blood, I knew we had a good take.

That was when the epiphany came. I mean, suddenly it all connected. A few weeks ago I had read a book about gay serial killer Bob Berdella (or Master Bob, as he liked his victims to call him) from Kansas City—a tall, over-weight ex-hippy Democrat (Why are most serial killers members of left wing parties? You may well ask), who picked up hustlers in the park, took them home, chained them up, clubbed them to within an inch of their lives, sent 11,000 volts of electricity through their bodies, injected Drano into their necks to retard their vocal chords and, keeping a journal of their responses, sodomized them at regular intervals. The objective was to turn them into utterly passive sex slaves so that they could be led around the house on a dog leash and provide oral gratification for him at any time; Jeffrey Dahmer, of course, would later conduct similar experiments.

In Master Bob's case, the training killed six of them, whose bodies he merely chopped up, stuffed into green garbage bags, and placed on the curb for pick-up. Now I've always been a dyed-in-the-warm-leatherette masochist myself, so I've often had sexual fantasies about similar scenarios, except that my Master would be in better shape, cuter, and he wouldn't let me die. And I could do without the Drano. (It's okay, it's the nineties—rape fantasies are back in style.) The point is, now that I have a dog to train, and a very dominant breed at that, I'm experiencing tension between my masochistic impulses and my identity as "master", and realizing that they are two sides of the same coin. What I'm discovering, of course, is that there are no absolutes where love is concerned. I guess that's why I impulsively put myself in the dog's position for that shoot with Ben Weasel (who, incidentally, would make a fine Master, judging by the way he controls his band members with an iron fist). And how, you may well ask, does this all connect with being in therapy? Do I have to draw you a picture?

Postqueer

Just got back from my Postqueer tour of New York, and boy are my dogs barking. Postqueer, for those of you in the don't know, is the latest fad in the homosexual underworld, so listen up if you don't want your face slapped.

To be identified as "Queer" today is definitely out—strictly five minutes ago. Getting back to your "gay" roots is where it's at. As you read this, untold numbers of young homosexuals are being processed by the new queer aesthetic, essential information about gay history and, well, how to be swish, for example, being systematically erased from their memory banks. Call it *The Manchurian Candidate*, faggot-style. Queers, with their cosmetically punk-influenced hairstyles and footwear, their incessant marching, and their cries of "homophobia" over every little thing, are really starting to work my nerves. They actually seem to want to rob all homosexual youths of their very birthright: an appreciation of latter-day Judy Garland, the fisting impulse, and the love of a good stiff drink, to name only a few. What follows are some examples of Postqueer behaviour I began to formulate in New York City. For those of you who insist on being homosexual, attention must be paid. For you heterosexuals, please feel free to participate. Separatism is definitely not our bag.

Far be it for Bruce LaBruce to dictate homosexual style, but I'm telling you right now, homosexuals must resist their obviously biologically determined drive to clone themselves. Do you really want to have the same look as everybody else, every day, for the rest of your life? If you dress like a queer all the time, people are just going to yell mundane epithets at you like "fruit" and "faggot". In New York, dressed in a fresh little black Chanel-like suede jacket, black suede boots whose buckles I'd cut off so they wouldn't scream the nineties (thank you once again, *Sassy*), an ascot, and big Tuesday Thursday sunglasses, street people yelled things at me like "Excuse me, are you famous?" and "Hey, I thought Hollywood was in California." Much more glamorous, no? Be prepared for rejection, though. When the leather-clad sling queens at the Spike got a load of my ascot, I was forcibly removed from the premises.

Although lip service has been paid to miscegenation in the form of

an occasional blow job, "queer" remains primarily a snow movement. Personally, as an unrepentant size queen, I must say I do sometimes prefer black men in bed. I know I may be crucified by the left for making such a statement, but in my extensive field research on the subject, black and South American men are generally bigger than other ethnic groups, if you catch my drift. Sorry. Anyway, I always seem to have a hot affair with a black man while in LA or NYC, and this trip was no exception. His name was Leroy, a strapping six-foot-two peroxide blond lawyer and frustrated fashion designer (only in New York, kids). He picked me up at the Bijou, an old movie theatre-cum-sex-club on the Lower East Side.

After sweeping me home and depositing me in his bed, Leroy informed me that he had a confession to make: he knew who I was on account of my Jodie Foster tattoo, and had chosen me because he'd "always wanted to fuck a porn star." "Me too," I thought to myself, although I did once accompany Vaginal Davis to a sex club in L.A. where Joey Stefano happened to be hanging out (literally), and she insisted that he was cruising me, which I find hard to believe, seeing as we're both hopeless bottoms. But I digress. Anyway, I don't mean to brag, and I'm only telling you because you asked, but Leroy did say that I was the best fuck he'd ever had. Say, isn't that what Carlton Stillborn, one of Madonna's Truth or Dare dancers, said to me once, or am I revising history again? Could be, considering I saw him recently at Sucker and he didn't even recognize me, the cad.

Hanging out with Sadie Bening was in itself an exercise in Postqueer pugilism. The pugnacious pixelvisionary pixie joined me and my good friend Glennda Orgasm on our Postqueer tour of the West Village—an event which we shot for "Glennda and Friends," her New York cable access drag show. On this particular "outing" (if you'll pardon the expression—I certainly don't mean it in the queer sense of the word), I was dressed as Judy Garland on the day before she died. Glennda and I bravely pranced the length of Christopher Street in heels, interviewing startled passersby about the new Postqueer movement that's sweeping the nation, while sniffing poppers.

Sadie, who blew off an Absolut Vodka ad and a *Mirabella* photo shoot to help with the show (and I'm not kidding, either), smashed into we two queens, knocking us over like so many bejewelled bowling pins, then viciously tore down several "March on Washington" posters before settling down for the interview. As it turns out, Sadie, the dyke James Dean, was as tired as we were of queers—not to mention Riot Grrrls—and didn't mince words in her condemnation of these failed movements. When Glennda told us a horror story about a legendary homosexual party in which a pig was provided for everyone to fist until, by the end of the evening, the poor beast had expired, sexy Sadie deadpanned, "And these people want rights?!" A truly Postqueer sentiment. Kudos, Ms. Bening.

Are you beginning to get a feel for the tenets of the Postqueer philosophy? Admittedly, it's a movement still in its infancy, so it may be difficult to grasp. But when it comes right down to it, it's really not a very complicated concept. Just trust your instincts for a change, and you'll be fine. Disassociating yourself from the established left and from orthodox feminism might not hurt either. Come on, kids. It's the nineties. As in fin de siècle. As in the millennium. As in—gay.

Spew You

Being a homosexual is a very complicated business. Since my debut, I've invested untold hours studying the phenomenon and feel no closer to a cure now than I did when I began. (Oh, lighten up. I'm only kidding. Besides, everybody knows they'll never find a cure.) My shrink (gay) informs me that many men who play for the pink team tend to be emotionally immature and thereby hyperintellectual by way of over-compensation. Well, kids, I hate to pull the newspaper out from under your Easter basket but he's absolutely right.

Believe me, I know because I wrote the book. Of course, I'm sure there are exceptions, and if you hear of one, tell him I'm dating again, would you?

I guess the reason I've been thinking about faggots so much lately (like I need an excuse) is the convergence of all these events: like Queersites–the academic conference at the University of Toronto–and *Spew Three*–the "queer" zine gathering. Of course, I attended neither of them because I can't stand queers. Well, that's not strictly true–I did attend the opening party for Queersites, at which I chased a scantily clad woman friend around the bar yelling, "I'm going to kill you," and ended up mock-raping her on the dance floor while biting her breasts. As a recovering academic, it really made sense at the time. Later, at the same international fanzine convention in New York. *Spew New York*, organized by my friends Glennda Orgasm and Christeen, was held at the Kitchen, a prestigious and very lah-de-dah art space in Chelsea where, indeed, parts of Madonna's "Deeper And Deeper" video were shot. (Apparently, she screamed all day for people to run and get her Hot Tamales, a type of candy , because she is a major sugar junkie, which is supposedly why her skin isn't as good as it could be.) At this fanzine convention, there were no queers or fanzines allowed–in fact, any brought onto the premises during the event were systematically confiscated and burned (the fanzines, that is).

function, I mock-raped a handsome young male acquaintance of mine (at least I think it was mock) on a table while a typically unre-sponsive Toronto audi-ence stood around and smiled politely. It's easier to embarrass your-self than others in this town, in my experience.

I borrowed the embalmed look from Warhol. Photo by Candy Parker.

Spew New York consisted of movies, videos and per-formances largely, but not exclusively, of a pornograph-ic nature. It was designed specifically to upstage the *Spew* held in Toronto weeks later. Perhaps you read about it in *The Village Voice*, where, incidentally, I was once again likened to Andy Warhol. What do I think of the comparison? Um, gee, what do you think?

Anyway, I didn't attend *Spew Three*, the third inter-national fanzine convention, partly because I hate queers, and partly because I had already attended the third

Some of the highlights of *Spew New York*, you ask? Well, the porno night was sick. Glennda and I, as master and slave, intro-duced the programme–I was ushered in on a dog leash, buck naked save for my size small Tom of Finland t-shirt. The show featured home-made, authentic skinhead porn that my gay photog skin-head friend John G. Byrne, who looks a lot like Donald Pleasance in braces and boots, sent me from Brighton, England. His work has attract-ed the attention of the likes of Morrissey, who used one of his images for a single, and the police, who recently raided his house and confiscated a large portion of his archives. Also included was a retrospective of some seventies blue movies from Hand In Hand Films, which were generously provided by my friend Bob Alvarez. Bob is one of the few surviving mem-bers of the company which produced, for example, some of the best Casey Donovan movies, like *Boys In The Sand* and *Back Row*. Featured at the screening were several Peter de Rome masterpieces, including *Underground,* a porno shot entirely on the New York subway in grainy, hand-held 16mm whenever no one was looking.

Another controversial programme during *Spew New York* was Christeen and Glennda's video, "Catfight: Just When You Though It Was Safe To Be a Feminist". It was girlcotted by a feminist organization called WAC who come by their acronym honestly. A third noteworthy night at *Spew New York* was "Revenge of our Fanzine Friends", a programme of work by recovering fanzine editors which included the debuts of trailers for upcoming movies by me, sexy Sadie Bening and candid Candy Parker whose *The Girls In The Band*, an ambitious super-8 re-make of *The Boys in the Band*, features the cream of the local dyke scene, not to mention yours truly as a waiter slash actor trying to worm his way into the latest Guy Wilbur play, coming to a theatre near you by the year 2000.

Enough self-promotion already. The only reason I brought up this whole mess in the first place is because one of my spies who attended *Spew Three* in Toronto informed me that he heard someone loudly threatening that he would like to punch Bruce LaBruce in the mouth for his last diary entry in *Exclaim* because "he always thinks he's eight months ahead of everybody else." Eight months, mind you. Apparently I have it down to an exact science. Yes, the gay trends I beget come to fruition, so to speak, in eight months like the arrival of a premature baby unable to wait out the standard gestation period in order to burst forth at the feet of an enthralled public. I can hear the nay-sayers right now, standing, so as not to appear gauche, the requisite distance away from the famous steps of the Second Cup in the ghetto, Toronto's very own version of the Castro, opining disdainfully, "Oh that Bruce LaBruce. He's so eight months from now." What can I say? To quote my good friend and confidante Christeen, "It's so exhausting being right all the time."

What Homosexuals Have To Be Proud Of

Don't get me started. I mean, Pride Day? Really. The nerve. What in the world do homosexuals have to be proud of? I mean as a group? The fact that they like to stick it to a man of their own gender? Please.

What it amounts to is a twisted patriotism based on sexual persuasion. I don't like it. This is not even to mention the notion that it is incredibly patronizing, this paltry symbolic gesture by the city that gays so desperately covet. Do we really need that kind of approval ? I don't. But then again, as you all know only too well, I'm Postqueer, or POQUE, as this fledgling movement has come to be known internationally.

Call me self-loathing. Go ahead. I know you do anyway. From New York to LA to Berlin, my spies are constantly reporting back to me the judgments, the denouncements, the condemnations of LaBruce. Well, to quote my dear friend Buddy Cole, every fag's a jury. Really, I've come to expect it.

If there is one thing homosexuals should be proud of, it's their insatiable, relentless, utterly unstoppable drive towards sexual satiation. Camille Paglia, who, incidentally, recently replaced me as guest co-host on the Glennda and Friends show in New York, has given us our due on that count: she surely recognizes the power of male pussy (it's in the back, you know). I mean, what other group has set up

an intercontinental network of bawdy houses in which free-thinking adults can choose from a selection of like-minded individuals to participate in a range of sexual antics at any time of the day or night, where free condoms are provided and there's easy access to safe lubricant, sex toys, mouthwash, beverages, a light snack, sauna and cable tv? What other group furnishes bars with back rooms for those standup sexual liaisons that just can't wait for the convenience of a standard bed? No other group, that's what group.

Of course there are other things for fags to take credit for and be proud of—the careers of Brenda Vacarro and Dyan Cannon spring immediately to mind—but on the whole, I don't think sucking dick is enough of an excuse for a parade, let alone an ideologically cohesive movement. On the day in question, in some—nay any—dark bar in New York, I will shout a silent hurrah to myself, but you won't be around to see it.

Now that I've thoroughly wetted that blanket, I'll tell you a little story. I recently accompanied a couple of my movies to the Gay and Lesbian Film Festival in our nation's capital. (If there's one thing a fag likes better that a parade, it's a festival.) The event happened to coincide with the Tory convention, so I was expecting to find some hot conservatives to have torrid sex with, right and centre. Unfortunately, this was not to be, for even in the midst of a hectic national political campaign, Ottawa is not exactly party central, so to speak.

Anyway, I was sharing my luxurious, all-expenses paid hotel room with a very handsome and sexy film-maker friend of mine, and one night we got all liquored up and found ourselves wildly dancing the night away at one of the two gay bars in the city (not the one with the country and western line dancing, the other one). As last call rolled around, my friend—I'll call him "K" because this does get somewhat Kafkaesque—handily took on the role of bait, easily attracting a small set of stylish homosexuals eager to play host to the glazed-eyed, disoriented out-of-towners. (As always, I attacked the Sandy Dennis part with gusto.)

Their ring-leader, Yves, a French dead ringer for Emory of *Boys in the Band*, arranged transportation for us to a club in Hull where we drank and danced to the respectable hour of three a.m. Before we knew what was happening, K and I were back at Yves' house (his boyfriend, Adam—and I'm not kidding, either—was of course not around) with seven of his closest friends, unreasonably strong rum-and-cokes thrust into our hands. Suddenly, we found ourselves perched precariously on a tiny piano bench, clinging to each other with eight hungry gay men facing us and arranged on a bed, virtually licking their chops as K and I turned into oversized roast chicken drumsticks before their eyes.

We were fresh meat, and the wolves were closing in. K was torn from my arms and ceremoniously unclothed by the small crowd, as I ended up on the floor with my shirt bunched up around my neck, two suspiciously similar looking fellows sucking simultaneously on each of my nipples.

"Have you ever had brothers before?" one of them asked lasciviously. The concept didn't turn me off, but I was more into another guy in the room who looked like the singer of *Faith No More*. After much manoeuvering, I was under the appropriate dude, and K had managed to pair off with a sexy little number of his own.

Well, that's all you get. I don't like to get too pornographic unless I'm being paid a lot of money for it. (That, in case you haven't learned to spot them yet, is an obvious lie.) I don't know what the point of that story was, exactly, except maybe as a kind of love letter to K, a very special friend, or so I thought. After our adventure, we did a post-mortem of the evening, holding each other under the starched sheets of a strange bed in a very straight hotel. It was oh, so romantic. Much later, K turned out to be one of the most notorious Eves I have ever encountered—an UberEve, in fact—but that's another sob story.

Jurassic Punk

I just have to get one thing off my hollow little concave chest. The person who wrote the anti-pit-bull-and-pit-bull-owner rant in a recent Toronto weekly must be punished. Believe you me, if I ever run into him in a dark alley with my pit bull, Cookie, I will not hesitate to let her off the leash. Of course, true to form, she will probably run over with her tail wagging and lick the fellow's boots as he stands quivering in a puddle of pee of his own making. This poor, sour, pussy-whipped soul is so out of touch with the cosmos, it's almost alarming. Nature, my friend, is not a walk in the park. She is more often than not a very brutal mistress, in case you haven't noticed, witness the various tornados and floods that have been ravaging the Midwest of late.

Pit bulls are nothing more or less than a force of nature, an aspect of reality one must either accept (try hugging one) or deny (try to have them banned, like pornography, another unhealthy manifestation of nature). When I feel the brute force of my little pit tugging at the end of her leash, I am awed by the unstoppable essence of life. One of my more fascist friends has tried to convince me that pit bulls also serve the purpose of thinning out the herd, Darwin-style, but I guess I'm still a bit too liberal to subscribe to that theory.

Anyway, everybody knows that love conquers all, and if you love your pit bull, your rewards will be great. Life can be beautiful.

Actually, Cookie has been reminding me lately of the raptors from Jurassic Park, one of those lovable man-eating dinosaurs that has been endearingly marketed for your pleasure this summer. Although I didn't like it that much, I saw the movie three times in its first week of release (to be fair, once was at the drive-in, and I really went to see *Dragon: The Bruce Lee Story*, with which it was playing), contributing significantly to its repeat viewing box-office cachet. All three times I boldly broke through the barriers of GLAAD protesters, who were

claiming that the movie is yet another stereotypical and hysterical representation of the psycho-killer dyke (the antagonists being an all-female dinosaur sect that somehow managed to breed). Au contraire–I think the film has a very positive message: lesbian separatism is dangerous.

In case you were wondering where the hell I was, I spent Gay Public Humiliation Day in New York, wondering how to avoid the festivities that festered across Manhattan and North America at large. I decided it would be appropriate to go see G.G. Allin, the real Last Action Hero, perform at the Gas Station on the Lower East Side. I strolled over to this indoor-outdoor, fenced-in space and saw a veritable herd of Jurassic punks milling about–you know, the unlaundered, panhandling, bemohawked behemoth that hasn't changed its style–nay, its clothes–in fifteen years. That was enough to turn me away from the inn–that, and the fact that Mykel Board, G.G.'s "manager", would be there, and he would probably introduce me on purpose to G.G. as the man who mercilessly trashed Mr. Allin in *Maximum RocknRoll* a few years back. This would undoubtedly provoke the pornographic punk performance artist–who shits and shoots up on stage and assaults and date rapes audience members at random–to murder me on the spot without batting an eyelash.

So I sauntered away and found myself alone in any dark bar, as promised, drinking to try to forget about societies of misfits who have become some of today's biggest conformists. Later that same day, I did manager to catch The Ron Athey Show. You know, he's the Modern Primitive gentleman with mondo tattoos who slices and dices and cattle prods and gives enemas and douches to fellow patterned pagans on stage. One girl, bravely named Pig Pen, gets blood extracted from both arms with hypodermic needles, and this, in turn, is squirted into her mouth, already sewn shut with surgical needles and thread.

I was filming part of the event on Super-8 for my friend Mark, a senior piercer at the Gauntlet, who was in the show with bells on (literally, sewn to his bare shoulders), so I got to meet Ron himself–a very nice and unassuming young man who was surprisingly into the show biz aspects of the performing arts. Backstage, I witnessed him sew his own mouth shut as if he were applying lipstick; on stage, his scalp was pierced by many alarmingly large needles, to form an ersatz crown of thorns, and his body was lanced from head to toe with spears in a San Sebastian-like finale. "My blood type is HIV," he declared baldly, blood spilling across the stage floor. Do tell. Well, if you're going to be proud, you might as well as go all the way.

I brought as my guest the friend I was staying with–I'll call her Glory Hole Domination, or Glory for short–who was cheered up considerably by the show; she had spent Pride crying alone in her apartment and wondering–as any sane person would do–if the suicide rate for that special day is comparable to that of Christmas. The previous evening, Glory had brought home a dyke in an advanced state of drink as I lay in a pull-out bed in the adjacent room; they thrashed and crashed around as pots and pans flew pell-mell and I feigned sleep. It was a scene right out of *Jurassic Park*: "If I don't move, they can't see me," I said to myself, balled up in the fetal position with the sheets over my head as the two female raptors ravaged the kitchen. I accidentally knocked over a bottle of Evian, drawing the attention of the dykes who, tipsy and tottering with their little T-rex arms curled in front of them, made straight for my bed and pounced, subsequently dousing me with beer and attempting to coerce me into questionable sexual relations involving strap-ons and such. Playing dead, I narrowly escaped the fate of all those other male victims of the Jurassic lesbian rampage.

Strangely, Glory, my dear friend and New York hostess, happens to be an in-law of one of the creators of *Jurassic Park*, but decency forbids me to name which. So the very next day, we decided to go shopping for a *Jurassic Park* t-shirt that she might pose in–wet, of course–for a photo shoot she was scheduled to do (by one R. Kern) to promote her latest video. As irony piled upon New York irony, we picked up a *Post*, only to read that G.G. Allin had died on Pride Day night of what was an apparent o.d. His final set with his latest band, The Murder Junkies, which I missed, had lasted but one song, after which he had picked a fight with someone and had gotten thrown not just through the drum kit, mind you, but through a plate-glass door as well. Glory and I remarked to each other how odd it was that Glory herself had recently been asked to appear in an R. Kern movie with G.G. Allin, but had declined, and the movie never got made. Oh well, it could have been worse. G.G. could have offed himself on stage, as he had so long promised, and then I'd have really missed something. But then again, that's show biz.

I, Judy LaBruce

Who was it that once said, "There are only three lesbians in the world—the rest is done with mirrors?"

It wasn't Queen Victoria. She wouldn't even allow one. When asked, after passing a law forbidding homosexual acts between men, about the question of lesbianism, she decreed, "it doesn't exist." Il n'existe pas, baby. Well anyway, whoever it was, let me add an adage from the gay male perspective: "There's only one homosexual in the world. And baby, it's me."

I'm not sure what I mean by that, but I know there's truth in it somewhere.

I'm not suggesting that I'm the original, and the rest are clones. Clones existed long before my debut, and I would not be so crass (like certain queers I could name) as to treat a clone like a member of a lower caste, an untouchable. Even at the peak of my punk posturing, I would eagerly have sexual relations with a man with a handlebar moustache, mutton chops, a single earring, white t-shirt and Levis, as long as he knew how to throw a good fuck. Neither am I suggesting that I am the only true homosexual in the world—i.e., the only one who desires sexual relations exclusively with other men, past, present and future. I know I am not the only poor,

deprived soul on that count although, being the eternal optimist, I have of late been identifying myself (like Suede in reverse) as a bisexual who has never slept with a woman. I mean, I can dream, can't I?

Maybe I'm inferring that all homosexuals are, by definition, narcissists. Don't you hate it when you see two gay lovers with identical style? Doesn't it positively make your skin crawl, to paraphrase Angie Dickinson in *Point Blank*? I've seen this one pair trashing around the baths who literally look like identical twins—both six-foot-two, with but exactly matching muscles and moustaches; one wearing a white t-shirt with black jeans, the other a black t-shirt with white jeans. One is always two paces in step behind the other, and they always trick together—double your pleasure, double your fun, i.e. All right, actually I have had them. The point is, however, that if they really are twins, more power to them—brotherly love is way in. But really, how into yourself can you get? Happily, all fags aren't like that, otherwise how would you account for us self-loathing types? Although, come to think of it, I guess I wouldn't throw myself out of bed for eating bon-bons.

No, I guess what I mean is, well, I don't quite know how to tell you this, but I'll just come right out and say it—I am the reincarnation of Judy Garland. Yes, on Saturday January 21, 1969—the exact date of my birth—the tortured soul of Judy left her spent body on that cold toilet seat in London, and a star was reborn. As the drag queens threw bricks at Stonewall in a frenzy of grief over the death of their idol, I, Judy, was suckling at my mother's breasts (we'll get to her lesbian tendencies in a minute), probably mistaking them for a couple of wet martinis.

I know what you're thinking—why don't I leave her alone? Please don't misunderstand me. As a co-founder of the Postqueer movement, I have a deep reverence for Judy Garland. I recently finished, feverishly and at four in the morning, the latest biography of the haunted chanteuse: *Judy Garland: The Secret Life of an American Legend*, by David Shipman. An hour later I woke up sobbing, such was the impact on me of the tragedy of her life.

Lately, all I've been reading are biographies or autobiographies of tortured beings on their slow and bitter descent to the bottom: *Neon Angel: The Cherie Currie Story*, *Nico: The Loves and Lives of an Icon*, *Thing of Beauty: The Tragedy of Supermodel Gia*, *Little Girl Lost* by Drew Barrymore and fag bios of the likes of Andrew Crispo, Roy Cohn, and Halston. But none can compare to the trials of Judy. Hooked on dolls at fourteen (fed to her by the greedy, slave-driving moguls at MGM), it was downhill from puberty. Multiple abortions, the constant struggle to keep the weight down, graduating from pills to junk—and I don't mean food, baby—five husbands, at least three of whom were gay... it just goes on and on. Of course, there were good times too: numerous hot lesbian affairs, passionate liaisons with such sexual dynamos as Yul Brynner and bisexual Ty Power, and finally, let's not forget two little blessings named Liza and Lorna. But let's face it, Judy could have taught the Greeks a thing or two about tragedy.

The most remarkable thing about little Miss Frances Gumm (her real name, to clarify for our straight readers) was her obvious identity as a gay man trapped inside a woman's body, which is why, I suspect, she chose yours truly as the next earthly suppository, pardon my malapropism, of her immortal soul. According to the *Book of Judy*, not only was her own father a known homosexual, but she also surrounded herself with fags throughout her entire life, not to mention her legions of adoring gay fans, who more than once kept her career afloat after she had been forsaken by the fickle heterosexual masses. She also had a voracious sexual appetite, and loved to get it up the ass (it's in the book). Why, when there were no straight men in sight, she was even known to order her gay male hairdressers to go down on her in the back of the limousine (ditto). Add to this her propensity to marry queens (obviously a genetic predisposition passed on to Liza) and her somehow mannish physique (the boxy torso, the sturdy legs), not to mention her trademark men's shirts worn over black tights...well, let's just say it's a duck.

In fact, it has always been my theory that Vincente Minnelli—one of Judy's fag husbands—directed his under-rated 1964 movie, *Goodbye Charlie*—in which a philandering man is murdered by a jealous husband and reincarnated in Debbie Reynold's body—as a direct homage to his ex-wife. But now I'm losing you.

Judy did, indeed, die on a toilet seat in jolly old London, England. In fact, when her fifth, much younger husband, club promoter Mickey Deans, found her there in the W.C., rigor mortis had already set in. This upset me a lot when I read it. In the last days of her life, her sponging spouse arranged for a sleazy Swedish film company to shoot a documentary entitled *A Day in the Life of Judy Garland*. In it, apparently, Judy is totally drugged out and incoher-

Festival, for which I will act as Grand Marshal. You may think I'm kidding, but I'm not. You may think this entire diary was meant as a tasteless joke, but it wasn't. Truth, after all, is stranger than fiction.

Very LA

So I'm standing in a decidedly gay café that is somehow appropriately located across from the mental institution, minding my own business, propped benignly against the counter, waiting for my take-out lunch that I'm about to have at the home of my editor who's off tomorrow to Peru for a month, when who should enter the establishment but a murderously old school homosexual acquaintance of mine, the kind they don't let you see in the movies any more. A real flame-thrower. A Molotov cocktail mixed with a third mischief, a third wit, a third contempt and more than a dash of bitter. You'd rather be dead than read by one of these queens.

We chat amicably for a few moments—laundry hints, his arts grant application—and for a moment I think that I might make it out of the encounter alive. Then he casually picks up a copy of *Exclaim* and declares emphatically that there is absolutely nothing to read in the joint. To give him the benefit of the doubt, perhaps he doesn't know I appear in it monthly. He is about to leave, but I notice him hesitating in the doorway. Suddenly a Grinchish grin spreads across his face. He turns, stating blatantly for all in the café to hear, "Oh, by the way. I just have to tell you. I hate your scarf. It makes you look like an American Airlines stewardess." He clocks me. I am taken so off guard that I burst into Dorothy-gales of laughter. Looking down at the admittedly garish silk scarf in question, I can only agree with his assessment. I drift off into a reverie about LA...

"Oh, that is so LA," I am wont to say at regular intervals during my most recent visit to the City of Angels. My companion, who lives there, at first assumes I am being derisive, as most outsiders are, of this much maligned city, but soon he realizes that my sincerity is sincere, and as Mia went to India, so Bruce goes to LA. It's not just the palm trees and bungalows pasted like cardboard sets against the artificial sunset. Or the googie-style diners and hamburger joints populated by hard-

ent, often naked and, in the final irony, unable to tell whether she is on stage or off. This treasure perdu, along with Jerry Lewis' masterpiece manque, *The Day the Clown Cried*, in which he plays a Borscht Belt comedian hired to lead the unsuspecting children in a Nazi concentration camp to the gas chambers, constitute, in my books, the two most coveted movie-watching experiences that never were.

So, in a week or so, I, Judy LaBruce, am off to LA to star in a remake of this lost film. They are also holding a parade in my honour along Melrose Place on Sunday, September 5: the Fourth Annual Post-Queer Judy Garland Memorial Parade and working hustlers and MAWs (Model, Actress, Whatever). Or all those Mustangs and T-Birds and Impalas, ranging from vintage to broken-down—prowling the boulevards and those Hollywood Hills at all hours of the day and night. It's not just that. It's the relentless urbanity of it all, the vast concrete blankness. Not to get too metaphysical, but Maria Wyeth, Joan Didion's alter ego in her prototypical LA novel, *Play It As It Lays*, got it right: When asked by a cop why she's driving with no particular destination in mind, she says of the freeway, "I mean, it just makes you feel like they had something in mind when they built it, you know?" That is so LA.

So after being picked up at LAX, an airport straight out of *The Tenth Victim* (whose soundtrack, incidentally, a friend gives me during my stay, and so it becomes the soundtrack of my visit), we head straight for Santa Monica Boulevard, which my host, Desi, lives just above. Desi is one of those LA faggots I love the best—Hollywood stylist by day (he was doing another Sassoon commercial during my visit, and had recently finished an Oxycute 'Em), photographer and videographer of hustlers and drag queens by night. Our little project during my stay was to find an appropriate hustler on the Boulevard for him to videotape me having sex with.

A lot of people, fags included, find Desi very intimidating, but he can actually be very sweet. Of course, he will read you to within an inch of your life if you let your guard down for a fraction of a second, not unlike the Toronto queen who induced this reverie, but that's part of his charm. He's into horoscopes and bondage and white magic ("The Dainty Satanist," I call him, although there are an alarming number of pentagrams in his bungalow), his cat, Pyewacket—for whom he had recently thrown a surprise birthday party, although I think someone had tipped her off because she didn't act very surprised—acting as his familiar. He has a particular fondness for amputees; after seeing *Boxing Helena* together at the Cinerama Dome, valiantly breaking through the line of feminist protesters, he keeps making me agree with him how cute Darren, his boyfriend, would look without arms and legs, while poor Darren smiles sheepishly.

Desi's New York stylist friend, known to all in the set simply as "Mommy", has called, so the next day we lunch with him at Ben Frank's on Sunset. Mommy is in town styling a Jack In The Box commercial to be directed by, of all people, Sam Raimi; afterwards he shows me the storyboards. Mommy is "ill", and is sometimes late because he's on the old i.v., but that doesn't stop us from cruising the Boulevard, in the Volvo he has borrowed from one of his debutante friends, to pick out our dream dates. It will become a daily routine, like breakfast.

That night, I attend a friend's surprise birthday party that he's known about for weeks. Gerald is a freckle-faced Idaho farm boy turned underground LA club promoter, and also one of the sweetest homosexuals you'd ever want to meet—witty, urbane and sophisticated. The party has been organized by Mrs. Glass, a black woman originally from South Central LA currently writing a book about Superfly culture—also a suave, cultured gay man with a sweet disposition. (The unmarried Mrs.Glass— no one knows why she is called Mrs.—and Gerald will later in the week accompany me to Numbers, the discreet upscale hustler bar on Sunset where Gerald swears he once spotted Jack Lemmon.) There are all sorts of gay celebrities at the party, from Roseanne and Patricia's little brother, Alexis Arquette, to Mod Prim queen Ron Athey, to sultry womandingo Vaginal Davis.

I am thrilled to finally meet Lance Loud, the lantern-jawed American Family son who came out on nationwide television and currently writes for *Us* and *Interview* magazines. There's Richard Glatzer, director of *Grief*, and his new discovery, Jackie Beat.

Here comes a famous model but no one seems to know his name, and there go a couple of queens working on a script based on the life of Monty Clift. I end up making out with the cute musician host of the party on a bed of coats until we get busted by his boyfriend and I leave posthaste, but now I'm kissing and telling again.

It's finally Sunday, the day of the very first Fourth Annual Postqueer Judy Garland Memorial Parade and Festival. The event has been listed in the *LA Reader* and *Weekly*, but one of them got the date wrong, so we're not sure how the turn-out will be. As we arrive at the designated spot, throngs (at least thirty) line the street. Ms. Davis, as Snooty Garland, greets me, the visiting Judy, as the crowd cheers. A cowboy hatted Gerald arrives on the hood of a Mustang, his float promoting his new club, Candy. Here comes Yves Montand, the famous video and tv commercial art director, in his pale green Mercedes. There's that well-known, stylish female Japanese stylist. And who are those pesky paparazzi? I manage a flawless string of one-handed cartwheels—my speciality—in heels, mind you, down Melrose Place as two parade participants, dressed as a bottle of uppers and downers prescribed by Sam Goldwyn and L.B. Mayer, respectively, walk on either side of me. It's so LA.

Oh, there is so much more to tell, but I'm getting a cramp. Desi and Judy go to Candy. Desi videotapes Judy getting drunk and picking a fight with a couple of very tall, very muscular drag queens. Desi shoots Judy crawling from the club on his hands and knees. But not before someone calls Judy a visionary and "the future". Desi and I never do get to shoot our intended porno flick: we can't find anyone who both turns me on sexually and Desi aesthetically. During the week, Desi has had a parade of middle-range hustlers through his house "auditioning" for a gay dentist ad he's doing—the kind of hustlers who don't work the street (their teeth usually aren't the greatest), but who haven't exactly found a gig with a Geffen or a Gallin yet, either. They all seem to have an edge of desperation to them, constantly hustling: off to the gym, off to acting class, off to meet another trick, off to A.A. or N.A. or their drug dealer's, whichever applies. One of them in particular, Desi says, since he last saw him six months ago, looks like he has lost his soul.

On the lower end of the scale, we interview a street hustler named Pike, on the Boulevard. He was the first baby of the new year in a small town in Minnesota in 1965. His parents moved him to Mexico and were murdered when he was twelve. His grandparents didn't want him, so he's been on the streets ever since. He's dealing now. He's got no one in the world. He's worried about a barefoot friend of his called Angel who's been selling himself for a buck a fuck because he's lost track of the value of money. He's really sweet. It's very LA.

Rape Me, Rape My Dog

I love my pit bull. I wish I could fuck her. But she is my dog, and that would be incest.

I have to tell you this story, though.

I'm walking Cookie off the leash in the park the other day, and this big, gross, ugly, dumb, unshaven male poodle starts trying to hump her like crazy as his owner, following behind, whistles half-heartedly. Even when Monsieur Owner starts calling him almost in earnest, the poor, stupid, obviously badly trained pooch keeps on sexually harassing my sweet, bright, affectionate best friend. Cookie takes it good-naturedly at first, but starts getting, understandably, a little pissed off, and I know she is about to go off on her assailant. Not wishing to witness the impending ugly scene of blood and fur, I put my foot against this dubious dog and push it firmly but not cruelly away with an adamant, "No."

At this point, the submoronic owner, finally starting to pay attention to the situation, runs toward me, barking, "Hey. This is how it works.You kick my dog, I kick you." His unwashed, hideous, broad little face is quivering inches from my calm, mildly bewildered pleasant one.

I respond, "I didn't kick your dog. I pushed it away with my foot. There's a difference." His already unfortunate, homely visage starts to redden gradually from bottom to top, like a rectal thermometer. "Just don't kick my fucking dog, or you'll be on the ground," he says again. I repeat calmly, "I didn't kick your dog, I put my foot against it and gave it a little shove. No biggie." By this time, his macho persona is getting a real workout, and his girlfriend is standing quietly quivering several yards behind me. After he yells at me some more, I finally walk away, saying, "Your dog has been harassing mine since it got here. I just wanted it to stop." And here's the clincher–are you ready?–the guy says, "Yeah, well your dog wanted it!" Yes, she was asking for it, all right, the little tramp.

So anyway, later that day I'm walking myself downtown, on the way to see the new Bob Altman movie, and this crazy lady starts screaming at me. She looks like a normal U of T student–sweats, pony tail, vinyl windbreaker–and yet she has obviously snapped at some point. After accosting another stranger, admonishing him for still being too attached to his mother's tits, she sets her sights on me. "Get off the heroin!" she screams at the top of her perfectly healthy lungs. "Get off the crack! This is Canada!" She pauses for a breath. Then, after studying me swishing away from her at an accelerated pace, adds, "Canadians don't walk like that!" And you know, she's probably right.

59

Okay, so that night I go bar hopping with a friend in the gay ghetto, working on my Postqueer credentials. Somewhere on Carlton Street, a flock of jocks, fresh from the Jays-Sox game, fall in step behind us. "Look at him!" yells one of them. "He sure got the colour right. He's a real flamer!" (By the way of explanation: having already had more than enough fun, I had recently dyed my hair back to red, from blond. It did turn out a rather more garish shade than I had intended, but still fell, I think, well within the boundaries of good taste.)

A few sheets and an electric blanket to the wind already, I turned around and blew a kiss to my verbal assailants, much to the dismay of my gay, if somewhat inconveniently pacifistic, companion. "Come here and do that,

faggot," yells another of them. "Kiss my ass," I offer instead, inspired, I have no doubt, no doubt at all, by Barbra Streisand in *The Owl and the Pussycat*. Very stupid, I admit. You might even say I was asking for it, in a way. Just like Cookie was, in the park. But apparently the brutes weren't up to a good bashing, and allowed us to float off into the night unscathed, dignity intact. As I entered the next bar, I crowed loudly within earshot of the bouncers about how I could have taken them all on with one limp wrist tied behind my back; the burly boys laugh and roll their eyes accordingly.

So, what do these three separate, yet not necessarily unrelated, incidents have in common, and what lesson might we garner from them? Clearly, each episode is predicated on some form of sexual panic and disapprobation, am I right? All three of my verbal assailants were making some kind of nervous comment, however veiled, about my (and by extension, my dog's) sexual "misconduct". Not only am I a drug abuser who flaunts his sexual deviance by walking funny and altering the natural colour of his hair, but I have also intentionally raised my pet to be a slut.

Now let me relate to you a fourth incident, albeit one reported to me second-hand, that might lead us to a little epiphany. According to my source, a certain lesbian couple was walking its prize-winning canine in a large public park in the wee hours of the morning, when, suddenly, they spotted in the distant bushes a pair of gay men in some state of undress, having furtive sex. The dykes in question, known in certain circles for their outspoken opinions about men as sexually predatory swine and women as victimized objects, were so affronted by the spectacle that they raced across the park with their large dog and chased the hapless homos from the vicinity, screaming about it being another case of men sexually harassing women.

And that's the moral of the story: how easily the oppressed become the oppressors. Armed only with an antiquated, orthodox, carved-in-stone feminist politic that posits all women as victims of male lechery, these sex police have no real tolerance for sexual difference and no appreciation for the dangerous thrill of a little harmless outdoor sex–a gay custom which itself originates in an attempt to steal a little pleasure outside the range of the probing eye of society's disapproval. Get with it, grrrls. Nobody died and made you Minister of Appropriate Sexual Behaviour. You're no better than the machos or the crazy lady on the street who kindly provided me with the fodder for this piece.

I'd been having a bad week already, as I'm sure we all had, but since the news, I'd been particularly despondent. So when my friend Bellini called me up and described the pink night he had planned for us, it was almost enough to bring me out my blue funk over River. When I told my shrink I was bummed-out about the tragedy of River Phoenix, he told me a lot of his clients had been mentioning it in their sessions that week (he does have, after all, a largely limp-wristed clientele).

Of course, I called my friends in the LA gay set to see if I could

The Essential Tragedy of Homosexual Existence

get any inside information. All they could come up with was that he had been miserable for a long time, hated the Hollywood system and had allegedly been a junkie since *Idaho*. No guff. Despite his convincing and sympathetic performance in *My Own Private Idaho*, River was, presumably, straight (although, if the grapevine can at all be believed, he did take the Method to its logical conclusion during its production); however, he was a gay icon of the highest order ever since his debut as Wil Wheaton's boyfriend in *Stand By Me*, and he will be sorely missed, especially by me.

Let me pull myself together. Where was I? Oh yeah, Bellini. First on the agenda was an amateur production of *The Boys in the Band* at the vaguely Soviet sounding Joseph Workman Auditorium. At first I mistakenly thought this venue was on the campus of York U., which would have been wildly appropriate since both Bellini and I and our companion for the Postqueer evening ahead, Thompson (no, not R.H., or Highway—the other Canadian celebrity Thompson) are either alumni or dropouts (or in my case, both, depending on which bio you read) of that fine institution. But no, the landmark gay play was to be performed at an even more prestigious institution of higher learning, and even more wildly appropriately—the Queen Street Mental Health Centre. The production was certainly engaging, and we all agreed that the underplayed Emory and the especially well rounded Bernard—who was better than the part—were standouts in the cast; one could not help, though, but be enthralled by the precise homage to Leonard Frey's Harold and the hunky casting of Hank—who got my vote for dreamboat of the night—and a smouldering Larry (Thompson's choice). I can hardly wait for Mart Crowley's promised sequel, *From Boys To Men*, to hit New York, because you know I'll be there.

Before we had a chance to hate ourselves so very, very much, Bellini whisked us off to the next leg of our fag field-trip—an audience with the Pope. Carol, of course. Unfortunately, we missed her show, but we did get to hang out with her backstage at the Queen's Bedroom. She looked great, but I didn't have much to say. I always grow silent in the presence of celebrities (except for some celebrities). It was fun, though. She's a fan of Thompson's and she sounded like she knew who I was when I was introduced, although maybe she was just being polite. Regardless, anyone who had a song on the *Cruising* soundtrack is okay in my books.

Next stop? The ghetto, where else? And the brand new Colby's II. It was kind of gross, but Thompson and I had an

61

interesting drinking contest, daring each other to confess the most disgusting thing we'd ever done, sexually speaking. Even though mine, involving penetrative sex with an unconscious stranger, was about a thousand times worse than his, he thought his was more vile and made me promise never to tell anyone, so I won't. I didn't have to ask my other companion about his worst perversion because we share the same therapist and so I get all the information I need about Bellini from him.

We were having a good time but I was a bit bummed because I saw this regular trick of mine whom I'd never seen in a bar before, and he was acting extremely queeny, even though whenever he fucks me he talks real butch. I gather he is a male model or something. It figures, on both counts.

The new improved Colby's reminds me of Katrina's, the gay nightclub that used to be in the same location many, many years ago before I was born, darling, which seemed to be consistent with the Postqueer theme of the evening: le plus c'est change, le plus c'est la même chose. Especially when it comes to faggots. The very next day I found myself belted into the Trans Am of one of my little sister's boyfriends on my way up north to my parents' farm for the first time in several years—just me and my sister and my dog. The long drive went smoothly except for Cookie throwing up her Chicken McNuggets in the back seat at Orangeville (Cookie—that's my dog, not my sister).

Soon I found myself in front of my folks' tv set watching "Kids in the Hall: Chalet 2000", the Buddy Cole Special starring Thompson and featuring Bellini. It was a strange sensation to be watching my two friends on the CBC after our gay escapades of the previous evening, with my dear courieur du bois father sitting beside me on the couch with his bespectacled face buried in the local newspaper. As Thompson camped it up to an alarming degree on the tube, my Dad did not look up once, nor did he even register the homosexual spectacle invading his living room. (Not me, you idiot, the "Kids in the Hall" show.) God bless him—he wouldn't know I was gay if he caught me modeling a muu-muu. It did strike me, though, how incredible it was that this groundbreaking, risk-taking show infiltrates the homes of millions of typical families like my own every week, and how inspirational it must be for all the gay kids out there.

When I wasn't helping my Mom wash the dishes like a good son, I spent the weekend reading the latest biography in my continuing search for the essential tragedy of homosexual existence: *The Gilded Gutter Life of Francis Bacon*, the famous poncey painter who died last year. It was written by Daniel Farson, an old alcoholic queen whose moist-eyed reminiscences about this monstrous man brought me to tears on more than one occasion. Bacon was a cantankerous old cunt who could annihilate you with one snide remark, but he could also be kind and generous in his own way. He believed that homosexuality was disgusting but that heterosexuality seemed no better, and claimed that "friends are people who can tear each other apart". A man after my own excuse for a heart. Bacon's many broken and failed friendships made me think of mine, how regrettable yet inevitable it all seems.

You see, I have this bad habit of comparing myself to notorious fags. Say, I'm not so bad. Look at Fassbinder. Three of his lovers committed suicide, he destroyed and humiliated his friends, and look at the great movies he made. Fortunately, I have a friend who frequently reminds me that next to Hitler, Stalin was practically a stand-up guy, gulags and pogroms notwithstanding. Or something like that.

When I finished the book, practically in tears, I started thinking about River again. How curious it was that a young, handsome teen idol could burn out at the age of twenty-three, and how an ornery old masochistic queen like Francis Bacon, who drank excessively every day until the bitter end and loved to be horsewhipped by young football thugs, could hang on ferociously until the age of eight-two. Bacon once said that after thirty, all that is left is death. You do the math.

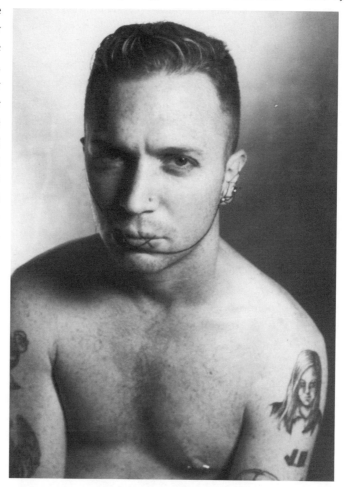

Mouthy LaBruce gets his lips sewn shut: the only way to shut him up, apparently. Affectionately note his Jodie Foster tattoo. Photo by Rick Castro.

Homosexual Is Criminal

Don't you get it? I mean, that's the whole point. Homosexuals are, by definition, outlaws and criminals. That's what makes it so exciting. I recently read something that explained to me my whole life so far. I quote it at length:

"Genet himself linked his pilfering to the first emergence of his homosexual desires. Heterosexual roles are reciprocal, not reversible (no straight boy wants to be his girlfriend), but homosexual roles are often redundant and a form of admiration or envy. For the classic homosexual sissy...the relationship to a sturdy, scrappy maleness is never a simple matter. The boy who is effeminé initially prefers the games of girls and the sociable, domestic activities of women to boys' squabbles and mens' competitive pursuits. Later he may respond to an older boy... but he responds not as a heterosexual boy with a trumpet call of comradely feistiness, but rather with breathless, charmed fascination and alternating waves of fear and attraction. The boy 'steals' the gestures of his idol. He repeats the beloved's expressions, models his actions on those of his friend.... The first act of homosexual love, then, is impersonation, but since he knew of the taboo, Genet links the guilt of theft to the guilt of homosexuality, which is another way of stealing, another form of forbidden appropriation."

There, you see? Homosexuality is built on the very concept of thievery–from the theft of ideas and aesthetics to the stealing of brief moments of forbidden pleasure that culture has deemed immoral and unlawful. No matter how hard we may try , we will never be "legitimate" citizens. So if you're gay, and you might as well be, go out and commit a crime today. It's only natural.

If I may be so bold as to make a suggestion, a good place to start might be a flagrant defiance of Bill C-128, the new anti-child pornography law, which I'm feeling more than a little freaked out by these days, if you want to know the truth.

Now you must understand, I'm not one to have ever really given a lot of thought to the matter of child pornography, having never been much of a chicken-hawk myself. Being slim and fairly hairless and, up until recently, young, I see myself as more chicken-identified. Why, just last week somebody characterized me as a butch bottom, thank you very much. Of course he was a representative from the Braille Institute, but never mind. Some of my movies have in the past been confiscated and/or destroyed at the border for such trifles as bestiality, bondage, nudity with violence, anal penetration, sedition and toe sucking. I'm currently working on incest and necrophilia, but I've never really aspired to what my good friend and confidante Glory Hole Domination refers to as "the last frontier": paedophilia.

However, now that this ridiculous, alarmist law has been passed, I have to admit the idea of having sex with high school students suddenly seems a lot more appealing than it did before. And as a homosexual, and thereby already having a predisposition to criminal tendencies, it's all I can do to refrain from running out and finding a couple of gay teens to make some porno movies with after school–as long as it doesn't interfere with their homework. You probably think I'm kidding, but I'm not. I never kid about homework.

There, I think I just broke several laws, like a good homosexual. For Bill C-128 makes it not merely an offense to publish or even possess child pornography–defined as "...visual representation that shows a person who is or is depicted as being under the age of 18 and is engaged in explicit sexual activity"–but it also makes illegal "...any written material or visual representation that advocates or counsels sexual activity with a person under the age of 18..." In other words, for me to write here that I think teenagers are sexy and that I'd like to lick one like a lollipop, or to confess that not very long ago I had torrid sex with a seventeen-year-old boy, could get me up to ten years in the "Holiday Inn—plus bars". The next logical step, of course, is to make thinking about sexy teenagers illegal—not good news for the Canadian branch of the Menudo fan club, for which I act as president, secretary and treasurer.

Let's face it, Menudo is just the tip of the iceberg. This Hispanic teen band, whose members are replaced, *Logan's Run*-style, once they hit the advanced age of eighteen, is emblematic of the cult of youth upon which the western entertainment and fashion industries are built. I recently saw the Elite Face of the Year contest on tv; the winner was a gawky, coltish nymphet of fourteen, dolled up like a Detroit streetwalker, whose prepubescent charm the media couldn't stop itself from slavering over. Michael Jackson is involved in a messy palimony case involving his thirteen-year-old male lover, who's taking him for everything he's worth. Child sexuality hasn't been this big since Freud invented it in 1912. It has been pointed out, however, that when a craggy, disgusting old Rolling Stone does what Jacko did, but with a thirteen-year-old girl, he gets a pat on the back. Homosexuality is still the crime that disgusts the masses (thank God) and, well, when it involves kids, it's heinous. There's no greater crime to aspire to.

I was a kid once. When I was eleven or so, I had the hugest crush on my incredibly sadistic, hypersexual gym teacher. With breathless, charmed fascination, I would watch him beat up other students, or sit animalistically and half-naked at his desk as he fingered his shockingly hirsute armpits. My favourite daydream involved being kept after school for delinquent behaviour, a locked building, a skipping rope, the cold cement floor of the equipment room, repeated rape...you know, the usual healthy fantasies of an eleven-year-old gay teen. Hey, I guess I could get arrested for writing down now what I thought then.

I hate the Wonderstuff. You know, that British band that recently came out with an anti-NAMBLA song (the North American Man-Boy Love Association, i.e.). It takes a lot of courage to single out the most hated organization in the world as the object of one's righteous rock'n'roll anger. Even law abiding homosexuals (you'd be surprised how many go against their true nature) save their most virulent intolerance for NAMBLA, who, along with drag queens (almost understandably) and leathersex people (even more almost understandably), must be kept at arm's length in order to preserve the integrity and respectability of gay life.

Now, I can't say I'm exactly an unconditional proponent of NAMBLA, since some members do seem a little creepy, but I'm sure there are some perfectly healthy and loving intergenerational relationships in which gay youths are able to express their sexuality consensually with the freedom they should come to expect. I'm not particularly worried that organizations like NAMBLA could make all homosexuals seem like predatory, sex-obsessed perverts whose sole purpose is to recruit innocent teenagers into the twilight world of depravity and lust, because to me, that sounds kind of exciting. (I mean, yes, it's a cliché, but clichés are, after all, merely overly ambitious truths, right? They're the Eves of truth.) I almost wish there'd been a chapter in my neighbourhood when I was growing up.

Anyway, I probably wouldn't even be thinking about hot, lean, young, sweaty, sexy, raunchy fourteen and fifteen-year-old boys wearing stained jock straps in smelly locker rooms if they hadn't passed a law practically forbidding me to think about them. But hey, I'm a homosexual, an outlaw, a rebel. I'll do or think whatever I want.

p.s. The entire text of Bill C-128 is reproduced, along with a nifty editorial that I just ripped off a little (must be my homosexual tendencies), in a cool punk fanzine called *Full Blast*, put out by Louanne. It costs two dollars plus postage. Don't be gay, order today.

Husbands and Wives, Homosexual Style

I don't know why I'm telling you all this. I mean, I am a homosexual (who knew?) and therefore anything I say can and will be used against me, probably by another homosexual, or a girl, so why do I even bother? Sure, whatever I say is bound to be entertaining because homosexuals, as you know, are all about show business, but why should I risk being laughed at and ridiculed by the masses for exposing the secrets of homosexual life? Shouldn't I be like a magician, guarding these secrets by some hypocritical oath? Why should I take on the burden of revealing trade secrets?

Because homosexuals are all about taking risks. You know the old saying "Live fast, die young and leave a beautiful corpse"? Well that goes double for homosexuals. Triple, even. Except lately the corpses haven't been looking so beautiful. But that's okay, because being a homosexual also means being a martyr. I mean, it's sort of a prerequisite. Actually, it's kind of relaxing, being stretched out like that, with your hands and feet securely nailed and everybody staring up at you and, oh, jeering, maybe. It feels right somehow, like you deserve the attention after all the bullshit you've had to put up with in this rotten heterosexual world. If I sound bitter, it's because I'm a homosexual.

Look, did I mention I'm a homosexual? Let's get that straight right from the start. I didn't exactly plan it this way, but here I am. Now, let's be clear about a few things. Homosexuals don't like women. That's the definition of homosexual. It means that you like other men instead of women. Heterosexuals like women. Is that clear?

I almost wish it were that simple, but of course, it never is. Because, you see, I am that particular style of homosexual who is actually as female-identified as a lot of women. And yet I am sometimes branded a misogynist because of my notorious fissions with the fairer sex. Well, darling, let me tell you, if I ever did get into a physical altercation with a woman, it would be a catfight, replete with bitch-slapping, face-scratching, and hair-pulling. I learned the technique by once observing two stunning punk women acquaintances of mine, one who dressed in the good-old fashioned, Exploited, bemohawked style, the other with a more Cramps-y, white-lab-coat-black-spike-heels-Racoon-eye-makeup thing happening, get into one of the goriest, whoriest fights I have ever seen.

It was in Pepper's old room when she and Spike lived with a couple of Goofs at Queen and Parliament and I lived in the condemned building sans central heating next door. Arguing over some indiscretion with another woman's husband, the two had at each other like proverbial Harpies, pulling out great clumps of hair and scratching at blood-shot eyes, peppered with some more butch manoeuvres like sharp, open-palmed jabs to the sternum. I tried to intervene, but they swore they would both turn on me if I didn't get out of the way, which I did posthaste, grabbing on the way Pepper's brand new colour tv that she had been saving up for so as it would not get prematurely busted. I and Pepper stood agog as one of the pair stomped upwards with her stiletto heel on the other's chest between her breasts, the skin bunching up in front of the sharp point of the ad hoc weapon as it approached her throat. This, I thought to myself, identifying like crazy, is the way to fight.

Sometimes I think I'm a heterosexual woman trapped in a homosexual man's body.

Historically, many of my strangest and strongest relationships have been with straight women. I guess that's because I am, after all, technically a man, but one who does not pose a sexual threat to the gals. Ursula Andress explains it best in *The 10th Victim* when she exclaims, upon spotting a group of homosexuals, "Oh, aren't they darling! I love effeminates! They're ideal friends for a girl! They're so amusing!" I am also reminded of Joan Didion's frighteningly accurate description of a variation of this particular category of friendship in *Play It As It Lays*. I quote it at length:

"There was at first that spring an occasional faggot who would take her to parties. Never a famous faggot, never one of those committed months in advance to escorting the estranged wives of important directors, but a third-string faggot. At first she was even considered a modest asset by several of them: they liked her not only because she would listen to late-night monologues about how suicidal they felt but because the years she spent modeling had versed her in the marginal distinctions which preoccupied them. She understood, for example, about shoes, and could always distinguish among the right bracelet and the amusing impersonation of the right bracelet that was merely a witless copy. Still, there remained some fatal lack of conviction in her performance, some instant of flushed defensive condescension. Eventually they would raise their eyebrows helplessly at one another when they were with her and be over solicitous: 'Darling,' they would say, 'have another drink,' and she would.

And who could forget the famous scene between Liz Taylor and her sissy hairdresser friend in *X, Y, and Zee*, wherein, after she finishes burdening him for days with all her troubles and woes over a couple of gin and tons, and he attempts at last to sneak in the recounting of a minor tragedy from his sordid little life, she snaps, "I've got problems of my own!"

Yes, the relationship between fags and straight girls is a complicated one. The fag-hag prototype is, of course, the most famous example, but it is by no means definitive. In fact, in my experience I have tended more to live vicariously through the sexual exploits of my girls, rather than the reverse. As an effeminate in high school, and thus exiled by the normals, I found myself hanging around with the girls who had the worst reputations in the entire school; the sluts, as it were, the untouchables. As it happened, they were also the most intelligent and entertaining and exciting, but no one else bothered to look deeper than their easy virtue.

68

Sometimes they would have ancient boyfriends, well into their twenties, who would chauffeur us around, buy us the liquor we were too young to get ourselves, and supply us with dope and mushrooms and Thai stick. The boyfriend would sit sullenly behind the wheel of his souped-up car as his girlfriend sat turned around in the front seat chatting animatedly with me, alone in the back seat, both of us ignoring him. Sometimes he would actually like me and stick up for me when I was threatened by some overzealous jock at the bowling alley, and sometimes I was merely put up with because I kept his girlfriend occupied so he didn't have to talk to her, just fuck her. Often I would have a huge crush on him, but this would remain only a fantasy imagined through her. And that, je presume, is why today I still act and feel like a high school slut.

Yes, I'm a sucker for wild women—the more neurotic the better. It's like the story somebody told me once about this girl in New York City, this debutante who lived Uptown. They found her unconscious in a gay bar on Christopher Street—naked in the piss trough at Boots and Saddles, a wrinkle bar, on New Year's Day in the morning, when they opened up at eight a.m. And this debutante, this exciting girl—I always cast her in my mind as a young Stockard Channing—gets assisted out of the urinal by a couple of gnarled old leather queens with handlebar moustaches, and she's like, "Where am I?" She must have had some wild New Year's Eve. Like before that night she'd probably never even met a homosexual before, and now she's waking up in a piss trough on Christopher Street, greeting the New Year that way. That's a girl I'd like to meet, or even marry.

Speaking of marriage, don't you just hate, loathe and despise those two gay male body builders on the cover of the latest *Out* magazine, the ones to whom Bruce Weber or Herb Ritts or one of those goddamn faggot photogs distastefully devoted an entire book? You know, the ones who actually took the marriage vows and became hyphenates? I mean, that's not what a homosexual husband is supposed to be about, in my conceited opinion. Oh yes, my Postqueer friends have husbands all right—a certain sports figure, perhaps, or a movie star or a porn actor, yes, but not a real person.

For example, I recently purchased a classic porno movie, *The Best Little Warehouse in LA*, by William Higgins, for five bucks off the street in New York, but accidentally left it at a friend's place there. When I asked for it back on a subsequent trip down a few months later, he pleaded with me on bended knee not take it away because, he said, it was the only video tape he had of his husband. You see, he had become inordinately attached, through repeated viewings, to one of the actors in the film, and had subsequently, in his mind, married him. And did you know that I was recently widowed? Yes, my husband, River, passed away only a few short months ago. That's my idea of a homosexual husband.

Which brings me finally, of course, to *Husbands and Wives* and Judy Davis, the ultimate neurotic heterosexual woman for me. Smoking cigarettes feverishly down to the filter, obsessing about her estranged husband in front of a nervous date while half-heartedly pretending everything is fine, yelling bullshit a lot, slamming down phones. She is my ideal wife. And coincidentally enough, she was co-starring with my dear departed husband in his last uncompleted movie, *Dark Blood*. I can just picture her, with a cigarette and stiff drink in hand, hearing the news that River was dead and the film to be left unfinished. "That's bullshit," she yells into the phone. Just the kind of wife every faggot prays for.

Your Movie Is Shit

Well, kids, it's been a helluva reel or two. (FYI, a reel, in gay parlance, equals a week.) Let's just say that the over-the-counter codeine Canada is so famous for certainly has come in handy lately, what with various lab disasters and post-production catastrophes, tv and radio appearances, print interviews, oh, and don't forget those pesky harassing phone calls. Yes, I think I may finally have that stalker I've always dreamed about, the one who proves you've finally made it. Sometimes it sounds like he is jerking off on the other end of the line; other times he says sweet nothings like "your film is shit" in a really scary voice; still other times he comes on like Chris Sarandon in *Lipstick* with some weird electronic-sounding shit. Maybe there's more than one of them. It's all too glamorous.

Now that I'm in New York, lounging around in a dear friend's tiny Hell's Kitchen apartment just a hop, strip and a jump away from 42nd Street, I let the events of the past few weeks dissolve in the stir of a pitcher of gin martinis. The various stress-induced ailments I always contract under high pressure circumstances—the hemorrhoid the size of a Cornish game hen, the ulcers, both duodenal and gastric—as welcome as inbred relatives at Christmas dinner, are finally getting the hint and begrudgingly leaving, and I'm coming about as close to happy as I ever get—which is probably closer than you might think. I'm even slowly emerging from grieving, over the loss of the second homosexual husband of my heart within a six month period. It was a whirlwind romance, but Kurt is gone. He once wrote in a letter to the *Advocate* of my "hilariously erotic films", so I wrote him a fan letter asking him to appear in one of them, but I never got the chance to mail it. Oh well. Twenty-seven doesn't seem that young to me anymore, especially considering, as I read somewhere recently, that the average life span of a gay male these days is forty-one. By that standard, Kurt, who claimed to be gay in spirit, made it to middle age, which is saying something.

So anyway, I'm sitting in the studio of a

quasi-famous fashion designer named Sylvia Heisel, in SoHo with a good friend and fellow film-maker who works for her, telling him the story of how I'd been talking to Gus Van Sant Saturday afternoon and he had asked me what I was doing that night. I told Gus about a big party for an underground music magazine I write for, and he said that he was going out to dinner with Tom and Nicole (Cruise and Kidman, dummy) but maybe they'd drop by later—but of course I never thought in a million years they'd actually show up, but they did. And as I'm relating this story, a famous stylist who is in the studio picking out clothes for an upcoming infomercial for Pantene Pro-V shampoo that he's going to be styling in Budapest in a couple of weeks turns to us and says, "You two sound like you should be sitting chatting over coffee on Rodeo Drive."

And you know, he's absolutely right, I have been feeling very LA these days. So later, I'm with a couple of friends at a relatively to-be-seen-at restaurant called the Odeon, and we are all dressed to kill, already slightly drunk, and boisterously catching up with each other's lives as only long distance best friends can. The waiters and wine stewards are literally fighting over us, bringing us sample after sample of wine—from other patrons' buckets, it seems—competing to see who will please our palettes the most. We gossip and yell loudly about sex and fame and the death of feminism and our analysts and end up paying the three-figure check with crumpled one dollar bills wrapped in bunches of twenty with elastic bands, the booty won that very day by one of my companions who works at Billy's Topless—the very strip joint that gave both Goldie Hawn and Madonna their respective starts in show business, and at which, most recently, tv star Kelsey Grammar was caught red-handed by the tabs ogling the burlesque beauties.

Later that night at a hot new nightspot called Squeezebox, run by another stylist slash designer acquaintance of mine, my New York hostess of the one dollar bills takes off her panties—the ones with Friday written all over them (it is Friday)—and gives them to designer Pat Field of the House of Field who, earlier that evening, held a fashion show at the 42nd Street post office because it's the final day to mail your tax forms and the hours were extended until midnight, so it was packed with people. Pat pockets the prize panties. Only in New York, kids.

A couple of nights later I sneak preview my new feature length motion picture, *Super 8 1/2*, along with my friend Glenn's short film, *Glennda and Camille Do Downtown*, featuring the irrepressible, fresh and supersexist, postfeminist guru Camille Paglia, at a fundraiser for the New York Experimental Gay and Lesbian Film Festival. Tickets are ten bucks a seat, but we still manage to draw a couple of hundred, including famous German filmmaker Rosa Von Praunheim—who afterwards, I am told, says my movie is "shit" (his films really suck anyway—say, you don't suppose he's my stalker, do you?)—and ex-Warhol superstar Taylor Mead, who loves it. Later, at the party at Flamingo East where a belly dancer is performing, Taylor autographs for me a photocopy he pulls out of his ubiquitous bag of press clippings of a letter he has written to the Warhol Foundation. Said letter chastises the Foundation for allowing Viva! to "buffalo" them into suppressing all six Warhol films she appeared in, five of which also starred Mr. Mead, because Viva! is now a stage mother in Hollywood where her youngest daughter, Gaby Hoffman, is appearing in an awful new sitcom and so Viva! is now ashamed of her illustrious film oeuvre—particularly *Blue Movie*, in which she has unsimulated sex with Louis Waldon, like I do in my movie. (Have unsimulated sex, that is, not sex with Louis Waldon.) Gee, I wonder if some day I'll be attempting to suppress my own oeuvre?

So along with his autograph, Taylor gives me four stars for my movie, saying that he had to admit that my precise homage to the Warhol film style in a particular scene "blew him away". I'm ecstatic, and I also feel pretty good; it's the ultimate kudos for me. Almost everyone seems to like it, including audience member Richard Kern who, the next day when I run into him on the street, thanks me for saving him from those antediluvian orthodox feminists who are always attacking his oeuvre. In my movie, I refer to his films as "sexy". Call it a gesture of solidarity between pornographers.

Well, it's off to Germany in a week or so for press screenings in Berlin and Hamburg. I'm a bit apprehensive, because German audiences are notoriously difficile. But it'll be a nice change from New York. My fag photog friend Ricky says New York is tired. In fact, Ricky says New York has been tired for quite some time. Anyway, I'd better sign off now. I'm feeling a little top-heavy. I'll talk to you when I get back. Love to the kids.

p.s. Postsensitivity is the latest movement for men, and reclaiming your masculinity is the order of the day. It may not be as easy as it sounds, however. On the way downtown to fax this very piece to Toronto (my portable fax is temporarily out of service), I was trying to affect a butch swagger while walking down Park Avenue and an Afro-American gentleman yelled out, quasi-admiringly, "Hey girlie-girl, girlie-girl, girlie-girl." Oh well, back to ye olde drawing board.

Meetings With Remarkable Fags

On KLM flight 642 to Berlin via Amsterdam, New York recedes in my mind like an old boyfriend's hairline. Some of the highlights, though, remain embedded in the postapocalyptic landscape that was once my memory. I'm so out of it–I totally forgot that someone told me Marc Almond was at my screening on Monday, but fortunately I am reminded when introduced to him at a club on Friday night. He loved both my movie and my friend Glenn's, who is starstruck upon meeting the former Soft Cell songsmith, one of his childhood idols. I've never seen Glenn speechless before. It's so cute.

Marc is a dreamboat: short and taut with great jailhouse and punk style tattoos completely covering his arms–somewhat more butch than I expected. He's totally unpretentious and sweet. We chat about various subjects, like the new album he's cutting in New York, sex dwarves, London, et cetera. Must ask him if he'll do a demented, dirgy cover of "Moon River" for the dream movie that Glenn and I want to but probably never will someday make: "Beyond the Boys in the Band". I have to tell you something. I stole that title, from Candy Darling.

I recall a great New York story told to me by Glenn, who works for fabulous fashion designer Sylvia Heisel–whose dresses we always wear when we do drag on the "Glennda and Friends" show on NY cable. Sylvia recently had a runway show during Fashion Week which of course was attended by many of the biggest magazines in the business.

Sylvia, a savvy, no-nonsense postpunk pixie, decides at a precise moment that the energy of the show is depleted, so she ends it fifteen minutes earlier than scheduled, at 2:45 p.m. At 2:55, who should stride into the showroom but Suzy Menkes, perhaps the most influential fashion writer-du-moment–whom I personally have been admiring a la distance for quite some time–the very woman Versace barred from a recent show owing to a scathing review she wrote of one of his collections. Menkes, who, of course, has a column in the *International Herald Tribune*, immediately pitches a Helen Lawson-calibre fit, ranting that the calendar clearly specified the Heisel show would be running until three o'clock sharp, and demanding to see her designs.

The bone-thin models already having fled for cigarettes and bread sticks, Sylvia has no choice but to show and explain each dress individually to the stern scribe, who is planted on a desk backstage with her legs crossed and a pad poised on her knee, furiously scribbling notes. I can just hear her barking to Sylvia, Susan Hayward-style, "Gimme a fountain pen, and not one of those lousy ballpoints," or "Sit down, Sylvia you're making me nervous." But it pays off: she gives Sylvia a rave review. I love legendary fashion world stories, don't you?

Speaking of legends, did I tell you about the Postqueer dinner party that Glenn and I held one Friday night at Rounds, the infamous Upper West Side hustler bar slash four star restaurant? Well, we decided to invite a few of our gay elders (while there are still some left) to an informal dinner party—homosexual pioneers who have paved the way for a new generation of artistes like us.

The honorees included: novelist and documentarian of the Spanish and Puerto Rican crack hustler underbelly of New York Bruce "Pretending To Say No" Benderson (who, incidentally, is also a confidante of Camille Paglia, who apparently gets a lot of inspiration from him); seventies pornography veteran Bob Alvarez, who edited all the movies made by Hand in Hand films, a company presided over by his late lover, Jack Deveau; and Miles White, the costume designer for the original Broadway productions of *Carousel, Oklahoma*, and *Bye Bye Birdie*, among others. Miles, who is seventy-nine years young and wore a black velvet smoking jacket, ascot and over-sized Swifty Lazaar glasses for the occasion, is a Rounds regular and favourite of the waiters, who all know him by name. Needless to say, it was a meeting of remarkable fags.

Oh, did I mention I have a new stalker? I'm at a nightclub in NYC that is partially dedicated this evening to my presence, and this odd, balding fellow with long fringe comes up to me hesitantly and asks for my autograph. In such scenarios I am always skeptical in the extreme, cautious lest it turn out to be some cruel prank in which the ersatz fan laughs derisively, crumples up my John Henry, and throws it in my mortified face. But the dude seems sincere, so I give it to him. He tells me that he loved my movie when he saw it at he sneak preview, and that he thinks I'm a "visionary"—there's that word again. I thank him, but the problem is he continues to stand at my side staring at me, even after I turn back to continue conversing with my companion. Sagely, said companion takes me by the arm and escorts me to the far side of the room. About a half hour later, though, I notice something, some suspicious speck, in the corner of my eye.

To my horror, it's the same deranged fan, facing me at a ninety-degree angle, not two inches away. I whisper to my friend not to look now, but to confirm that it is, indeed, My Stalker. He does so, gravely, and grabs my arm yet again to extricate me from an awkward, maybe even dangerous, situation. Before I have a chance to amscray, however, the weird one thrusts into my hand a piece of paper containing his vital statistics, muttering something about wanting to be in one of my movies. Not wishing to end up with a hunting knife jammed up under my rib cage or something, I accept it politely. Ah, the price of semi-celebrity. Actually, my Toronto stalker is more glamorous. Lately he's been leaving messages telling me I'm going to die. I hate to break it to you, baby (I informed him one evening), but we're all gonna die.

Well, I've just finished my delicious airplane meal—second only to hospital cuisine in my books—and am about to nestle into a cognac and my new book, *Obsession: The Lives and Times of Calvin Klein*, so I better sign off for now. Or should I watch the in-flight movie, *Mister Wonderful*, starring Matt Dillon, Annabella Sciorra, and Marie-Louise Parker? Decisions, decisions.

p.s. While in NYC, someone told me an LA story related to her by the effeminative Vaginal Davis that is simply too good not to pass on. It's about this infamous drag queen we know, named The Goddess Bunny, naturally, who was like, a thalidomide baby or something, so her arms and legs are all withered and crippled and she's really short with an oversized head and a

74

LaBruce and the Goddess Bunny: legends in their own minds.
Photo by Klaus Von Brucker.

face that looks kind of like a cross between Mercedes McCambridge and a T-rex, and she lip-synches to "Vogue" and does a great tap dance routine, although she's mostly confined to a wheelchair. She's been in several underground art films by this guy I met called John Aesthetic-Nihilism (Aes-Nihl to his friends), and yes, it is my duty to report, some pornos.

Only in LA, kids. Strangely, she always has a bevy of beauhunky hustlers around her, and sometimes she works the streets herself. She's even fathered a child in her day, as I understand it. Anyway, she recently gets evicted and needs a place to stay, so she wheels on over to an AIDS hospice and checks herself in. Thing is, she doesn't have AIDS. So she has a nice big bed and clean sheets and three squares a day, but it seems her hustler harem keeps dropping by and shaking down the real AIDS patients in the joint, relieving them of their last remaining worldly possessions as they sleep.

The understandably upset victims threaten to have the Goddess unceremoniously thrown out, so in the middle of the night, she rolls silently into their rooms in her wheelchair, puts a knife to their throats, wakes them up, and promises to give them an ear-to-ear happy face if they rat her out. This is my new favourite gay story, replacing the one in which a certain jilted lover in New York, who only wears endangered species, sent out an international press release revealing that his ex-boyfriend had AIDS. "Full-blown AIDS," that is.

Have you ever had one of those hangovers where the entire right side of your body seems to be somewhat paralyzed and you feel like you're going to swallow your tongue so you have to keep gulping spit and occasionally you have to consciously remind yourself to breathe and you appear at times to feel like you may be about to experience one

Danzig Needs A Blowjob

of those acid flash-backs that Art Linkletter always used to talk about but which you were convinced up until now didn't really exist? That's the kind of hangover I'm having today.

Last night I went to a literally underground gay punk club in East Berlin called Subversiv. Their logo has a picture of me and another guy on it, but the two guys, Bastien and Louis, who run the joint didn't know

Me and my drunk doppelganger. Notice the blank space where my Jodie Foster tattoo now resides.
Photo by Candy Parker.

it was me when they designed it—even though they have it on t-shirts and everything, and even though they've met me before and I've actually slept with at least one of them—because I'm bald in the photo and look like a skinhead, whereas now I look more like a French Nouvelle Vague director circa 1965.

Anyway, I was getting free drinks all night because if there's one thing in this world I can't turn down, it's a free drink, and I ended up talking drunkenly to Wolfgang, who is the recently exed boyfriend of Reinholt, the cute Bavarian boy I had a fling with last time I was in Berlin. I met Wolfgang at a crowded little Kreutzburg bar called Drama (oh, those Germans) where I went to rendezvous with Reinholt and another friend of mine, Marc, who is doing his M.A. thesis on Derek Jarman (but we won't hold that against him) and always makes fun of my nasally Canadian voice because he's a real Anglophile and kind of speaks with a pseudo-Cockney accent, which sounds way funny because he's so German.

So, Wolfgang is getting a little hot under the collar because Reinholt and I are spending so much time getting reacquainted, and then Reinholt and Marc and I get a taxi together to a club in the East called Plush—which is in a former restaurant where the Politburo used to dine after a hard day of Marxist revisionism—and Wolfgang is left to come in a separate cab with his friends who, frankly, seem extremely piss-elegant to me, I have to say. So at Plush, Reinholt and I are talking up a sturm, but finally I say enough is enough already because I no longer knowingly sleep with other people's boyfriends, ever since my karma kicked

in and it happened to me with a vengeance, and I don't want to be responsible for breaking up a relationship as I have done so often in the past, I must confess.

So I leave Reinholt alone, and later I notice him and Wolfgang having a long argument, and the next day I see Reinholt at a DIY sushi party at Marc's place, and he tells me that he and Wolfgang broke up that morning. (Are you getting all this? I feel like I'm giving dictation. How's your short hand?) So when I ran into Wolfgang at Subversiv the following night, I wasn't surprised when he virtually snubbed me. Later, though, when we were both drunk, we started acting like long lost army buddies, and he turned out to be a pretty down to earth guy, for an actor. That's the beauty of liquor. But I got a bit too beautiful and started to slur my words like a Bowery drunk, which I hate, but Basti didn't mind because we were both suffering from depression and besides, he's an Autonome (Mary, don't ask).

When the club closed at eight in the morning, he dragged me home in broad daylight, stopping for a peasant's breakfast on the way. We could have gone to another club which opens around ten a.m. (only in Berlin, kids) but I was already smasherooed. I'm literally sitting here writing this with a cold compress plopped on top of my head in front of Basti's tv, but I stop at one point to jerk off to a Danzig video (the one about his mother) because he is so hot, steroids and all. As far as I'm concerned, Sugar Ray is right: Danzig needs a hug—from me. Not to mention a blowjob. And of course everything connects, since, as we all know, Danzig is the German word for the northern Polish port of Gdansk.

I've also been trying all day to think of the name of the actress who played Michael Burns' sister in *That Cold Day In The Park* because I love her so much, the incestuous little bitch, and it finally comes to me through the funny shortwave haze of my liquor absorbed brain—Susanne Benton—and I wonder whatever happened to her and why she didn't become a big star, looking, as she did, like a cross between Elizabeth Montgomery and Ann-Margaret. Now I'm wondering if I can get enough money out of my producer to buy some leather chaps when I go back to New York. Probably not. Scheiss.

So Berlin is really different this time, because last time I was here the wall had just come down and there was a lot of optimism in the air, but now there's a depression and you have your rise of neo-Nazism and all, so it's a bit of a downer. I still like it, though. The thing about Europe is, it's so civilized. I feel like I'm a loud crashing Texas bore compared to all these demure, well-mannered Germans. One good rule of thumb to remember about German men is that the ones who you might think are straight are actually gay, and vice versa, except, of course, for the queens, because, baby, a queen is a queen is a queen, lisping "fierce" and snapping her fingers wherever she goes.

There is very little mixing of dykes and fags here, which is very Postqueer, in a double reverse with a half twist kind of way, and I hear the dyke bars, which don't let men in (good for them) are really dangerous, with lots of Prussian bull-dagger shot-putter types trying to rip each other apart with their bare hands. It reminds me of those exciting bars like Chez Moo and Togethers in Toronto in the eighties where somebody once whipped a billiard ball at local lesbian warbler Bratty's head, and where I once witnessed a diesel reach up and grab a light bulb, smash it against the bar and brandish it at another Sapphist who was getting a little too cosy with her girlfriend. Those were the days. Although I do like the new wave of power dykes. They don't get angry; they get cross. They're very Catherine Deneuve in *The Hunger*.

Faggots here are far better dressed and turned out and whatnot than their North American counterparts (except for the drag queens, who are hausfrau messes), have better taste in music, and they all chain-smoke and drink a lot, so I fit right in. I'd probably move here, but there's no call-waiting or twist-off caps and hardly any American tv, so I couldn't possibly. I could never live in a country that is still showing last year's episodes of my favourite shows. I mean, let's be realistic.

The evening I arrive in Berlin, my producer, Jürgen—who always teases me for being bourgeois—whisks me off to a gala presentation of the latest Claude Chabrol film called *Der Holle* in German and *L'Enfer* in French, but any way you translate it, it's "Hell". The movie is about pathologically obsessive jealousy, so I can easily relate. Afterward at the ritzy reception, I notice that the actor who plays the jealous husband and ends up killing his wife (luscious Emmanuelle Béart) is really nervous as he talks to important people like the German cultural attaché; he keeps playing compulsively with his cigarette, his hands fidgeting nervously behind his back. This gives me an odd feeling, like when I

77

was recently reading *Obsession: The Lives and Times of Calvin Klein* in the toilet of a jet airliner and I looked down and noticed I was wearing Calvin Klein underwear. I want Jürgen to give the invitations for my movie to all the important people there, like filmmakers Volker Schlondorff and his ex-wife, Margarethe von Trotta, and Ulrike Ottinger—who has just made an eight-hour movie about the Siberian tiger that I'm sure is really riveting—but he's chicken and I'm not drunk enough yet. Oh well, fuck them.

Germany is so advanced. Everyone is so adult. The U-bahn (subway to you) is based on the

LaBruce puts the camp back in concentration camp. Germany circa 1994. Photo by Michael Brynntrup.

trust system—there are no monitoring systems or turnstiles—so I'm riding totally for free. You can sunbathe nude at public swimming pools, and they just sort of decriminalized hash (their word for all types of grass, dope, what have you. It can also be used as a verb, e.g. "would you like to hash?") But it frightens me that despite all of these freedoms, it is still a very tightly-wound country. Everyone seems to be controlling themselves like crazy, in case they transform into a Nazi overnight or something, I guess. There are tell-tale signs. A cab driver won't let me roll down my window. An entire subway car is completely silent for an unusually long time. And everyone smokes, smokes, smokes, as if it is the only vice left going. One of my hosts smokes four packs a day, for Chrissake.

Apparently Italy is going fascist again, so I think everyone's a little on edge here because of that. I've also noticed that you can't make jokes about the Holocaust (not that you'd want to, mind you). I thought I'd crack a few jokes about the Holocaust, just to see how it would go over. Trust me, it was strictly lead-balloonsville. There are exceptions, however. Andreas, who works at Kinos Eiseit—the cinematheque where *Super 8 1/2* will be showing—has currently programmed a series of obscure movies that feature Hitler, and the logo he chose to promote the event is a happy face with a little Hitler moustache. Andreas is such a camp, if you'll pardon the expression.

The Berlin press conference was a bit of a nightmare. Sixteen journalists came and sat soberly and silently through my entire introduction, which was supposed to be screamingly funny so as to butter them up. Similar material had them rolling in the aisles in New York. There were a couple of scary celebrities there like Ulrike S., the Lothar Lambert star of *Fraulein Berlin*, and Jorge Buttplug, director of *Necromantic*. Many of the references in the movie are so specific to both North America and the American porn industry that I might as well have been showing an Earth sex-education film to a group of Venusian castratos (if, indeed, they have a boys' choir on Venus). Some people call it a masterpiece, others call it a piece of shit. God, I really need money for subtitles. Got any?

Time to sum up. Try to imagine a gay Canadian film-maker in the nineties dressed like a French New Wave Auteur from the sixties attempting to pick up a sturdy heterosexual Bavarian lad straight out of the forties with rough leather knee-length lederhosen and very little English, at a bar called Drama, and you might come close to understanding my most recent trip to Berlin. I was trying to make him because I thought he was a neo-Nazi, but when he told me he wasn't a fascist, I lost interest. (Mary, d.a.)

Miscellaneous, Not To Mention Gratuitous, Celebrity Items

Trent Reznor, front man for industrial act-du-moment Nine Inch Nails is, apparently, in an advanced state of style denial. Recently, at the neurotic New York nightspot, Jackie 60, I ran into up-and-coming fashion designer Walter Sessna, who doubles (who doesn't) as a stylist. Trent was, until recently, one of his clients. Walter had just returned from a disastrous two-day business trip to LA, where he had a major fight and final falling out with Trent. It seems the morbid musician (who had, incidentally, until a few months ago, been staying at one of the sites of the Manson Massacre—which he claimed, by the way, not to know had once been the former Tate-Polanski home. "Oh, that's why the rent is so cheap," he was heard to say disingenuously) accused Walter of leaking to the press that he was, indeed, employed as his stylist slash image consultant. (Walter denies any indiscretion on his part.)

Please, Mr. Reznor, there is no shame in having a stylist. After all, the entire entertainment industry complex is built on the backs of hard-working, style-wise, trend-spotting homosexuals. And I mean, it's not as if you're not already perceived as a tad cocksuckerish yourself. Smells like an advanced state of style denial to me.

During Fashion Week in New York, gorgeous Kim Gordon pulled a Monika Treut by showing her new Riot Grrrl Resort collection on the street between the locations of two major fashion shows, thereby snagging some of the attention from the fashion hounds dashing from runway to runway, including Fashion Ford Coppola and his fashionable daughter

Sofia. Kudos to Miss Gordon who, judging from her memorable Gap ad, certainly knows how to manipulate the media while coming out smelling like a rose: the savvy songstress got more attention for doing the ad than the ad itself generated. Good luck to Miss Gordon on both her new X-girl fashion line and her other new project—baby Coco. Love to Thurston.

(The expression, "pulling a Monica," by the way, means to sponge off other people's publicity, which is what Ms. Treut did at the press screening of one of my movies in New York. We happened at the time to be sharing the same publicist, who told her to get her German carcass over to the lobby of the theatre where my movie was showing to a full house of press, to talk up her new movie. I know this because she happened to rustle up as her date a certain famous gay novelist whom she pulled out of the theatre and made leave with her after only ten minutes, having already accomplished her task. Sounds like something I would do, but I suppose that's no excuse. I bear her absolutely no grudge, however.

Recently I allowed Monica to hire someone to impersonate me for some performance piece at an anniversary celebration for the Toronto International Film Festival, as I was in San Francisco at the time and could not attend in person. I'm sure the imposter did a better job of doing me than I could have. After all, as we all know, celebrity impersonators are amongst today's biggest celebrities.)

True R. Kern story. Recently, while I was over at Richard's in New York, being photographed with a big, thick candle shoved up my ass for possible use in *Future Sex* magazine—which I hate, p.s., but I felt I owed Richard a favour after he appeared so gamely in my movie—he told me that he recently had a "model" over being photographed, and he had her hung upside down from her feet in bondage but the rope broke and she fell right on her head. She could've broken her neck. And just try to explain that bondage gear to the cops. Fortunately, she was okay, and she didn't even sue. By the way, Richard was afraid to come to my post-screening party with all those damn homosexuals there. He's so cute.

True Glory Hole Domination story. Glory Hole was almost fired from Billy's Topless for a) flashing her pussy; b) licking her tits; and c) being intoxicated while working. The rumours about her drug use started when she showed up for work wearing the hip hop hat with "DRUNK" plastered across it that I bought her, not removing it for her performances throughout the evening.

Glory Hole also lobs her purse unceremoniously onto the small stage before she mounts it, and that same evening, the purse flew open, spilling out the contents of a bottle of Canadian aspirins (think Codeine) that I had also brought her from Canada (along with the "DRUNK" chapeau). The management and customers raised their eyebrows in unison as she tottered over in not much more than her stiletto heels and G-string and gathered up the pills, exclaiming, "My dolls, my dolls!"

The perpetual, completely natural smile adorning her face as she does the burlesque also may have contributed to the drug rumours. Anyhow, the owner of Billy's called her into his office to give her a severe reprimand. Glory Hole denied both the charges of drug use and pussy-flashing ("Why would I want to?" she asked, wide-eyed), and as for the tit-licking question, she promised never, ever to do it again.

Lucas Haas, child star of such Hollywood movies as *Witness* and *Ramblin' Rose*, was recently caught shoplifting a rap tape at Tower Records on Hollywood Boulevard in LA. The manager of the store, a rancid queen, took several Polaroids of the poor boy as he sat locked up in the back room waiting for the cops to come, telling him it was standard procedure for shoplifters, but actually snapping the shots because he thought the young actor was so cute. Excuse me, but if he was that cute, why didn't you just let him go? After all, Lucas was just carrying on a long tradition of star shoplifting, pioneered by Hedy Lamaar in the sixties. Kudos, Mr. Haas.

How Bret Easton Ellis Can You Get?

It's been one of those hauntingly debauched summers, the kind perhaps not seen since Geraldine Page played Miss Alma in Tennessee Williams' *Summer and Smoke* back in 1961 opposite the perpetually dissolute Laurence Harvey—an obvious role model of mine, to be sure, considering his sunken-cheeked presence in such great movies as the slatternly Elizabeth Taylor vehicle *Butterfield 8*, and *Walk on the Wild Side*, which also featured the delightful yet tragic Capucine (pronounced "Capoo-seen"), who not too many years ago, threw herself out of a turret in Paris in a fit of despair. (But then, you always did get her mixed up with Anouk Aimee, didn't you?) Anyway, I know it must have been a broken heart that made her do it because that's exactly how I felt when it happened to me.

When my heart broke, I mean. The closest anyone has come since then to touching my heart was when I got fisted recently—speaking, of course, both literally and metaphorically, which I am known to do with some frequency.

You see, I spend a lot of time trying to forget. In lieu of languishing in warm oceans or lakes, even in lieu of a Jacuzzi, I lie in the bathtub for hours reading magazines, magazines, magazines, magazines, magazines. Not to mention magazines. And the occasional book; although the only ones that make sense anymore are Bret Easton Ellis novels, whose style, of course, was influenced by Joan Didion, whose novel, *Play It As It Lays*, I recently based a movie on. And I occasionally manage to drag my carcass out of the water to attend an Antonioni film festival. Treatises, all, on emptiness and futility, set against barren modern landscapes.

Nothing matters. Love is elusive. Nothing ever seems to happen.

News that a friend is considering buying an $800,000 boat that must be moored exclusively in equatorial regions excites only momentarily. It actually makes me feel a little inadequate, if you want to know the truth. Reminds me of the time I went out onto a bay near a nuclear plant with a sturdy German friend named Gunne in a rowboat which sprung a leak, and she deftly plugged it with a hefty wad of gum she was chewing. Reminds me of my $500 fucking phone bill. I was kind of hoping that Jupiter would have been knocked off its orbital path by that celebrity comet that's been in the news recently and have hurtled towards Earth, sending us crashing into the sun so I wouldn't have to pay it. Didn't happen, though.

82

A little child, a wild little boy of four, recently came up to me in a restaurant and told me that I'm going to die soon. His mother assured me that he'd never said anything like that before to anyone, and that he's also very psychic. That made me feel a lot better. Coincidentally, the day before, on a whim, I'd watched *The Exorcist* on video. "You're gonna die up there." At least this kid didn't pee on the rug. I whispered to him that I predicted he would not be making it to his fifth birthday if he didn't bugger off. The little bugger. I went home that night and watched five hours of "Little Rascals" reruns, which were incredibly violent, all those poor children prodded and tortured for the amusement of adults. I laughed so much I thought I might be going a little crazy.

The next morning I wake up, and there is blood everywhere—the floor, the walls. In a panic, I feel myself all over—something I normally wouldn't do—to make sure it isn't mine. It isn't. It's my dog's. Somehow she has managed to slice open one of her hind legs.

Three days earlier, I awaken in the morning not knowing where I am. I turn my head on the pillow and there is the crazy Frenchman again. Fuck. I told myself that I wouldn't let this happen. Not that he isn't beautiful—I'm a sucker for a nice, deep scar, especially if it's on the face—it's just that I swore off violent, self-destructive indifferent men a long time ago. He also happens to be a pervert. I mean, getting your ass eaten out for two hours straight isn't exactly my idea of a good time. Well, at least not every fucking day. Christ, that's all he ever wants to do. Definitely a one-track mind. And the kid on the couch has still never been sufficiently explained to me, although he is cute, too, I have to say. Nevertheless, I bail. Aloha, with a steel guitar.

Blur is the only band that makes any sense anymore, and you can quote me wildly on that. They're all so pale and skinny—but out-of-shape skinny—and kind of, I don't know, passive and listless, and they're always hung over and throwing up a lot and complaining about PJ Harvey singing about her monthly all the goddamn time. They're awfully fucking cute, like a ninety-eight pound weakling version of Take That, minus one member and the West Hollywood posturing.

A Japanese fan slash friend of mine who lives in Osaka used to worship Take That, but currently he's fixated on Ricky Nelson, to the point where he dresses like Ricky did in the late fifties and combs his hair in a ducktail and even wears blue contact lenses. My little friend, Kee. He's so fucking adorable, I can hardly stand it. He used to go out with another friend of mine who is in a band that recently got signed to a major, but I don't want to tell you who it is because he's kind of in the closet, and I respect that a lot. I'll give you a hint, though. His band, unhappily, has a song on the *Airheads* soundtrack.

Anyway, where was I? Oh yeah, Blur. You know, they actually kind of turn me on. Maybe I have some potential for paedophilia after all, although I guess they're getting a bit old for that. Oh well, you know what they say. Be young. Have fun. Drink Pepsi.

Speaking of Blur, as in it's-all-a, I can't remember much about California, since you asked. You see, I went on the wagon for the entire three weeks—not a single drink—so it's all kind of hazy. I recall my friend Manuel driving me around San Francisco to all the sites where they shot the movie version of Armistead Maupin's *Tales of the City* (which, incidentally, my friend Miss Davis, who has a little cameo in my latest movie, has a little role in), like Seal Rock and Seal Rock Inn and the Windmill and Lombard Street—the curviest street in the world, also featured in a lot of Hollywood movies like *What's Up, Doc?*, which I and Manuel actually drove down like a couple of crazy tourists. And we went to Anton LaVey's house on California Street, which was painted black in the midst of all these quaint pastel abodes and had barbed wire around it and kind

The auteur with nuclear missile, left, and the big guy who babysits the nuclear missile, right. Photo by Marc Geller.

of had the same vibe as Glen Danzig's house, which we would later visit in Hollywood. Manuel told me that in his Misfits days, Danzig used to live with Jayne (or was it still Wayne?) County—you know, of "and the Electric Chairs?"—and that one of Manuel's ex-boyfriends used to fuck him. Fuck Danzig, that is, not Wayne slash Jayne. Then again, rumour has it that I once gave Nick Cave a b.j. in NYC. I guess anything is possible.

I and Manuel and MarcandKevin, the adorable gay couple we stayed with in swishy San Francisco, also visited a nuclear missile site one day, descending down into the silo on the hydraulic lift to see all these stealth missiles and everything. Very *Dr. Strangelove*. I and Manuel also spent an inordinate amount of time in MarcandKevin's outdoor Jacuzzi, with the cool California breeze rippling through their Anna Madrigal garden and against our exposed skin. It reminded me of a line from a song off the last Eagles album: "And still my Jacuzzi runneth over." I always loved that line. Something so debauched about it.

Still, I'm glad that when I and Manuel had been over at his friend's—the famous porno star Peter Berlin's—place earlier and Manuel had invited him back for a Jacuzzi, Peter declined. I mean, I'm so shy, I didn't even want to go in naked with Manuel—which he teased me mercilessly for, seeing that I'm supposed to be a world famous porno star and all—and besides, Peter had said that he never enters a Jacuzzi unless it's for the purposes of sex and, well, Peter is at least fifty by now, not that I haven't had sex with lots of people older than that but, well,

he's a legend, and trust me, you should never have sex with a legend. You'll only end up disappointed.

I and Manuel drove down to LA in his Cougar along the PCH (Pacific Coast Highway, darling). Actually, it was his mother's Cougar, which is all white, which he traded her for his Cougar, which is white with a black top, for the trip because hers is in better condition. I remember this because when we stopped for lobster sandwiches, Manuel yelled at me for sitting on the hood of his mother's clean, white Cougar with my allegedly dirty boots and showing no respect for him (or her). I accused him of being mean. It was the first fight of our trip. I love Cougars. They're like nobody else's car (I used to love that ad line), except maybe your mother's.

I was enthralled when we drove through Big Sur because, of course, that's where Vincente Minnelli's *The Sandpiper* with Elizabeth Taylor and Richard Burton was shot. I love that movie. We ran across a group of about fifty beached sea lions which we stopped to examine quite closely. That was Manuel's favourite part of the trip. The reason I know this is because he told me. He is quite the nature lover.

As I was saying, I can't remember much more about my trip to California because I wasn't drinking and all. But I looked great. Oh, I suppose I did show my new movie at the Castro theatre, which was sold out, fifteen hundred fags, and friends of fags, and friends of friends of.... And I suppose it was a big hit. And I guess when I introduced it, I said, "Hello, San Francisco," then paused, and added, "You old whore." And I suppose they were rolling in the aisles. And I understand I got a good review in *Variety,* and I guess it was the pinnacle of my career. Too bad I can't remember much about it.

A couple more things I remember, not that it matters. I'm in LA at a friend's house trying to watch the NBA finals, cheering rather too loudly, in a temporary fit of butch assurance, for the Bulls, when all of a sudden, the game is interrupted by an advertisement for a white Ford Bronco, but it's shot kind of funny, from a helicopter, and it turns out to be the whole OJ bonanza, which reminds me a lot of *The Sugarland Express* for some reason, probably because the onlookers are cheering for the criminal. If I was with Manuel, who is an excellent driver, we would go in his Cougar (or his mother's) to the freeway and watch OJ drive by because it is history in the making and all. But I happen to be with Miss Davis at the time, who is a Nip Driver (sorry, that's terribly lacist, I know, but it is the name of one of the all time great SoCal punk bands, which is why I couldn't resist), and well, she's in drag at the moment because she's about to play a gig downtown with her band, Black Fag, which also has Beck's mother as a member, Bibi, Bibi Hansen, who's a scientologist, I think.

A lot of Hollywood Jews and fags are. Look at Seinfeld, whom everyone says is involved in a long term relationship with a black comedian, which makes sense because his girlfriend, Rosh Hashana, or whatever her name is, is the ultimate beard. She's the beard of beards. But this is all heresy. I mean hearsay. I always get those two mixed up, which could get me in trouble some day. Anyway, like I was saying, Miss Davis also kind of looks like OJ, so the police might think she's him in disguise trying to get away while AC drives someone else in the white Bronco as a decoy. I know she's a bad driver, by the way, because just yesterday in the parking lot of the Hollywood IHOP she had to get a perfect stranger to park the truck she had rented to move with because, she said, "The parking space is too small," batting her eyelashes at him and acting like a damsel in distress even though she is six-foot-seven in heels, speaking conservatively, although she wasn't in drag at the time, but she might as well have been.

Incidentally, Miss Davis just wrapped a movie in which she plays a pool cleaner, and one of her co-stars, Kim Cattrall, says Andrew McCarthy, with whom she worked on *Mannequin*, is an asshole. But we all knew that. Although I have to say it was that very quality that suited him so perfectly for the role of Clay in the movie version of Bret Easton Ellis's *Less Than Zero*. Do you see how everything connects? Very six degrees of separation.

Anyway, two nights earlier, I and Manuel are driving our friend, Glory, in one of the Cougars—I can't remember which one—back to her sister and brother-in-law's estate—who are also famous, but I'm tired of dropping their names—in Brentwood, where she is staying during her visit to LA. She is here to teach a class called "How To Drive Your Woman Wild in Bed" at the Learning Annex—which I and Manuel end up attending, strictly for anthropological reasons—and we decide to pop by OJ's house and Nicole's condo, which are quite close, just to say we'd done it. When we get home very late, we can hear the queen with Tourette's who lives in the bungalow behind Manuel's yelling, "mothering cunt" and "cocksucker" and "mothergrabbing nigger" just like Linda Blair in *The Exorcist*. I wonder to myself how you can tell a queen with Tourette's Syndrome from a regular, run-of-the-mill queen.

Two days earlier, I and Manuel are sitting in his "office"—the Astro Burger on Santa Monica—which serves an amazing pastrami taco, although he is thinking of changing locations to the Yukon Mining Co. a little further east, but I tell him not to because too many transsexuals hang out there, and you know how they are when they prowl around in packs—and as we're dining al fresco, watching all the hustlers saunter by, I notice some city workers chain-sawing down a couple of dead palm trees on a side street, and Manuel says they have to because rats build their nests up inside dead palm trees in LA, and I think to myself, wow, how Bret Easton Ellis can you get?

Gay As In, You Know, Stupid

A dream. I am riding in an elevator with a girlfriend and an unknown Chinese girl to the penthouse of a skyscraper to visit my shrink. When we arrive at the top and the doors open, I discover the elevator has stopped short so that I am forced to climb up to the desired floor. As I am doing so, the cable snaps, and I fall backwards into the elevator as it hurtles toward the bottom of the shaft. While we are falling, the floorboards begin to break up so that there are only three planks left, one for each of us to stand on. The Chinese girl is getting hysterical, so I pull her over to my plank and talk to her calmly, even as we plunge

closer to certain death. Miraculously, the elevator stops at the last minute, and we are saved. Later, I am riding in a van or bus with a group of friends, among them Helena Christensen, my current favourite supermodel (along with Lucie de la Falaise and, of course, Amber Valetta). We are watching a videotape of the elevator incident, which had been recorded by a surveillance camera. I ask Helena if I can kiss her, and she says yes, so I do, deeply. Michael Hutchence be damned. Her lips are soft and full.

Interpretation. Well, I've seen *Speed*, so the elevator reference is obvious. In fact, I saw it at Graumann's Chinese Theatre on Hollywood Boulevard, which is the perfect place to see it because at the end, the subway car that bursts out of the unfinished tunnel lands squarely in front of Mann's Chinese. This probably explains the circularity of the dream, watching the beginning of it at the end, on video and, significantly, in a bus, just like the video monitor on the bus in *Speed*. It also may partly explain the presence of a Chinese girl (i.e. Graumann's Chinese), although clearly, this is also a reference to the China Girl who appears on the countdown at the beginning of most movies, an obvious allusion for any cinephile. The China Girl, therefore, probably represents my latest movie, a subject which I have been covering rather thoroughly lately with my shrink, to whom, in the dream, I was taking her.

The whirlwind of the crashing elevator thereby represents the recent film festival through which, for the most part, I calmly navigated my movie. As for Helena Christensen, the Christ analogy is palpable. Once again, I have martyred myself for the homosexual cause and, might I add, once again, thanklessly. The fact that I kissed her full on the mouth may well be an unfulfilled wish, because frankly, I'm tired of being gay.

Not so long ago, a fey friend and I were swishing across Park Avenue in New York when suddenly, out of nowhere, two straight boys, catching our routine, opined loudly, "Stop being gay; get a real life." Both being Postqueer, we merely laughed ribaldly and continued on our Mary way (as opposed to the queer route, which would have been to have called an emergency bake sale or some goddamn thing to protest verbal homophobic abuse). But lately, that phrase has been coming back to haunt me, with reverb, as in a German Expressionist dream sequence: "stop being gay, get a real life, stop being gay, get a real life" as I sit bolt upright in bed drenched in sweat. It's unnerving. And no, it's not AIDS, despite the rumours circulating—most recently, at a queer anarchist gathering in Minneapolis–that I am in the final stages of dementia and body-withering syndrome or whatever the hell you call it. I swear, what Michael Stipe and I have to endure as gay men in the public eye.

Now you must understand, it isn't the actual fact of homosexual desire that has become for me so unwholesomely jejune, but the state of the art itself. It's the way the gay establishment and media present the homosexual experience that makes me want to tear up my membership card. It's like what one of my little sisters says whenever I use the term, "gay". She goes, "Do you mean gay as in, like, homo, or gay as in, you know, stupid?" Increasingly, the distinction becomes purely academic.

So of course, whenever I find myself in this kind of dilemma, I turn not to Christ–because the cross gets so dull after a while,–but to Nietzsche, whose fascist underpinnings are a little too close for comfort for most queens. *Twilight of the Idols* certainly comes in handy. During the Toronto International Film Festival, it reminded me to appreciate the apparent world, to revel in its absurdities, to take its deceptive flatness for what it is: reality. You don't have to ascribe anything transcendental to it, no need to look for the deeper, hidden meaning. It's all right there on the surface in its glimmering splendour. Caviar is its own reward. As to the perplexing issue of being a tragic homosexual artist, I'm sure Nietzsche would be the first to point out that my suffering and indulgence in the questionable and terrible side of life is, after all is said and done, an affirmation of existence.

Hey, nobody said it would be all glamour, but then again what could be more glamorous than the torture of everyday life? But more to the point, Nietzsche's whole ubermensch thing is invaluable when you're trying to lift yourself above all the inanity that is gay culture, the rank conformism cosmetically packaged as rebellious individualism. It kind of makes you want to revisit Ayn Rand.

Look, let's just drop this pretense about all getting along like some big, happy, gay family. As Neil Tennant, the soi-disant songsmith of the Pet Shop Boys, recently opined in *Attitude* magazine, there is no gay community. Il n'existe pas, baby. Sorry to break it to you. Because outside of same-sex attraction, we really don't have anything in common with one another, unless the gay media establishment tricks us into believing that we do.

In the current issue of *Rolling Stone*, a bunch of female musicians can't seem to get by the fact that at some point or other, they have been majorly fucked over by another member of their own sex. Newsflash. Disenfranchised groups are not immune to such appalling behaviour. In fact, we probably invented it. But that's okay, because at least it means we're human, precisely what the Feminist Orthodoxy and its trickle-down sister, the Gay Community, want to rob us of. Well, I for one, don't want appear in yet another remake of *Invasion of the Body Snatchers*, homosexual-style. I want to make out with Helena Christensen. Call me a modelizer. Go ahead.

I hardly go to concerts anymore because I'm too old to stand up for that long, but I had to see Blur. I mean one simply must see the Next Big Thing from England, even though they're already Next To The Next Big Thing, i.e., Oasis. And I'd seen Suede last year, when they were the first Next Big Thing from England since, oh, The Smiths, I suppose, if you don't count that whole Madchester thing, which was all engineered by some large international drug cartel, I imagine. Oh, and I forgot about Primal Scream, but then again, so has almost everybody else. I love Suede. If you ask me—and nobody has—Brett Anderson and Bernard Butler are more than worthy successors to

88

You Can't Beat A Good Pair Of Tits: Blur Vs. Suede

Morrissey/Marr, the other husband and wife songwriting team whose marriage finally fell apart over jealousy, competitiveness, and unfulfilled desire—a trajectory I can certainly relate to.

And believe me, it's a harsh toke. I never really liked The Smiths that much (no, fuck you!) except for "How Soon is Now?", which is one of the greatest pop songs ever written ("Oh shut your mouth/how can you say/I go about things the wrong way/I am human and I need to be loved/just like everybody else does" was practically my mantra for several years), but otherwise I always found their music kind of thin and disengaging and, I don't know, jingly or something.

Okay, Morrissey is hot, in an onanistic kind of way, and he did pioneer the whole poncey boy thing, but nobody does it better than Brett. Brett like channels Oscar Wilde, man. By way of Joe Orton. I mean, okay, Bobbie Gillespie is skinny and gaunt and strung out and claps his hands like Joan Rivers imitating a seal when he performs, but Brett is so much more tortured, so much more Paul Jones in *Privilege*. The fans reach out for his hand as if his touch will send them to heaven, like all those over-dosed, suicidal, crashed-out waifs he sings about seeing in the next life. And I don't care what you say, I like the way he sings about astrological signs and "Pantomime Horses," and that every song of his must contain a reference to sleeping pills. I'm sorry, that's what I like.

Anyway, getting back to Blur, I think Damon, the lead singer, is really, really cute, and he's also really fey and poncey, but in a much different way than Brett. While Brett is all lethargic and pasty and pointy and boney and weak, Damon is more elfin and bouncy and coy and short and bratty. Whereas Brett is a man, Damon is a boy. Whereas Brett is heroin, Damon is beer. While Brett prances and pirouettes his hour on the stage, Damon pogos and parades his boyish charm. Both styles appeal to me. Actually, there's more than a little homosexual one-upmanship going on between the two—

recently in *Vox*, Damon opined, "I'm more homosexual than Brett Anderson. Always have been. As far as bisexuality goes, I've had a little taste of that particular fruit. Or I've been tasted, you might say. But...when you get down to it, you can't beat a good pair of tits."

Hear, hear. Of course Damon is referring to the famous Brett quote about his being a bisexual who has never slept with another man, but if you read between the lines, it appears that Damon is not above receiving a good blowjob from one of his adoring fans. That really turns me on. It gets really complicated when you consider that Damon is currently living with Justine of Elastica—next year's Next Big Thing from England—ex-girlfriend of Brett. Two guys fighting over the same girl while simultaneously arguing about which of them is the most gay. How delightfully twisted and twirled the Brits are.

Incidentally, where drummers are concerned, Justin of Elastica is the cutest, but I imagine he's straight. And I'm sure you already know that Simon Gilbert, the drummer of Suede (or is it the London Suede now? I can't keep up) recently upped the auntie by coming out of the closet as a boner fide, dyed-in-the-chinchilla faggot. Not celibate. Not theoretically bisexual. Not bisexual. Gay. As in cocksucker. But we won't hold that against him. Let's just hope it doesn't ruin his career.

As for the exact Blur show I saw, I spent most of it staring, at very close range, at Damon's cute little basket and the little hairy patch running down from his navel to his pubic hair over his little embryonic beer belly that you could see when he lifted his shirt up to tease the girls who love boys who want boys who like girls at the front of the stage. The little prince anointed them with much mineral water as they squealed in delight.

I was enthralled when they played "There's No Other Way" from "Leisure"—one of the best pop songs of the past ten years—but most of the songs were from "Parklife," which a bit too, oh, I don't know, *Harper's Bazaar*-sy by way of XTC filtered through EuroDisco or something. But I'm not complaining. And the rest of the band is cute too, especially the painfully thin guitar player who appears briefly in drag in the "Parklife" video (it's only okay now when straight guys do it) and who seems like a perfumed ponce. And I also liked the way Damon would put his palms together and place his fingers under his chin and tilt his head bemusedly to one side or the other, or hug himself in a very come-hither, NAMBLA newsletter coverboy kind of way.

Oh, and by the way, I haven't heard Oasis yet, but they're not even in the running, I suspect. The singer was recently quoted as saying, "I know I'm a lad. I can tell you who isn't. Anyone from fucking Blur." Jealous.

Austin

I just got back from Texas, if you must know, and I'm on a layover in Toronto before jetting off to Vancouver, so I have a few minutes to tell you about it, if you're interested, and why would you be? Austin, to be exact. You know, where *Slacker* was shot, and its director, Richard Linklater, still lives. Also the home of ex-Hüsker Dü-de Bob Mould, Butthole Surfers Gibby Haynes and King Coffey (sounds more like a couple of Hollywood-western character-actors to me), *El Mariachi* director Robert Rodriguez (I still don't believe it was made for seven thousand dollars) and, perhaps most famous of all, Charles Whitman, the Tower Murderer who, in 1966, shot forty-six people from the three-hundred-foot-high observation tower of the Austin campus of the University of Texas, where *Super 8 1/2* was shown as part of the seventh annual Austin Gay and

Lesbian International Film Festival. Fortunately, my movie was well received, so I was not compelled to re-enact the Whitman incident.

The capital of Texas, Austin is also very much deserving of the epithet "Capital of Slack": the long-haired, slightly vacant, oft-stoned characters of Linklater's movie are omnipresent, shuffling around the health food supermarkets, holding up traffic in their sloppy jalopies at the drive-thru bank, or dropping off their slacker off-spring at the drive-thru day-care. Yes, as you may have gathered, Austin, like LA, is definitely a car culture (did you know their are no subways in the entire state of Texas?), but it has somehow managed to combine this modern attribute with the unmistakable sloth of the Northwest. So, indeed, it is a slow car culture in which nobody seems to be in a very big hurry to get anywhere (O.J.'s white Ford Bronco chase must have seemed to them like a scene out of William Friedkin's production of *The French Connection*, I'm sure) and the southern drawl is less an accent than a philosophy of life. The eternal heat is partly responsible. I gather their winter is practically negligible; when I arrived in early October, it was still ninety degrees in the shade.

My guide was a fellow named Heyd (pronounced "Hide") who works as an art director in film and video (he had just done a couple of Sugar videos)–a native of Louisiana whose brother is a well-known rodeo cowboy. Heyd once dated King, the Butthole Surfer's drummer, so I was suitably impressed. He took me to see Bob Mould's house, a rather shockingly large estate in the quasi-upscale Hyde (pronounced "Hide") Park district. It kind of looks like a miniature castle and apparently it is in fact run by a real Queen–Bob's long-time companion, if you get my drift. Of course, Bob's homosexuality is no secret, but neither is it particularly his favourite topic of conversation in interviews. But as you know–and I shouldn't even have to tell you at this point–I support the closeted lifestyle one hundred and sixty-nine percent, so I don't even know why I'm bothering to mention it.

From all accounts, it appears to be the typical gay bourgeois marriage–you know, antiquing on weekends, boozy dinner parties, a little henpecking from his significant other just to keep his ego in check, that sort of thing. I think it's absolutely charming. Yesterday's punk hero has turned into an Edward Albee play. Couldn't be more charmed. Incidentally, perhaps Mr. Mould is about to become a little more forthcoming about his sexual associations–he has just completed a soundtrack for the upcoming screen adaptation of Dennis "The Menace" Cooper's novel *Frisk* (no, it's not about a cat).

Not that I think he should. Be more forthcoming, that is. It could ruin his career. As per usual, you probably think I'm kidding. As per usual, I'm not.

As soon as I arrived in Austin, Heyd whisked me off to the University of Texas radio station, where I did an hour-long interview for their gay program. The interviewers were two v. intellectual queer types whom I liked a lot in spite of their politics—very big of me, I know. Actually, in some ways the brand of queer activism they espoused makes more sense down there, owing to the pervasiveness of Christian fundamentalism, something which I was to experience first-hand the next day when the radio boys—a gay couple—invited me to drive up with them to Waco to visit the site of the Branch Davidian compound. As soon as we left the city limits of Austin, we were engulfed in a sea of Whataburgers, Baptist churches, used trailer lots, and sprawling Bible campgrounds the likes of which I have never seen. Unfortunately, time did not permit us to make a slight detour to Killeen to visit the famous Luby's Cafeteria where George Hernan gunned down numerous fellow Christians, but we did have lunch at an identical Luby's in Waco where only months before one of my companions sat while a swarm of Feds in quasi-fascist black uniforms with cute little matching black caps descended to dine before heading off to blow up David Koresh and his merry Branch of Davidians.

After lunch we got really, really stoned and followed the instructions given to my compatriots by a friend of theirs named Brother Russell who is known for his clever prank phone calls to fundamentalist Christian phone-in radio shows, collected on cassette tape under the title "Radio Jihad". Brother Russell had just been up to the compound the week before and said it was well worth the trip. His instructions started out innocuously enough—turn off the Interstate at Highway such-and-such, hang a left at the next exit—but as the roads became smaller and smaller and the farmhouses increasingly few and far between, they started sounding more sinister: you will come to a fork in the road, turn right at the water tower onto a gravel path. More and more, the landscape began to resemble Tobe Hooper's production of *The Texas Chainsaw Massacre*: remote, brushy, isolated, unmapped.

When we finally reached the compound, it was so nondescript that we drove right past it. We turned around and reluctantly pulled into an open clearing populated by a few craggy trees, a couple of shacks, a portable toilet, and several Japanese tourists with cameras. The actual site of the compound and bunkers lay behind in the near distance, fenced off and guarded by rent-a-cops. The shacks had been built by some of the surviving Branch Davidians, who sat quietly on one of the porches passively observing us tourists.

We talked to the woman who seemed to be in charge. She had a kind of Georgia O'Keefe thing going—brown, leathery skin, draped Indian fabrics—and turned out to be the widow of David Koresh's archrival, the one he had allegedly shot to death long before the siege and destruction of the Compound. She apparently remained a member of the cult—or rather, sect, she was quick to correct us, the Branch Davidians actually being a sect of the Seventh Day Adventist Church—and returned to try to set the record straight. Her side of the story, surprisingly loyal to Koresh, considering he killed her husband, was scribbled in Biblical fire and brim-

91

stone language and posted on the sides of the shacks and on the fences the government erected to keep anyone looking for evidence away from the Mount Carmel Compound.

In her version, which a lot of people in Austin corroborated, there was no "crisis" which precipitated the intervention of the federal agents (actually the FTA–Bureau of Firearms, Tobacco, and Alcohol–always my favourite combination); no evidence of the manufacturing of illegal drugs, which was the Fed's official excuse to intervene; and no proof of abuse or forced confinement of the women and children. In fact, videotapes of the children denying abuse were repeatedly suppressed. The woman spoke calmly with the slow deliberation of a martyr, and when I told her I was visiting from Toronto, she informed me that she had lived in Cabbagetown for ten years.

She also maintained that Koresh had a secret bunker below the underground com-

pound replete with hidden escape tunnel, which made her wonder aloud dramatically, and I quote, "Whose teeth are really buried in David Koresh's grave?" It was all very mythic and bigger than life. The area was littered with abandoned, half-buried buses which the Branch Davidians had acquired to use as underground bunkers; rather than go to the trouble and expense of pouring concrete, they merely buried the buses.

The warm wind blew dust across the buses and through the ancient trees as the setting sun illuminated the little army of crosses the woman had erected on the government fence to commemorate each dead Davidian. It was heavy. But like I said, I was way stoned, so maybe I'm making it seem more glamorous than it actually was. On our way back to Austin, we noticed that there were a number of other compounds of other sects, some of which, my friends informed me, speak in tongues and handle snakes as part of their religious ceremonies–even wackier than Waco, waiting for their own private apocalypses. Texas is so exciting I'm almost sorry I missed the floods.

The next day Heyd picked me up and drove me around to more historical sites in Austin, like the frozen yoghurt shop where several years ago four sisters were murdered in a bizarre, possibly Satanic ritual. Although the incident was reported nationally, few people know the true story–that the girls were chosen because they were all virgins, and each was discovered with a sugar cone deposited in the obvious region. We ended up at the Dobie Theatre on the UT campus where my movie was to be shown. In introducing it, I commented on how butch Texans are, but immediately retracted the statement based on the audience seated before me. (If you can't think of anything nice to say when addressing your public, say something really mean.)

Later at a house party held in my honour (Austin is anything but pretentious, and never underestimate Southern hospitality–I don't think I paid for a single meal or drink the entire time I was there, although they both would have only cost me about half as much as in Toronto), I chatted with lots of local artistes, including half of the apparently well-known dyke band Two Nice Girls, who was, and the fellow who is playing Leatherface in the upcoming feature film *The Texas Chainsaw Massacre, Part Four,* who also was. Said film should be interesting as it is directed by the writer of the original Tobe Hooper classic which haunts me still.

My radio friends also introduced me to the editor of the infamous Austin punk fanzine, *Sluggo,* a large, bearded, middle-aged man who had lots of fascinating stories to tell about the Austin punk scene–the Dicks, The Big Boys, et al. Currently a librarian at the university, he was actually a student there when Charles Whitman pulled his famous sniper routine, and remembers a professor crawling into his classroom to tell everyone to get down on the floor. It was a fun party, especially since everyone there seemed to be either a cult member or former cult member, and quite forthcoming about the details. Why, one fellow, a fundraiser for the United Negro College Fund, even admitted to being a former Amway representative.

Unfortunately, the trip kind of went downhill from there because the next night I was obliged to attend an awards ceremony for the festival which reminded me that wherever you go in this ugly, ugly world the banality of the gay community follows you like an overly ambitious cologne. I thought it might be mildly amusing considering it was the very first time I ever presented an award, but the event was so unintentionally camp, complete with antediluvian drag queens, rivalling Toronto's for sheer brainlessness (tits, I'm afraid, are not ends in themselves, girls) and frightening dominatrix dancers whose choreography made Juul Hallemeyer look like Agnes DeMille.

When I presented an award to a scary Dallas fag (you can easily distinguish them from the Austin variety by their big hair and facelifts, which actually makes me want to visit Dallas, and quick) who apparently loved my movie but said I should cut out all the sex parts, even though he couldn't stop talking about my dick, I announced that the proceedings reminded me of the Oscars as depicted in George Cukor's version of *A Star is Born* starring Judy Garland. Nobody seemed to appreciate the irony.

Later, at the post-awards party, and at the only gay bar in Austin that even remotely verges on leather, several fags made comments on my apparently infamous member, one going so far as to say, in a Southern-fried accent, no less, "Now you make sure you don't let that big dick of yours go to waste tonight, y'hear?" as if it were some sort of precious commodity, or if it were not exercised nightly, it might atrophy and fall off. This despite the fact that I purposely included a scene in my movie, which he had seen earlier, parodying such incidents in order to ward off this very type of interloper. Oh well. Back to the old drawing board.

On the trip home I had a stopover at the Dallas airport where I purchased a magazine, called *Texas Monthly*, with none other than Anna Nicole Smith on the cover, the Playboy Playmate of the Year and budding actress who recently wed J. Howard Marshall, an eighty-nine year old Texas oil man worth five hundred million. The accompanying article, which I devoured on the plane, described in detail Miss Smith's rise from her incarnation as Vickie Lynn Smith, Red Lobster waitress and single teenage mother, to high class stripper with extreme breast augmentation in such Houston hot spots as Chez Paris, Puzzles, and Gigi's, to famous model, to one of the richest women in America. More recently, she has been slapped with a sexual harassment suit by her female secretary and almost killed herself with an overdose of dolls. And somehow, as I flew back to boring little old Toronto, I found myself already missing the Lone Star State.

It's All Coming Back To Me Now

I may not be a completely successful alcoholic, or even a rather parochial or somewhat dilettantish one, but I have discovered a crucial paradox of the life: the more one drinks, the more intense and theoretically unforgettable adventures one experiences, but the less one remembers of them. It's like that Nirvana show I was once at but never attended. An acquaintance of mine, whom I run into from time to time, frequently reminds me of the time that he and I and forty or fifty other lost souls were privy to an intimate

Nirvana gig at Lee's Palace just before they went celestial; apparently, he and I, after God knows how many cocktails, were jumping up and down on top of a table like a couple of school girls. I do have a vague recollection of the year in question, but no conscious memory of this particular event, although I'm sure my unconscious had a ball.

Oh well, I guess that's how Kurt would have wanted it. In fact, I told him about it in a letter I wrote asking him to be in one of my movies after he had written in a postscript to the *Advocate* of my hilariously erotic films quote unquote, as I may have already mentioned several thousand times. I never got to send it, though.

Anyway, I've written this introduction as a kind of caveat because since falling off the wagon yet again, I can't promise to remember much about my latest tour. But I will try to dredge something up for you, not that you care.

What can I say about Vancouver? I hated it. To be fair, I was ensconced in a four star hotel for the first four days and, suffering as I do from occasional bouts of agoraphobia, confined to bed and bathtub. I did manage to order room service for the first time in my life, believe it or not. A steak sandwich and a shrimp cocktail. A peeler friend of mine once told me that whenever a client takes a stripper to his hotel room for a private, she always orders a steak sandwich and a shrimp cocktail—protein, I guess—so that's what I got. I wish I could have ordered the Chateaubriand for Two, carved in your room, with Béarnaise sauce, but it was sixty-two dollars, and I'm not exactly Howard Hughes yet. (I suppose, in order not to date myself, I could have said Bill Gates, but he's so dull. You have to have a license to be that dull. It would be kind of like saying, "And kilometres to go before I sleep." Mais je me divague.)

I guess I expected Vancouver to be more like Seattle or Portland, not that I've been to either of those places, but you know what I mean. Sort of a post-hippie, slacker thing going, a *Generation X* vibe. After all, it is the home of Douglas Coupland, who, incidentally, from all reports, is as big a closet case as Bret Easton Ellis, if you can believe that one. But that's okay, because, as I've probably mentioned so many times that it has become a running gag, I support the closet. Anyway, my fantasies of Vancouver have always revolved around two movies: Bob Altman's *That Cold Day in The Park*, which was not only shot but also set there—and which I remade once myself (not to brag or anything, but when I met Richard Miles, the author of the original book, he said he preferred my low-budget, pornographic, trashy version)—and, of course, *Hookers On Davie*. I half expected to see Sandy Dennis scouring the parks for forlorn, mute male waifs to lock up in her guest bedroom, or to run into one of the transsexuals who says "severe" a lot in that fine Canadian documentary. But alas, Sandy Dennis fell victim to the Big "C" several years ago, and the hookers are probably all dead now, or worse. The prostitutes of Davie Street have been subjected to the same diaspora as those of Yonge Street, which has been mildly gentrified and sanitized since its seventies heyday, and the era of the great gay bars (the Paramount, the St. Charles Tavern, the Quest, and Cornelius). Wait while I wipe a tear from the corner of a bloodshot eye.

Ah, well. Onward and downward. The two highlights of my Vancouver experience were: a) hanging out with my cute little Japanese distributor, Suzuki-san, getting tipsy and bowing to each other politely as if we were stuck in a racist Jerry Lewis movie; and b) being asked at a highfalutin' Film Festival party if the salsa was too hot by—you'll never guess—Stella Stevens. Yes, Stella Stevens. One of my idols. Star of *The Nutty Professor* and *Where Angels Go, Trouble Follows*, not to mention *How To Save Your Marriage-And Ruin Your Life* and *The Ballad of Cable Hogue*. I was so starstruck, all I could do was mumble, "No, I think it's okay, actually." I could have at least asked her how Andrew is doing.

Later, at a Q and A after one of my screenings, the first question—in front of five hundred people, mind you—was, "You have a lot of white cocks and black cocks in your mouth in that film of yours, but this is Vancouver. Why were there no Asian cocks?" It is true, I did not realize that Vancouver, owing to its closer proximity to the Far East, does have a rather large Asian population, and it is also true that while making my movie, I neglected to take into account that at some point in the distant future it might be playing in Vancouver where the lack of Asian representation could very well disappoint some rancid old rice queen. But, always the diplomat, I merely replied that my mouth is only so big, that I can only fit so many races into it at a time.

My overall, albeit limited, impression of Vancouver was of a rather provincial city trying desperately to be cosmopolitan. Kind of like Toronto. But at least in Toronto you don't get attitude based on not having any attitude. Wow, I think I just read an entire city. I'm feeling a little top-heavy.

New Orleans and London I can't remember at all. I vaguely recall painting my nails with silver varnish in a bubble bath in yet another four star hotel while listening to "Come As You Are" from "Nirvana Unplugged in New York" on my Walkman—a practice that I had previously disapproved of for men (nail-painting, not bubble baths or listening to Nirvana) until Kurt started doing it. That must have been London, because they call it "varnish" in England, as opposed to "polish" in America. It's all coming back to me now. New Orleans was very *Interview With A Vampire*, obviously. (A great movie by the way, which proves, once and for all, that having two gay Dads simply does not work.)

I spent a certain amount of time in grave-yards, where, owing to the city's proximity to sea level, the corpses must be buried above ground in tombs and mausoleums. The gay scene is a bit grotesque, because it spills out onto the streets in the ghetto every liquor-ridden night, as if every day is Pride Day, a "Night Gallery" episode if ever there was one. My movie was playing at a small art house theatre in the middle of nowhere, and could not be publicized in the *Times Picayune*—the only New Orleans daily—owing to its policy of not promoting smut, even though the film reviewer, who is gay—not to mention the brother of Chi Chi Valenti, proprietress of Jackie 60 in New York City—told me he liked it a lot. Nevertheless, a surprising number of brave souls made their way to the screenings.

Oh, and I did fall in love, sort of. I mean, I've been falling in love a lot lately—well, twice in two months, if you must know. Maybe it has something to do with the fact that I've grown tired of the gay male handshake—i.e., introducing yourself to someone by fucking them, rather than getting to know them more intimately, in increments. Or maybe it has something to do with meeting two handsome, sweet, intelligent Englishmen who aren't professional gays. I don't want to reveal too many of the details (to protect the innocent); let's just say there was a lot of snogging involved. I spent Hallowe'en with one of the gentlemen in question in a supersleazy joint in the Latin Quarter, a bar actually quite reminiscent of those defunct Toronto establishments I was mentioning earlier.

Death was there, living it up: a person of indeterminate sex dressed in a black hooded robe and skeleton mask, complete with scythe, snapping His fingers and dancing groovily to the astonishingly comprehensive jukebox. Apparently, a few months earlier, He had claimed a victim in a particularly dark back room at another gay bar in town; the corpse—which, theoretically, could have been sexually active all evening—was not discovered until daylight. Back in the land of the living, the old shooters and alarmingly stiff bourbons ensued until, baked, at six in the morning, my new friend and I stumbled arm in arm back to my hotel. Unfortunately, I was to be picked up in two hours for the airport.

96

The next thing I remember, I was on a Detroit-bound airplane and, I noticed, glancing at my reflection in the window, I had somewhere acquired a white baseball hat with a black eight ball on it. Later, I discovered that when I left, still dead-drunk, I had inadvertently locked my companion of the previous evening in my hotel room—influenced subconsciously, I have no doubt, no doubt at all, by Sandy Dennis—and stolen his prize hat. Quite feasible, considering I can't even remember getting on the plane—a feat I had not accomplished since a flight from San Francisco to Los Angeles in 1992. Fortunately, my friend was more than understanding, and since Fed Ex-ing him his chapeau, we remain tight.

London is coming back. The last time I was there it seemed rather dismal and depressed and bleak and hopeless, but now it seems really upbeat and happening and exuberant and fin de siècle. Or maybe it's just me. It is too crowded, though, and the traffic is abominable. In fact, one day I spent an hour in a car for a trip that should have only taken ten minutes, and missed the Q and A for my press screening. Oh well. They probably thought I was just being princely.

After one of my public screenings at the National Film Theatre, an elderly Egyptian married couple cornered me aggressively and said ominously, "We are from the East, and we must know. What is your movie all about?" The husband added, "I have been to San Francisco. I know of your people." They weren't being mean or rude, just curious, having never seen blowjobs and buggery before, I suspect, so I filled them in. It was kind of like two tribes coming together.

Marc Almond came to see the movie again, having already attended a screening in New York, and he invited me over one evening to watch some videos with friends at his home—a huge converted church with a fireplace you could park a car in. We watched The Bad Seed, which Marc had never seen before, and bonded over our mutual identification with Rhoda Breedlove.

Apart from that, I mostly hung out with a small group of artistes and journalists who, like me, are starting to believe more strongly every day that the gay community must be destroyed. In fact, one of my London friends is editing an upcoming anthology entitled Anti-gay, to which, you can bet, I will be the first in line to contribute. As for my romantic interlude, might I remind you that discretion is the better part of valour?

Let me just say that he was a devilishly handsome rockabilly gentlemen and painter with a broad Lancashire accent; that there was no sex involved, but he did end up with what he referred to as the biggest hickey in London; and that I fell in love the moment he said of my Farrah Fawcett-Majors t-shirt (given to me by my dear friend, Grief), "That's a fetchin' top you 'ave on." I will also reveal that we did a lot of snogging at the Market Tavern—the very bar where Freddie Mercury met his longtime companion and Burt Reynolds look-alike, Jim Hutton (not to be confused with Timothy's late father), but that's all I'm going to say. I really don't have time to tell you about my codeine overdose.

You see, after pulling a dirty stopover with the rockabilly dreamboat, I had a Joan Didion-calibre headache, and I figured the codeine pills he offered me were the same strength as what my American friends call "Canadian aspirins" (over-the-counter Tylenol with codeine), which each contain eight mg, so I took three of four, but they actually each contained thirty mg, having belonged to his longtime companion who had recently died of AIDS. Then I had to go directly to the Institute of Contemporary Art for an on-camera interview for their archives. It should be quite an archival moment, as I was stoned to the brink

of coma. Good thing I had my Terminator sunglasses with me. God knows what I said, but I don't.

Anyway, I must go now, as my pizza is here (delivery of which, by the way, has only recently come to London), and "Barbra: The Concert" is about to begin. Having enjoyed a guilt-free double bill of *The Way We Were* and *On a Clear Day You Can See Forever* with my Postqueer host in England, I feel compelled to watch. After all, with Judy gone, she is our leader.

Bruce LaBruce: Why Not?

If you must know, I just finished watching "My So-Called Life," or "Life," as I and a couple of my friends call it. As in, "Hey, how was "Life" this week?" or "I will be so bummed if "Life" gets cancelled." It really is the best show on television, even if it does fail miserably from time to time. And although I'm not feeling very Left-identified these days, the introduction of the gay high school teacher was, I have to admit, a stroke of liberal genius. And so what if the show is inconsistent—there's always Jordan Catelano to stare at in awe. Anyway, now, I suppose, I'm expected to tell you about my so-called life, or "life," as I like to call it.

Well, speaking of non-Left-identified faggots (i.e., me), did I mention I was at Paul Morrisey's X-mas party in New York several weeks ago? You know the gay arch-conservative Warhol alumnus and director of such classic, self-loathing, unwholesomely thinly concealed gay subtextual movies as *Flesh*, *Heat*, *Andy Warhol's Frankenstein*, *Andy Warhol's Dracula*, *Forty Deuce*, *Mixed Blood*, *Spike of Bensonhurst* and *Beethoven's Nephew* (in that order)? Well, I was. Of course, I wasn't really invited per se; a friend of mine, also a film-maker and part-time drag queen, happens to work for M. Morrisey's niece, a top fashion stylist, who invited him, who in turn dragged me along. Being the social-climbing, Neely O'Hara-style faggots that we are, we were appropriately excited by our little window of opportunity and, dressed in smart suits, headed for the Townhouse for a pre-party, self-congratulatory cocktail.

The Townhouse is the kind of gay bar that Toronto needs desperately: situated in the East 50's, and without so much as a placard to alert passersby of its existence, it is a very upscale, very discreet establishment (Queers may want to take a moment to look up "discretion" in the dictionary although, ironically, I suppose they won't find my picture beside it) catering to gay professionals (as opposed to professional gays) who congregate to talk of stock options and palimony suits and, oh, who is keeping which Broadway chorus boy at what cold water flat in Chelsea. The decor is decidedly, and probably somehow appro-

Ciao, Manhattan. Bruce does his Edie routine. The future is the bottom of a swimming pool.
Photo by Eric Johnston.

priately, funereal in tone, conjuring the old adage, "You show me a happy homosexual and I'll show you a gay corpse". The atmosphere is subdued, with occasional bursts of deranged, queeny laughter or the forced mirth of show-tune dementia at the piano bar. The carpeting is beige and so thick as to suggest soundproofing may have been in mind when it was chosen, neatly reinforcing the closet-y ambience. Small alcoves replete with tasteful end tables and kitschy knick-knacks complete the picture.

As we sat on what could only be described as a divan and looked out at the sea of expensive suits before us, my companion turned to me and inquired blithely, "I wonder if a lot of these men are married." Without thinking, I replied rather wistfully, "Yes, I suppose they are," and then added, after a thoughtful pause, "Oh, you mean to women." I then opined that there were probably a lot of both types of married gentlemen present.

Seated near us was a typical, if somewhat on the young end of the scale, Townhouse patron: a youthful man in his early thirties sporting a really good camel's hair coat (it's almost impossible to get a really good camel's hair coat these days), a shopping bag from some expensive department store tucked compactly between his loafer-ed feet. After no doubt just spending hours elbowing his way through hysterical X-mas shoppers to buy his hateful parents several pricey, tasteful, soulless gifts, I'm sure he wanted nothing more than to sit and have a quiet, private drink in the anonymous company of his peers.

Hovering over him, however, was an already-drunk-by-dinner fortysomething faggot in a vicuna sweater who, having spotted his young prey, proceeded to sit on the delicate glass coffee table in front of us, all the better to chat up the young refugee shopper. After listening to the drunk deliver a series of unsuccessful pick-up lines to the stony face of the Log Cabin Society Member, we could not help but notice that the little table on which the former was planted seemed about to give way beneath his not inconsiderable girth. When my companion pointed this out to

99

him with as much tact as possible under such circumstances, he lumbered to his feet muttering apologies and then, as if in a screwball comedy, started to teeter, teeter, then fall towards us, accompanied by a phony-sounding "Whoa-oh-oh".

For a moment I was reminded of Holly Golightly yelling, "Timber!" at the stoned, about-to-topple Mag Wildwood. The drunken faggot fell just shy of the table but in the ensuing confusion managed to spill our martinis, and his, all over us. Disdaining even a pretense of concealing our disgust, we brushed vigorously at our suits and made our way silently to the front bar, leaving the young conservative dreamboat to fend for himself.

Sufficiently fortified by several more martinis, it was time to hail a cab and ascend to the Upper East 80's where the Paul Morrisey soirée awaited us. Following our grand entrance–observed by no one–into the ancient brownstone and the antique elevator, the doors opened up to an apartment luxurious by any standards: a high-ceilinged affair taking up the entire story and crammed full of expensive early American furniture and international objets d'art, although, suspiciously, without a Warhol in sight. (My guess is he's living off them, since he hasn't made a movie in quite a few years.) On a gilt table, I noticed an X-mas card from John Waters, consisting of a grisly photo of facial plastic surgery accompanied by the filmmaker's loopy autograph. (I had just seen John Waters–or, as Russ Meyer called him in a recent issue of *Detour* magazine, which, incidentally, I had just done a photo shoot for the day before (more on that later), "That kid, what's-his-name, who had the flop movie with Kathleen Turner"–a few days earlier at a club called Squeezebox run by a friend of mine who told me that when he told Mr. *Pink Flamingos* of my movie, *Super 8 1/2,* Waters said it was the best movie title he'd ever heard. So when they start giving out awards for titles.... But back to our story.)

Of course, we knew no one there (the niece was on vacation in California), only recognizing the waxworks–aged film stars like Sylvia Miles and Monique Van Vooren who have appeared in the Morrisey oeuvre, and several high profile gossip columnists, such as Richard Johnson of the *New York Post*'s Page Six. You know, the one who once challenged Mickey Rourke to a boxing match. So we mainly stayed to ourselves, complimenting each other on our suits and loading up on the hors d'oeuvres and free booze. Finally, my companion said that it would be rude of us not to introduce ourselves to the host, so we approached him delicately, as one does with celebrities.

After chatting to Mr. Morrisey about his niece and her connection to him, my companion turned to me and said, anticipating at least a glimmer of recognition, "And this is my friend, Bruce LaBruce." Mr. Morrisey, who had the bearing of a weekend yachtsman, looked at me and repeated the name, "Bruce LaBruce," almost as if to himself, then paused, and, perhaps in the spirit of the season, added generously, "Why not!" I'm not sure precisely what he meant by it—perhaps it was a holdover from the "anything goes" mentality of his Warhol period, although somehow I think it was more likely dismissive—but before we could figure it out, some other faggot came up and whisked him away to charm other guests. I love that story.

If you want to know what else I did in New York, you might consult *New York* magazine—although by the time you read this it will be off the shelves—for a little item in the "Gotham" section under the heading "Activism: A scene in two acts". It seems my dear friend, Glenn(da)—actually, if truth be known, my companion from the Morrissey story—arranged for a reporter to be present when we descended, in drag, upon the Aesthetic Realist Foundation to ask the members to cure us of our homosexuality. The Aesthetic Realists are some strange art cult

Designy Living: LaBruce in Gaultier for a quasi-glamorous photo shoot. Polaroid by Eric Johnston.

who, apparently, are not unlike the scientologists in certain respects, particularly regarding the good sense—both socially and financially—of functioning heterosexually in the world, even if only as a public demonstration of decorum and good faith. Several prominent people—including, I think, William Atherton, talented star of some excellent movies of the seventies such as *The Sugarland Express*, *The Day of the Locust* and *Looking for Mr. Goodbar*—once claimed to be cured of their homosexual affliction by this fine organization whose philosophy, as I understand it, is based on the harmony of opposites. The punch line of the piece, of course, is that the two drag queens (including yours truly) ostensibly haranguing the group are also anti-gay, albeit in a slightly more complex, or perhaps less complex, way.

Actually, to quote a line from the underrated Paul Schrader movie, *Light Sleeper*, "it's TCTE"—Too Complicated To Explain. You'll have to watch "Glennda and Friends", for which we videotaped the event, to figure it all out.

As to the *Detour* photo shoot alluded to earlier, I thought I should mention it because it was the first time I actually got to wear designer clothes—Gaultier and Dolce & Gabbana, to be exact—and had my very own stylist and all; although I'm sure they'll end up using the haggiest, ugliest shots, and I'll be mortified, or else they'll probably drop the idea altogether. But for a moment there, it was almost glamorous, on the verge of being glamorous.

Sundance, Bloody Sundance

Okay, it's true, I did go to Sundance. I did. I'll be the first one to admit it. But I didn't want to go. They made me. When I asked Telefilm Canada for the cash to fly down, a) I didn't really think they'd give it to me, and b) I thought if they did, I could just pocket the dough and maybe buy that new stereo I need, or that laptop, or maybe even a trip to London or something. But of course there were conditions attached. Not only would I have to provide proof that I had been on the plane to and from Salt Lake City,

but it would also be specified that I must adhere to the following conditions: 1) I must pledge to promote not only my movie (which I am so sick of), but also the Canadian Film Industry in general (because I'm so ambassadorial by nature, as you can plainly tell); and 2) I must submit a written report of all my activities and contacts made at the festival. Gosh, does that include that line of coke shared with a semi-famous actress in the ladies room of the hospitality suite? Anyway, I'm really busy so this diary entry will have to double as my report. I hope that's okay.

I was in Park City, Utah, home of the Sundance Film Festival, for exactly forty-seven hours, which seemed like forty-seven days, if you want to know the truth. Grasping for a simile to describe the experience, I might say that it was not unlike sharing a Jacuzzi with a school of sharks, albeit sharks with cellular phones and the most painstakingly chosen casual clothing I had ever seen. What can I say, it was brutal. A war zone. Every man for himself. It was very entertaining. I mean, they don't call it show business for nothing.

To begin with, I had come down with a nasty cold the day before I was to leave; the only way I could pull it together for the airport was to stop just short of an overdose on Theraflu or Neocitron or whatever the hell you call that dangerous chemical cocktail with vaguely hallucinogenic properties which is designed to make you so stoned you forget you're ill. (Let there be no mistake, it's a potent brew—don't forget, there's been some speculation that River's fatal o.d. was compounded by the presence in his system of some such cold medicine.) As a consequence, I can't really recall the flight down, although I seem to remember listening in my delirium to Oasis on my Walkman ("I know a girl named Elsa/She's into Alka Selza/She shoots it through a cane on a supersonic train/And she makes me laugh/I've got her autograph"). It was very trippy, because under the influence of those medicinal white crystals I was Elsa, except on a plane, not a train.

Actually, I had just spent the previous week listening obsessively to that song, tottering around on my new platform shoes which I hadn't brought with me because they would have taken up half my suitcase, and I figured they might not be so practical at a ski resort—which turned out to be true, since the streets of Park City were mostly at a forty-five degree angle and covered in ice, with cellular phone people falling on their asses all over the place, non-stop, the whole time I was there. So instead, I took a Polaroid of them—my platforms, i.e.—before I left to give to my friend DJ in case he wanted it for AMOS, his gallery (the American Museum of Snapshots) in Portland, Oregon, where he had come from via LA with his ex, Gus, another friend of mine. I had arranged to meet them in Salt Lake so I could bum a ride with them to Park City because otherwise it would have cost me nineteen US dollars and I was a bit skinned at the time, as per ushe.

They had come to see the sneak preview of the movie called *Kids*, directed by Larry Clark, the famous American photographer—which Gus had executive produced and which had been shot by Gus's usual cinematographer, Eric, who is really sweet, especially for a d.o.p. (Actually, come to think of it, d.o.p.'s are usually pretty nice.) So we had a cute little reunion at the airport before heading up the mountain. I of course almost immediately asked them, with charmed, breathless fascination, how Joaquin, River's little brother, was doing, as I had made friends with him when he was with Gus in Toronto shooting *To Die For*. He is really, really cool and nice and cute and if I didn't know him personally you can be sure he would be my latest theoretical homosexual husband.

We also reminisced about the time I and Gus and DJ went up for a weekend to my parents' farm in Gus' big truck and when we were sitting at the dinner table with my Mom and my Dad—who is kind of like Jed Clampet, only not quite so sophisticated, but really sweet and gentle and calm—at one point during a lull in the conversation he leaned over and looked out the picture window and said very quietly to my Mom, almost as if talking to himself—as people who have been married for fifty years are wont to do—"Are those goat's whiskers, Mother?" referring to a particular cloud formation which presages rain. It sort of really captured the essence of my childhood, and I even had witnesses.

Later, DJ, a hardy Dutchman with rosy cheeks and a gorgeous disposition, asked my Dad to pose for a photograph, and as he was about to take the shot, he said to my father—who practically doesn't even know I'm gay or anything—"Sir, has anyone ever told you you have a beautiful face?" My father turned beet red and said with his typical modesty, "My face might break your camera." I and Gus, naturally, were very bemused by the whole scenario. DJ kills me, he really does. Once when we were rough-housing on the street whilst drunk on the way to a rave we never did manage to locate, I fell off his back and broke one of my two front teeth in half, and DJ felt so bad he started to cry. "Don't cry, DJ, it's only a tooth," I comforted him, but he was disconsolate. So now whenever I lick my chops I think of my friend DJ.

Flying into Salt Lake was like setting down on a desolate, uninviting planet, so it was nice to spend the first night of my forty-seven hour experience getting the princely treatment because I was with an A-list Hollywood director—who, incidentally, is the nicest guy you would ever want to meet and remains remarkably untouched by all the bull-shit—tagging along to a somewhat-lavish-under-the-circumstances, all expenses paid dinner held for anyone involved with *Kids* by Miramax, who bought the two million dollar feature for three and a half (it was financed by a couple of young, rich kids who own a record company in New York City), and I had the salmon and one tee many martoonis. DJ and I tried to order our drink of choice when we're together—Long Island Ice Tea—but they are illegal in Utah where you can only order one shot at a time (i.e. no doubles) and you can't mix more than two kinds of liquor together in the same drink (sorry, folks, no tiny drop of scotch in that perfect martini).

Also the legal drinking age is twenty-one, so Harmony, the eighteen year old kid who wrote *Kids*, couldn't order a drink, but DJ and I kept them coming and slid them over in front of his nose. After dinner, Gus and DJ and Harmony and me (we're pretty good company) went back to my hotel room with a bottle of Mescal so that I could shower before the big *Kids* premiere. Harmony, a child prodigy who has already seen every European art film ever made, told us that on the trip from New York a certain director known for his gritty New York movies starring Harvey Keitel sat beside him and did coke on the sidebar in first class and yelled at the stewardesses the entire way.

We went to the screening, and of course *Kids*, as you will soon hear, is not only a masterpiece, but destined to become one of the most controversial films of the decade, if not the century. It's kind of like moving Larry Clark photographs by way of Godard's *Masculine/Feminine* times x-rated "Little Rascals," if you can get your head around that one. We drank mescal through the entire screening, which intensified the feverish feeling of watching history unfold before your eyes.

Afterwards, Gus and DJ and this guy that once sued Gus for $170,000 and I went back to my hotel room and finished off the mescal and talked animatedly until the neighbours complained and I swallowed the worm.

• • •

My two illustrious friends left early the next morning, so the Sundance Kid (surely not Butch) was on his own for Day Two and, without high profile companions, just another piece of independent trash. I started the morning off being interviewed in pixelvision by the very charming and sincere director and producer of the low-budget, black and white vampire movie *Nadja*, featuring Peter Fonda, who I had seen at dinner the previous evening replete with his cellular phone and his pony tail—apparently the Hollywood look-du-moment—for a documentary they were making about the people of Sundance. As my American distributor slash executive producer had not deigned to contact me or help me get oriented in the least since my arrival, I guess I did inadvertently refer to him as a bitch in the interview.

After I informed him of this, he was nicer to me, I suppose, and he did usher me around for a little while and introduce me to all sorts of journalists and producers and agents and whatnot. The nice woman who has a movie column in *Mirabella* told me that she had not only heard good things about my movie—which she obviously hadn't seen—but that I was also a swell individual to work with, so it seems my publicists had already been doing some damage control. A reporter from *People* magazine promised me she would see my movie that evening (as Richard Carpenter says to his sister Karen in *Superstar*: "Oh, you liar!"); another, from the *LA Weekly*, said it was one of her favourite films of the year (I believed her).

My distributor guided me around by the arm as if resigned to some mundane task, introducing me here to cranky Graham Fuller of *Interview*; there to Mr. *Details* who is oh, so interested, I'm sure; there to a photog from *Detour*, who just adores my hat; here to an agent from William Morris, who's seen it, loves it, we must do. Alonso, the charming director of the Dallas Film Festival, extends me an invitation with my movie to the Lone Star State, but subsequently doesn't follow through, boo hoo.

Unable to locate a film party, I end up at a shindig for *Unzipped*, where, unbeknownst to me, I just happen to be seated back to back with Isaac Mizrahi, the famous designer, the paparazzi elbowing and jostling me out of the way to get his picture. At one point, my pushy distributor virtually jerks me and my chair backwards for a photo op with the fag-du-moment. As the flashbulbs pop and the shutters click and we both smile like old friends for the camera, Miss Mizrahi asks me through Elsa Klensched teeth who the hell I am. "Bruce LaBruce," he ponders. "Never heard of you." I wanly explain that my movie will be opening in New York in a month at the Cinema Village; he claims it's two blocks from his house and maybe he'll check it out, although somehow I don't believe it's exactly Les Miz's cup of hemlock. There's Parker Posey, Independent It Girl of the Year, crawling under my table, ostensibly to retrieve a sentimental scarf—not, I expect, to re-enact the corresponding Julie Christie scene in *Shampoo*.

"Look at you and your cute pants," she opines of me and my brown and blue striped, flared trousers.

A reporter from an internationally syndicated movie television show drags me outside for an interview. He has the wild look of Dennis Hopper in *Apocalypse Now* in his eyes—less like an entertainment reporter than one caught in the middle of the war-torn, breakaway Republic of Chechnya. I've seen the same look in my distributor's eyes, who had stared at me blankly without recognition the night before when I had run into him at the *Kids* show, only registering bigger game, bigger fish in the protoplasmic pond of independents. "It's social Darwinism run amok," I hear myself tell the reporter. Or maybe I'm just being a sissy.

Later that night I go to the premiere of a movie by one of the big independent gay filmmakers and it sucks really,

really hard. That's what you get when you put a loaded gun in the hands of an infant, especially if it's for the cover of *Vogue Bambini*. My screening is afterwards at the Egyptian theatre at midnight. At this point I am so tired of introducing and talking about it that I find myself really past the point of caring. It all seems a little anti-Clamato. I get a ride to the bad party of the bad gay movie with my, um, distributor, and David Ansen, film critic for *Newsweek*—with whom I chat about Edward Albee's new play, even though he thinks I'm a pervert. (Ansen, that is. Albee, who was not so long ago charged with indecent exposure, might be a little more forgiving.) After the party gets busted by the local gendarmes, my distributor

arranges a ride for me back to my hotel with four gay publicists from LA, if you'll pardon the redundancy.

As we are about to pull away, one of them rolls down the window and yells, "Yoohoo, Jared, do you need a ride?" A handsome young man squeezes into the back seat. Much to my amazement, it's Jordan Catelano, the self-same teenage heartthrob from "My So-Called Life," that amazing tv series which, alas, has been cancelled since I mentioned it earlier. He looks and talks and is dressed but exactly like he does on the show, which I somehow find reassuring— although the fact that an eighteen year old straight boy already knows, by name, four extremely gay publicists from LA and does not hesitate to squeeze into a mid-sized car with them makes me worry vaguely about his future. I am introduced to him, our eyes meet, and my heart flutters just like Clare Danes'.

I go back to my lonely hotel room.

I won't tell you much about Rotterdam, which followed immediately. I didn't do much because I was almost certain that I'd picked up a dose somewhere along the way (alas, not from Jordan Catelano), and I didn't want to be a Typhoid Mary or a Patient Zero or anything. (It's okay, it was only chlamydia which, I am unhappy to report, like the song says, is not a flower.) There was a big café in the Hilton where they put up blow-ups of all the directors and such, and somebody stole mine, which was very complimentary, I'm sure. Someone also removed one of the numbers from my hotel door, the three of twenty-three, and we all know what that means—or am I just being paranoid and conspiracist.

One person asked for my autograph. There was a marathon of the third season of the "Real World" on European MTV, so I spent a lot of time in my hotel room watching that as we are not blessed with MTV in Canada. I got invited to Helsinki, Bogata possibly, Japan maybe, although I doubt it. I stole a white terry-cloth Hilton bathrobe, made some deals. That type of stuff. Nothing to write home about.

Hell Is Other Faggots

Okay, once and for all, I am not self-loathing. I hate other homosexuals. There is a difference. Or, to paraphrase my existentialist pal, J.P. Sartre, "Hell is other faggots." Recently, in an interview in a straight (read: "real") magazine, I brazenly claimed not to be gay-identified. Of course, it was a blatant falsehood. I'm about as gay-identified as you can get. I mean, can you think of anyone gayer-identified? I'm always going on and on about it, gay this and gay that, gay, gay, gay. But the point is, I'm not one of these people who insist on mindlessly supporting gay events or gay agendas, or, well, gays in general, just because they're gay. Especially some gays. Especially those petit bureaucrats and Pharisees, those gaylords who pompously dictate the rules of gayness.

Of course, these sentiments are far from new. Uncle Gore said it best a long time ago: there are no homosexual people, only homosexual acts. Neither is this philosophy confined to an underground sect of malcontents completely out of touch with the mainstream. The recent inclusion of an article in *Details* magazine called "Queer and Loathing," subtitled "He's here, he's queer, and he's over it" suggests that these ideas may be gaining some popular acceptance. (If I weren't so modest, I might add a footnote to the effect that a profile of yours truly in the *Advocate*, an internationally distributed gay magazine, appeared four or five years ago under the heading "He's here, but don't call him queer", but as my dear friend, Glennda Orgasm, recently opined, "Bruce is so far ahead of everything that he's even over himself.")

The author, a self-proclaimed recovering Queer Nationalist, goes so far as to label himself "postgay". I recently contributed to a book being compiled by a friend in London to be called *Anti-gay*, based on a show I did with Miss Orgasm on Manhattan Cable tv about identifying with ex-gays. Something is obviously afoot. I've said it before, and I'll say it again: the extant gay community, largely a fiction concocted by the pink media, anyway, must be destroyed. Destroy all monsters. Let's start with Pride Day, shall we? All the heterosexuals line up to see the freak show they have booked in this season, mothers covering their children's eyes as if at the scene of a gruesome car accident. It brings to mind Jane Wyman's line to Hayley Mills in that classic Disney film: "Don't stare at the orphans, Pollyanna".

Now you may think, as the sister of Mary Todd says to her in *Abe Lincoln in Illinois*, that I'm "speaking with a degree of irresponsibility that is verging on sheer madness." (Can you tell that I've been watching the Family Channel a lot lately, even though I'm a fag?) But what can I say? I'm a provocateur. A rabble-rouser. A common adventuress. It's a dirty job, etc., etc., standard closing.

As I write this, perhaps stoned out of my mind, perhaps not, I'm listening to Elastica, the new NBT from England, and I'm daydreaming that Justin is gay. (The drummer, naturally.) He is super cute, kind of like Damon (Justine's boyfriend, in case you weren't paying attention), but more faggoty. I've been trying to get into more faggoty gays lately, to counterbalance my obvious homophobia, but it isn't easy. Not for an unrepentant heterophile like myself. (Put that in your Apocalypse Culture and smoke it.)

In fact, Me and Miss Orgasm are thinking of putting out a new fanzine called Mongoloid (Mary, d.a.) which would consist entirely of representations of married heterosexual couples having sex in the missionary position. Despite the presumably pejorative connotations of the title, it would be paradoxically pro-procreation.

Yes, I'm afraid the days of breeder-bashing are long since over. Then again, even though Trent Reznor admitted in another recent *Details* (that oh-so-cutting-edge publication) that he thinks practically non-stop about sucking cocks, he doesn't do a thing for me. He reminds me of that old joke: a horse walks into a saloon and sits at the bar. The bartender looks at him, pours him a drink and says, "Why the long face?"

108

Why, indeed. I guess this latest in a series of anti-gay rants was inspired by an incident I witnessed recently while making a rare guest appearance on the public transportation system. One late, rainy afternoon, I found myself trapped on a crowded streetcar, sardined into a seat directly behind the rear doors as the closed, dripping umbrellas of disgruntled standing passengers poked and prodded my meager ribs.

I had already noticed the young queen standing before me with the eyebrows plucked to oblivion and the arm-load of Le Chateau shopping bags at the streetcar stop—she had dumped a frightening amount of refuse from her purse into the gutter, then glared around daring anyone to say anything about it. Clearly a reject from *Paris is Burning*, her favourite expression, used with neurotic frequency in her one-sided conversation with her mousy companion, was "Drama!" Now don't get me wrong, I have nothing against mincing, nellie-queens who provide shade for anyone within reading distance, having a provisional membership in this club myself, but sometimes being a bitchy diva is not enough.

Witty sophistication, timing, aplomb and a certain ability to mock oneself as well as others can transform one from pathetic spectacle into sparkling entertainer. Believe me, all drag queens are not created equal, and if one is being particularly obnoxious and rude and cruel, you have my permission to sock her in the jaw, gay-bashing statistics notwithstanding. (Actually, I have to confess that when Camille Paglia recently claimed in her *Playboy* interview that incidents of gay-bashing are isolated and rare, I didn't bat an eyelash.) Now, the queen in question was definitely a hate crime in the making, so it did not surprise me when a by-the-numbers Toronto hoser, replete with plaid shirt, squirrelly moustache, and work boots so worn the steel toes showed through, picked a fight with her.

Lost in her oblivious blather, she failed to notice that she was squeezing the poor short little Canadian everyman into a corner. A heated exchange occurred, in which the hoser was eventually driven to the obvious, but rather funny under the circumstances, remark: "Stop stepping on my foot. You're gonna give my boot AIDS." The queen responded with a tired tirade about how the hoser would never have the privilege of contracting AIDS from her, if, indeed, she did have the disease, because she wouldn't touch him with a ten-foot pole, etc., etc., as her silent partner pursed her lips and rolled her eyes in support. By this time, the entire back half of the streetcar was riveted to the unfolding drama, which seemed posed to escalate into an exchange of blows. Serendipitously, the queens' stop came up and they were obliged to make their grand exit, the big one snapping and spitting a path through the crowd. Not to be outdone, the hoser called out after them, "Bye Tutti, bye Frutti," as the crowd tittered. I have to confess, in this instance I felt no sympathy for the oppressed minority.

Let me leave you with a little anecdote that was related to me by a friend of a friend of Miles White, the famous Broadway choreographer who counted amongst his friends Miss Judy Garland. (Miles, incidentally was the friend whom Warhol was supposed to have met at a bar across from the Factory the day that Valerie Solanas cracked; Miles didn't show up; Warhol returned early to the Factory and was shot.) Miles once attended a gay party at which Miss Garland made an appearance shortly before her death. She got stinking drunk, climbed up on the piano, and started yelling at the crowd, "You're all a bunch of fucking faggots! Get a life."

Listen to Judy. Judy knows.

Whatever Happened To Season Hubley?

Los Angeles is a little like Alfred Hitchcock's production of *The Birds*: oh, you may look very glamorous in your fur coat and pearls and your little silver sports car, but disaster could strike at any moment. Because of the constant threat of disasters both natural and oh, so unnatural, there is a particular "après moi, le déluge" attitude which makes everything seem just a little bit reckless, a little out of control. Drinking and driving, for example, is de rigueur; you see, if you can survive earthquakes, fires, riots, and mud slides, you should be able to navigate an automobile through the wide, cool, evening streets, even if you are blind drunk. Besides, the police are too busy harassing hustlers and prostitutes and other street habitués to worry about an inebriated starlet weaving down Sunset. Yes, there's just something about the city that makes you say to yourself, "Ozone layer, be damned," and replace your sun block with baby oil as you sit out baking in the sun beside your kidney-shaped pool. Because if you're going to meet your maker, you might as well have a tan. You sit and calmly smoke your cigarette as the birds silently congregate behind your back. It's very liberating, in an apocalyptic kind of way.

And so it was that I recently made my way back to Gomorrah (Sodom being somewhat further up the coast), mixing business and pleasure in a nice, stiff cocktail that kind of sneaks up on you if you're not careful. There were agents to see, movies to promote, and pre-production to accomplish, all in a town where you are hard-pressed to find a really good cup of joe. I don't want to bore you with all the gory details. I'll just run over some of the highlights, like road-kill.

The pre-production I alluded to was for a new movie I would soon be shooting in LA with my friend Ricardo to be called *Hustler White*, a romantic comedy with documentary overtones about hustlers on Santa Monica Boulevard. I and Ricardo hung out at our various offices around town—Numbers, the upscale hustler bar on Sunset, the Yukon Mining Co. and Astro Burger, both on Santa Monica—scoping the local talent. The auditions—consisting of a videotaped interview with a minimum requirement of underwear, a sexy Polaroid, and a casting form—lasted several days, and bore only a passing resemblance

to the corresponding scene in Paul Schrader's *Hardcore* in which George C. Scott poses as a porno director casting a new picture while searching for his daughter, played by Season Hubley, who is lost in the seamy underworld of the adult entertainment industry. (Whatever happened to her? I loved her.) It was much more benign and cozy. Hustlers and porno stars, you must understand, are people too.

Not to mention us pornographers. It's just that our pleasure is our business, that's all. At least, that's what Xaviera Hollander once told me. I can't reveal the details of the auditions, because most of it will end up in the picture and I don't want to blow my load, if you'll pardon the expression, but let's just say I came this close to falling in love several times over. You see, I'm a sucker for a hard-luck story, espe-

The Mellifluous Mrs. Glass slips me the tongue. Photo by LaBruce himself.

cially when it's attached to the body of death. I was particularly enchanted by the Hungarian refugee, but it was the bald amputee, despite his paranoid delusions, who came closest to capturing my heart.

My dear friend and confidant Mrs. Glass, fearful that I might be working too hard, decided to hold a party for me at her groovy Mid-Wilshire digs. It was a gay affair, with a potent punch the likes of which has not been seen since Jonestown. Among the usual LA suspects were a couple of muscle queens whose masculine exteriors dissolved as soon as they opened their mouths, an Atlanta queer whose handshake consisted of a sloppy tongue kiss, some obscure Scandinavian lesbians and their aloof Eigil Vesti-look-alike male model friend, and what party would be complete without an assortment of modern primitives with day jobs at various upscale agencies?

One shirtless muscled Queer Nation casualty sporting a huge cross with "HIV" on it tattooed on his back, replaced party palaver with one long, uninterrupted diatribe about various conspiracies involving pharmaceutical companies and the CIA. As the party progressed, an aging actor slash producer and his significantly younger German protégé, who, it seems, was the former protégé of Thierry Mugler, pulled out a couple of joints masquerading as Cuban cigars and proceeded to play musical blow-jobs with the local gentry. Workaholic that I am, I spent the evening casting, but without much success. Sometimes truth is much too strange for fiction.

I and Mrs. Glass ended up in the vintage Mercedes of the producer who, after the party broke up, invited us, along with his protégé, over to his place for a night-hat. If we hadn't been so drunk we might have been terrified as the car squealed around corners at sixty mph and narrowly avoided smashing into parked cars. Once at his charming West Hollywood home, with undistributed (and not very good) Bruce Weber movies on the VCR starring several adorable little Dillons (younger brothers of Matt and Kevin), he danced a little jig for us and showed us the photo albums of his early acting career. After a few more joints, out came the photos of unconscious teenagers in bathtubs. Time to go, Mrs. G.

A few days later it was off to Palm Springs and Joshua Tree with Ricardo to write our script. It was just like Kirk Douglas and Dick Powell sequestering themselves in a hotel at Arrowhead to write a screenplay in Vincente Minnelli's production of *The Bad and the Beautiful*. Well, something like that. I'd wanted to go to Palm Springs ever since seeing Robert Downey, Jr. blowing youngish tanned gay men there to support his freebasing habit in the underrated *Less Than Zero* (a scenario which, I have been assured by people who know the actor personally, was strictly autobiographical). On our way out of town in Ricardo's '67 white Cougar, we stopped to do a little extra casting on the Boulevard. I'd already bought a hustler several nights earlier—strictly for research purposes—and now we talked to one who begged us to take him to the Poison Palms.

He looked pretty rough—probably on the lam from the law—so we thought better of it. Ricardo later teased my mercilessly for my lack of experience, because the whole time we were talking to him my wallet was sitting on the dash, clearly in snatching distance. I told him to shut up. At the Springs we stayed at a little pink bed and breakfast run by a fat, leathery-skinned Auntie who had a mat of gray hair on his chest and a little Mexican houseboy who served us breakfast in bed in a Speedo. We sat by the pool in bathing suits and sunglasses, sipping strawberry margaritas and writing on my adorable little laptop. You couldn't get much more Palm Springs unless former Mayor Sonny Bono joined you for a script conference.

The architecture of the city—low, one-story, sixties-style buildings snuggled amidst the Sierra Mountains—is just my style. One restaurant, designed by Frank Lloyd Wright and built into the side of a hill, was right out of "Thunderbirds." And the lighting there is definitely for my age. Joshua Tree was much more rustic, more Ricardo's cup of twig tea. (He's a real nature nut.) We were going to but didn't stay at the hotel where Gram Parsons committed suicide. Ricky had stayed there once with his ex-boyfriend in the very room where the tragedy occurred, and the management insisted that anyone sleeping there had to write down in a special book any sightings of or experiences with the ghost of the famous musician. We had already encountered a ghost in Palm Springs. Sleeping in the same bed, we both thought in the morning that the other had been jerking off but, as it turns out, neither of us had. The bed had been shaking, and it wasn't one of the vibrating variety. Instead, we stayed at the 29 Palms Inn, located on an oasis in Joshua Tree, where rabbits and lizards and roadrunners

and other woodland and desert creatures wandered amongst the quaint cabins. Here, in the company of a six-toed cat, we finished our script, got drunk, and confessed dark secrets in the Jacuzzi.

Back in Los Angeles while scouting locations, I experienced my first earthquake. It was only 3.0 though, so I only found out about it later on the news. In the last two days of my trip I went to five parties, don't ask me why, representing an odd cross-section of the city. The first was at the Silverlake abode of Ron Athey, the controversial performance artist whose work caused Jesse Helms to call for the total abolition of the NEA. Ron, who mummifies and slices open people on stage and makes like a human pin-cushion, is the sweetest man you'd ever want to meet. The party was full of dykes, including his muse, Pig-Pen, and those omnipresent modern primitives.

The second party was a big homo blow-out, with every style of fag in the book present and accounted for and the occasional celebrity thrown in for good measure, Donita Sparks springing immediately to mind. I ended up at the Taco Bell drive-thru at sun-up in a car full of drag queens. The next night it was off to the opening of Exene Cervenka's store called You've Got Bad Taste, in Silverlake. There were a lot of former SoCal punks there. I probably should have known who they were, but I didn't. I only recognized Flea.

This was followed by the birthday party in Beachwood of a co-worker of my friend Jeffrey who works at ICM, the agency Madonna left William Morris for after only a month and a half. It was upscale, very industry, with Melrose Place-style faggots, straight female models and young career women.

The final party was supposed to be an alternative queer music party, and indeed it was—LA-style. The band played the requisite (read: dull) music, but everyone seemed to be dressed how they supposed alternative rockers should look, with carefully pressed plaid shirts and brand new Doc Martens. When Mrs. Glass went to take a beer and was told it was "private," we split. Anyway, it was all very anthropological.

Did I mention that the bungalow in West Hollywood I crash in when I stay in LA , and to which I will soon be returning to shoot the movie, was once the office of a famous shrink who specialized in former child stars and had a clientele which included Lucille Ball and Judy Garland? Well it's true. Do you think I'd make something like that up?

I Don't Want To Be A Homosexual After All

Okay, so here's the thing. Remember Ben Weasel? He once sent me a letter asking me to place an ad in my fanzine *J.D.s* to promote a band called Sloppy Seconds who had a new single called "I Don't Want To Be A Homosexual". I went totally post office and challenged him to write a song called "I wanna be a Homosexual". He rose to the occasion and wrote a brilliant number (sample lyric: "I wanna be a faggot a mincing ninny a prancing fairy merry little queer a Bruce LaBruce").

Ben and I stayed in touch, and when he recently formed a new, more commercial band called "The Riverdales" (yes, it's an *Archie* reference), he flew me down to Chicago for a week to shoot his first music video for a single called "Fun Tonight," the money coming from his label Lookout, famous (not to mention rich) for producing the first two Green Day records. The three members of The Riverdales are straight, although their drummer, Panic, recently toured with the jejune queercore band, Pansy Division, when they opened for Green Day, whom the Riverdales will also be touring with at the end of the summer. Ben left the entire concept of the video up to me so, of course, while staying well within the conventions of MTV, I tried to make it as pervie as possible: the video babe, a gorgeous cross between Drew Barrymore and Betty Boop, has a black eye for no apparent reason (I was inspired by the old Terryton "I'd rather fight than switch" cigarette ads), and the two nubile young boys who drench each other with squirt guns and get into a pillow fight and a wrestling match in their white briefs, end up under the sheets together.

The boys were straight, but very co-operative, especially considering they were neither getting paid nor laid. The production company I worked with, Ripchord, and the band were totally supportive of the idea, although the bass player was concerned that the homosexual angle was too trendy, and one female gaffer found the representation of a woman with a black eye "problematic". (Personally, I find people who find things "problematic" problematic.) "I think black eyes are sexy," I responded blandly, and I do.

Anyway, one reason I decided to essay the video was to get back behind the camera again before starting a new feature. The movie is to star Tony Ward, who modeled for Ricardo long before Tony hooked up with Madonna and did the "Justify My Love" video, as well as feature porn stars Kevin Kramer (recent coverboy of *Freshmen* magazine), Alex Austin (recent cover-man of *Rump* magazine), Wolf (recently featured in the awful Tom of Finland video *The Wild Boys*—Wolf's the one who got the billiard balls shoved up his ass) and black porn superstar Ryan Black, as well as real hustlers of various socioeconomic and racial backgrounds.

Johns will include gay Canadian country musician Glen Meadmore, hot off the success of his latest album, Hot, Horny, and Born Again; controversial NEA slice 'em and dice 'em performance artist Ron Athey; and, if scheduling permits, "Kids in the Hall's" own betowelled Bellini. The movie will feature no women, no drugs, no AIDS and no drag queens, except for one surprise. Why? Because I say so. Relax, there'll be more than

113

enough of all of the above in my future feature, *Homicidal*. (Except for drag queens. Don't get me wrong. I love all drag queens. Except for some drag queens.)

The soundtrack of *Hustler White* will feature music by Japanese noise band The Boredoms, possibly a tune or two by Smoke, especially their love ode to Luke Perry's feet, as well as a song and a tie-in music video with Toronto band Rusty, which I will also direct, for their Canadian anthem rock classic, "Misogyny".

After the shoot, I hope to be going up to Portland to observe the filming of a Gus Van Sant movie, *Binkie*, in which I have been promised a very minute, very minor, virtually non-existent role. So anyway, directing music videos is really fun. If anyone out there wants to hire me, I'm interested. Call me.

114

Hurray for Hollywood! Detail of hustler's stomach, Santa Monica Boulevard, 1995. Photo by Bruce LaBruce.

Hustler White: The Shoot

LA is not only a great big freeway, as Hal David would have it, but it is also the biggest movie set in the whole, wide world. I don't understand why more people don't take advantage of this gorgeous town as a movie locale, before it takes advantage of them, which it inevitably will, darling, just you wait. Of course there have been some great movies set in this my favourite city in the world, but mostly—as in *The Day of the Locust* and *The Last Tycoon*—to demonstrate its depravity and decay (albeit no less beautiful for it). Even *Shampoo*, the film that comes closest to capturing all the subtle gradations and degradations of late afternoon Los Angeles (photographed so beautifully by my favourite cinematographer, Laszlo Kovacs), while designed as a cautionary tale, cannot help but make the mod metropolis look as fresh and stunning as a brand new tit job. Anyway, allow me to share with you a few of the highlights of shooting a movie in, of all places, Hollywood, CA.

Before I proceed, a word about my co-writer and co-director, the fag photog Ricardo. Ricardo has been shopping the Boulevard for many, many years now, both for pleasure and to cast for his bondage photographs, many of which have appeared in such magazines as *Drummer* and *Mach* and in his very own *The Bondage Book*. Whenever out-of-towners like yours truly or the late great stylist George Byron (or "Mommie", as we affectionately called her) came to town, Ricardo would dutifully drive us up and down the

Boulevard, waiting patiently for a little hustler white to catch our eye. Mommie is gone now, RIP, but Ricardo and I have continued the tradition, and decided on one of my visits that we should make a movie about hustlers on Santa Monica Boulevard—a romantic comedy, of course, what else?

Jürgen Bruning and I rounded up some of the money at the Rotterdam Film Festival this past January thanks to the various international distributors who handle my two previous features, *No Skin Off My Ass* and *Super 8 1/2*: Strand in the U.S., Stance in Japan, Dangerous To Know in Great Britain, and Swell in Canada. After scouting locations and conducting screen tests, I and Ricardo wrote the script together, inspired by his extensive experiences with rent boys and mine with my hustler ex-boyfriend, Joe the Ho, who was the first boy to break my heart, but not the last. The script also incorporated many of the true-to-life tales of the hustlers and johns whom we auditioned on video, proving once again that truth is raunchier than fiction. Anyway, what follows is my account of what went on beneath the making of *Hustler White*; I'm sure Ricardo's version would be very different, but hey, I'm the one with the laptop. I magnanimously gave him veto power, but he, equally magnanimously, said leave it all in, so here it goes.

I'm going to gloss over pre-production because it was so boring and businessy, in a stomach-churning kind of way. Suffice it to say, we jammed three weeks worth of it into one, and there was a lot of wailing and gnashing of teeth and endless meetings and arguments and power-plays and internecine rivalries and ego-trips and anxious producers wringing their hands and our adorable little Prince Alberts (our affectionate diminutive for Production Assistants) already starting to fuck like rabbits and it looked like the whole shebang (or, more accurately, he-bang) was about to be called off a couple of times there, but it wasn't.

There was the requisite hob-nobbing with our star, Tony Ward (the ex-I.T. coverboy, international model, one time lover of the likes of Madonna and Christina Applegate, and featured hunk in music videos by Miss Ciccone, Belinda Carlisle, and George Michael, nevermind), with me and my directing partner, Ricardo, attending his birthday barbecue the day before shooting was to begin. There we met his charming tattooed live-in girlfriend, Dede, a dead ringer for Elizabeth Taylor in *The Sandpiper* except with far more enormous breasts (think about it) and her adorable year-and-a-half-old, bemohawked son, Rocko, who

would subsequently make his big screen debut in our own *Hustler White* (more on that later). Tony turned out to be a truly marvelous, enthusiastic, and talented co-star, working, for less than peanuts, above and beyond the call of duty–i.e., he would even hang around the set when he wasn't in a scene just to lend moral support or something. He is also a great kisser, as I will expound upon when I get to "Shooting Day 8", our big love scene on the beach. The day after he was wrapped, Tony was off to Paris to appear in a beer commercial for Ellen Von Unwerth, and to do the fall runway shows in Milan. Quel star.

115

Previously unpublished production stills from "Hustler White" by shutterbug Bruce LaBruce.

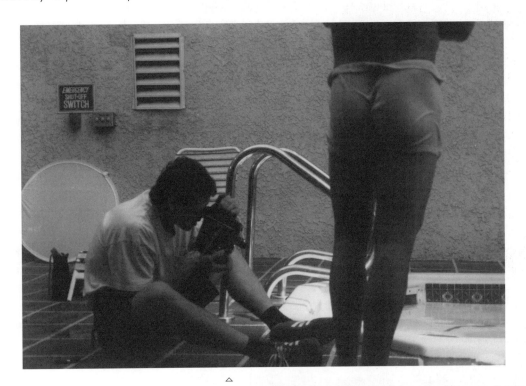

△

James Carman, our dedicated d.o.p., left, and Tony Ward's bubblicious butt, right, on set in Marina Del Rey.

Rocko and Tony in the tub, a direct ▷ homage to slash rip-off of the analogous scene in "Flesh".

Tony Ward butches it up between takes in the usual jacuzzi.

And still
my jacuzzi runneth over:
Tony Ward between takes.

James uses his trusty Bolex to shoot
the anti-climactic head bump with
Tony Ward.

The Wonder Years: A black hustler yanked off the Boulevard literally minutes before shooting a scene for "Hustler White".

Alex Austin, gay porn star, and straight as a shot of Kentucky bourbon, I might add.

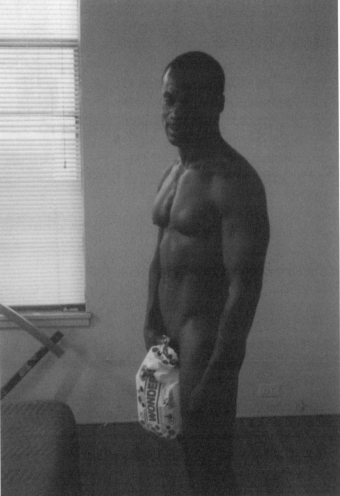

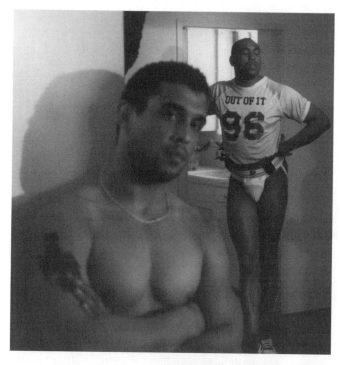

Penultimate, pectacular porn star
Ryan Block, foreskin - I mean, foreground -
and the vestigial Vaginal Davis, background.
Miss Davis is obviously taking a breather from
her butch role as Buster Boote.

The top bottom in the business: porn star
Kevin Kramer displaying what could only be
described as the male pussy.

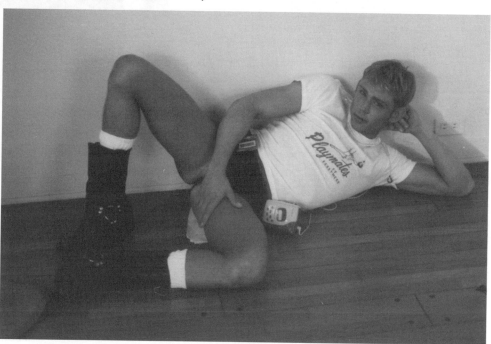

Born for porn: ▷
Ryan Block leads the
chain gang while Kevin Kramer
takes his directions like a man.

Next! Keven Kramer (white, horizontal)
prepares to get ploughed by, in order, a
porn star, a hustler, a porn star, and a hustler.
▽

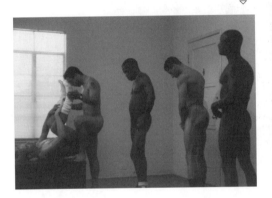

James Carman, our dutiful d.o.p., dons Kevin Kramer's ▷
white tube socks for the all important p.o.v.

Mrs. Glass and her hustler harem share a laugh on the friendly, sincere set of "Hustler White".

Josh, our first ▷
a.d., lurking
behind what I
come to be able
to identify, dur-
ing the course
of the shoot, as
a grip stand.

△

Glen Meadmore, the infamous
gay born again Christian country
and western singer, as Stu Blake, in
front of one of her numerous John
Wayne Gacy paintings of herself.

◁ Emily, a.k.a Embryo, our shockingly
young Prince Albert (production
assistant) who could have
got us all busted for
the corruption of a
minor lesbian.

◁ James, our kamikaze cameraman, on location.
Gladly note the John Wayne Gacy painting
of Miss Meadmore in the b.g.

◁ I guess you could say not knowing how to operate a camera worked to my advantage. Seymour reappears over our Clint Eastwood look-a-like prop master, Steve.

I accidentally double exposed a roll or two, creating a rather unsettling effect: an appartition of Seymour Kasabian (Ron Athey), our murderous mortician, appears over Tony Ward. ▷

Another eerie double exposure. If you look carefully behind the morbid mortician Seymour Kasabian/Ron Athey, you can see his naked victim, Eigil Vesti/Kevin P. Scott, reclining behind him.

Mrs. Glass in Heidi's Mercedes convertible. Fondly note ▷
his kaftan sticking out the bottom of the car door a la
Shelley Duvall in Bob Altman's "3 Women". I and Josh
coincidentally appear reflected in the door.

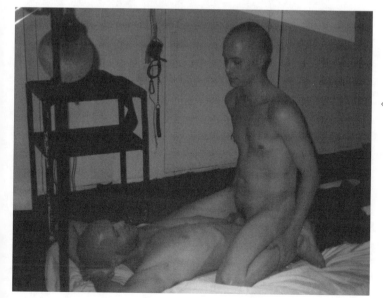

◁ Piglet (Ivar Johnson) sits upon Eigil Vesti (Kevin P. Scott) in
the autoerotic asphyxiation scene in "Hustler White".

◁ *On the Boulevard: Piglet surrounded by a bevy of beauhunky hustlers, not to mention our soundmensch, Søren, foreground.*

Hustler Nelson: Our hustler twins sing the ballad of Hustler White.

▽

△

*"I have a little proposition for you, Mr.
Ward." Tony Ward as Montgomery
Ward and Bruce LaBruce as Jürgen
Anger in "Hustler White". Publicity
still by Rick Castro courtesy of
Strand Releasing.*

*The "Whatever Happened To ▷
Baby Jane?" sequence from
"Hustler White" Publicity
still by Rick Castro
courtesy of Strand
Releasing.*

"Denied!" Bruce LaBruce as Jürgen Anger.
Publicity still by Rick Castro courtesy
of Strand Releasing.

The longest gay kiss in screen history. Bruce LaBruce and Tony Ward in "Hustler White". Publicity still by Rick Castro courtesy of Strand Releasing.

The Shooting Diary

With our tight little crew of ten hardcore members not yet quite so tight, we set out to shoot a 16mm feature film on an eleven day shooting schedule plus two days of Hi-8 for good measure. It is a rag-tag group composed of trust fund kids with scientologist parents (two crew members actually attended an all-scientologist High School); cute, wealthy young film students with famous boyfriends; and hot, ambitious baby butches who don't seem to think twice about sleeping their way up the lesbian food chain to get this film made and further their own careers in the process (and more power to them). Everyone on the crew—

which begins more and more, in cultural and class diversity, and in its tragi-comic circumstances of isolation and the impossible reckoning with the forces of nature, to resemble one of the less pedestrian episodes of *Gilligan's Island*—seems to have either a short film of their own on video to show us, or a script on the back burner to expound upon, so I guess there'll be no shortage of Eves on this shoot.

Except for Søren, our adorable sound recordist from Berlin, who claims to be heterosexual but in denial, and who seems to have no ambition beyond fathering an Aryan brood in the Fatherland (and more power to him). It's okay, though—a little Eve-age is only to be expected. It's an occupational hazard, especially when the crew is young and eager and underpaid. Besides, no Margo is complete without her Eve. It's a Hollywood tradition. But I digress. Our handsome, swarthy art director slash prop master, Steve, who looks not unlike a young Clint Eastwood circa *Rawhide* (make that *High Plains Drifter*: although only twenty-six, the man looks at least ten years older, and he knows it) arrives from San Francisco a day late, and every homosexual on the crew—which, roughly translated, means tout le monde—is immediately smitten with him, except for me: it's not that I don't find him attractive, it's just that I seem to have lost my sex drive somewhere, and can't locate it for a gander. (By way of overcompensation in the wrong direction, I scarcely say a word to poor Steve for the first three or four days, save for a few mumbled commands—er, requests—on set, but then again, my social skills are hardly on a par with Amy Vanderbilt's, as you may have noticed.)

To be fair, our director of photography, James Carman, from Berlin (whose girlfriend, incidentally, won an Oscar last year for best short subject, and who, I can't help but notice when I meet her at the wrap party, looks more than a little like a Weimar Republic Tracey Ullman) is technically bisexual, having slept with other men only in that trashy, decadent, European avant-garde kind of way, but, I mean, I think you can safely say that the crew is pretty gay, let's face it. Even Søren, only begrudgingly bisexual, will be caught making out with Wash, our slow loris assistant cameraman from Leeds via New Orleans who—as it turns out, has a lot less camera experience than he had led me to believe, putting me in hot water with the d.o.p. Are you starting to get the picture?

DAY ONE

We set off, after a six a.m. wake-up call, for LAX to shoot the scene in which the character I play, Jürgen Anger, arrives at the airport and arranges to be driven immediately to Santa Monica Boulevard, where he spots the man of his dreams, Montgomery (Monti) Ward (played by the Tony of the same name). Obviously not being able to afford a car-clamp on our absurdly meager budget, this means that whenever we are shooting any car interiors we have to squeeze in not only the usually two characters involved and the soundman, but also the d.o.p. and the assistant cameraman as well (to pull focus and/or hold the sun-gun). It is a minor blessing that the car that Jürgen drives in the film is a maroon Lincoln Town Car with a spacious interior–generously furnished by our sexy young amazing Malaysian dyke production manager, Annie.

Having decided that we cannot afford any kind of permits for shooting on location, we begin to practice our guerrilla-style film-making, setting up quickly and getting the shot before the airport authorities arrive. James, our d.o.p. is, thankfully, a consummate kamikaze of the Haskell Wexler school who actually seems to enjoy working under adverse conditions. But then again, it's only the first day, right?

Oh, a note on the choice of monikers of the lead characters. Monti, the name of Tony's character, is a remnant from casting; it is the real first name of our original choice for the lead before Tony became available. This Monti came to our attention through one of the johns in our cast, who happened to be semi-keeping the boy at the time. When he came over for his audition, Monti looked extremely street, wearing, as he was, nothing but a pair of cut-off track pants, sneakers, a tan, and a shit-eating grin. Although obviously having been through the wringer a few times, and still elbow-deep in substance abuse, he was still a looker, hovering somewhere between a young Gregory Peck and Desi Arnez, Jr. When we arranged to meet him for a follow-up interview at a suspiciously up-scale restaurant of his choosing in Santa Monica, however, suddenly he looked like a gigolo straight out of central casting, replete with an Armani knock-off, a French vest with no shirt, slicked-back hair, and snake-skin cowboy boots.

Obviously he mistook I and Ricardo for a couple of directors with a budget, and decided to work us for all it was worth. Boy, did he have the wrong bank account number. As we did not even have enough money to spring for lunch for the poor boy, we ended up driving him around LAX as we scouted for locations and tried to determine if he was reliable enough to carry our movie. We decided he was, with reservations, and gave him the role. As it turns out, in the three weeks between pre-production and production Monti ripped off our friend with whom he had been staying (including his electric guitar and four Gacy paintings), had a separate warrant out for his arrest for grand theft auto, got one girl pregnant, married another, and disappeared. I guess you could say he wasn't very reliable after all.

But he was what *Hustler White* is all about so, when God gave us Tony Ward for the part, we named him Monti, as an homage. As for the name of my character, Jürgen Anger, it is an amalgamation of the name of our co-producer, Jürgen Bruning, and the infamous gay avant-garde film-maker, Kenneth

131

Anger, a litigious son of a gun who will much later catch wind of the picture and be none too amused. Neither is Jürgen too pleased that we're borrowing his name, considering my character is a bit of a pompous fool with a temper, and rather pathetic, but he forgives us for our little jest. The real Jürgen flies in from Berlin for pre-production and provides us with a few good Jürgenisms, like contemptuously naming off several fellow producers and film festival programmers and then, putting thumb a centimeter from forefinger, saying, "I knew zem ven zey vere zis little! Zis little!" He really cracks me up. Like the last time I was in Berlin I asked him to translate the menu for me, and when I pointed to the veal he said, "Zis is little dead cow." Thanks Jürgen. You make it sound so appetizing.

132

Anyway, as the script for *Hustler White* borrows heavily from such Grand Guignol Robert Aldrich classics as *The Killing of Sister George* and *Whatever Happened To Baby Jane?* (ironic, considering our movie includes no female characters whatsoever), Ricardo, the co-director, feels that my character, Jürgen, should be made to look as grotesque as possible. I have other plans. During pre-production I had had a little meeting with our d.o.p. (or d.p., as Americans say, consistently ridiculing me for the indigenous Canadian use of the extra "o") at The Source on Sunset (the self-same Health restaurant where Diane Keaton took Woody Allen when he visited her from New York in *Annie Hall* and he ordered a plate of mashed yeast and subsequently played inadvertent bumper cars in the parking lot), convincing him of the exigency of making me look as attractive as possible in this movie, despite Ricardo's perverse insistence to the contrary. Now it pays off, as James slips a filter in front of the lens and prepares for my beauty shot, as he wisely refers to it (wise, i.e., if he expects to see his pay cheque–not much of a threat, I know). He shoots me against the barren b.g. ("background", darling, in film parlance) of the oil derricks on our way from the airport back to the city. Well, God bless him for trying, anyway.

The next location is the Marina Del Rey apartment complex of one of our john stars, Glen Meadmore, the infamous expatriate gay Canadian Born Again Christian country and western singer whose latest album, "Hot, Horny, and Born Again," as you may recall, is poised for national release. Miss Meadmore–who, with Vaginal Davis, used to be a member of the hardcore drag band Pedro, Muriel and Esther (which, incidentally, recently reunited to make a Steve Albini-produced album) and has appeared in women's clothes in several videos including "The Drift," John Aesth-Nihil's updating of Tennessee Williams' *The Roman Spring of Mrs. Stone* (Glen, of course, playing the eponymous Vivien Leigh role)–refuses, on principle, to do drag anymore (can you blame him?), which is perfectly consistent with our *Hustler White* "No women, no AIDS, no drugs, no drag queens" policy which all in good time we will be crucified for, I'm sure, darling. Instead, Glen plays Stu Blake, a character not unlike himself, who picks up porn star Alex Austin (straight as a shot of Kentucky bourbon, although he's from Wisconsin) in front of Hunters, a hustler bar on the Boulevard, takes him home and, after listening to his tragic life story and serenading him with a little post-coital Christian ditty of his own composition, throws a saddle on his naked body and rides him like a bronco.

Like most of our interior locations, space is very tight, and with a minimum of two actors and a crew of ten, things tend to get a little, shall we say, high-strung, to be euphemistic about it. Earlier that day, at the same location, we are to use the Jacuzzi in Glen's open concept courtyard (think low-rent Melrose Place) to shoot the crucial scenes in which Jürgen and Monti (me and Tony) finally connect romantically just prior to Monti's tragic Jacuzzi accident. A tense moment on the set as Tony fails to arrive at his call time and I wonder anxiously if he has come to his senses and decided not to throw his career away on this trashy project. Luckily, bad judgment prevails, and he shows up—not the first time the sweet man will get lost on his way to a set. (He also has the charming habit of locking himself out of his Silverlake digs and having to break into his own apartment.)

We brazenly don't even ask the building supervisor for permission to shoot, but with equipment that includes huge silver light reflectors on grip stands, cameras, a dat, and a small crew, not to mention an almost naked Tony Ward, we are hardly inconspicuous. Most of the occupants are curious and surprisingly friendly, and when we lie to the building manager (you know he's a closet case) that we are shooting a music video for Glen, one of his tenants, he enthusiastically gives us his blessing.

I'm so preoccupied with attempting to act and direct at the same time that I am virtually oblivious to the beautiful glistening intercontinental male body posing beside me. A strange asexuality begins to set in, but trust me, this will change by the end of the shoot, with a vengeance. By the time we are finished at this location it is approaching midnight. Our tired little crew dutifully begins to pack the equipment into the vehicles we have rented, for an employee discount, at the car rental agency Miss Meadmore conveniently works at as her day job. Because the crew is so small and working for so little, I will find myself doing all sorts of little jobs during the duration of the shoot, from gripping to loading equipment. No leisurely poker games in the director's trailer for me, I'm afraid.

DAY TWO

Getting out of bed on the second day of production of an impossibly low-budget shoot is not the most pleasant sensation I can think of, particularly when the call time is six a.m. once again, and a substantial amount of the production money, from Great Britain, predictably, has still somehow mysteriously not arrived, putting the entire enterprise in jeopardy. At least this is one of the rare days on which I have no scenes as an 'actor' and therefore don't have to trowel on the make-up and the greasy hair product which turns my hair a very *Death in Venice*-y shade of Auschenbach black and which will also, by the end of the shoot, have stained all my clothes and played havoc with my manicure. The first exterior of the morning is on the Boulevard across from the Hollywood Cemetery. When we set one foot on the cemetery driveway to position the camera for a shot across the street, a severe matron comes running out to inform us that we must stay off the property unless we want to pay the going rate of five hundred dollars an hour.

This does not bode well for our planned use of said cemetery as a future location, but never mind. The droning relentless traffic makes sound recording with our crude equipment dodgy at best—I mean, a dat is a dat, but the recordist is not that experienced, and apparently we can't afford a wind sock or something. We also can't afford, but desperately need, walkie-talkies for shoots on the wide, crowded Boulevard; in lieu of this, we will have to make countless trips back and forth across the street, everyone on the crew at one point or another almost getting unceremoniously mowed down by some sociopathic LA motorist. Owing to the intense noise and our budgetary limitations, I'm thinking the scene, in which three hustlers—Monti, Eigil, and Piglet—yell at each other across the Boulevard, may have to be subtitled or dubbed or something, but that's okay because the dailies from the first day of shooting—the only

ones we will be able to afford for the duration, mind you—are very sixties European Nouvelle Vague in colour; I'm thinking Eric Rohmer, I'm thinking Chabrol's *Les Biches*, I'm thinking Antonioni's *The Red Desert*, you get the picture—i.e., subtitles, albeit English ones, might not be inappropriate. (I can rationalize anything, baby. I'm the prince of rationalization.)

Thankfully, the next exterior takes place in the parking lot adjacent to Ricardo's bungalow, so we don't have to organize transportation and can relax a little, even—although I'm a bit nervous because the production office of a rival gay film-maker who shall remain nameless is right across from Ricardo's bungalow and I just know they're spying on us. Kevin P. Scott, our adorable amputee actor slash hustler with mild paranoid delusions and the body of death (that means "hot"), has arrived for his first scene in which Tony, having stolen a john's wallet, tears off in a stolen car and accidentally runs over Kevin's character, Eigil Vesti. This name, of course, is stolen from the infamous Andrew Crispo murder case in which a rich art dealer into heavy S & M fails to acknowledge the safe word in an encounter with a young Scandinavian model slash FIT student and kills him, dumping the body in upstate New York with the leather mask still on its poor beautiful head. Steve, our handy prop man, has made a very cool prosthetic foot complete with exposed bone and hamburger, as we are pretending that Kevin, a real-life amputee, gets his foot ripped off in the hit-and-run. So it's all special effects this morning, darling.

Since virtually the entire movie takes place during the day, the general rule of thumb is exteriors during the daylight hours; interiors, lit to approximate an afternoon ambience, in the evening. Tonight we venture to a location on Cherokee Avenue just north of Hollywood Boulevard, a low-rent apartment building whose live-in superintendent, Paul Bateman, aka Superhustler, is to play Billy Ray Jaded, a murky character who subscribes to the magazine *Amputee Times* and wants to be stumped by Eigil. Paul is another of Ricardo's bondage models that he has photographed and videotaped before (ditto Kevin, our amputee; Piglet, a Ron Athey acolyte; Zoltan, our piss model; etc.).

Superhustler is fascinated by the film-making process (ours, at least), and after some initial resistance, wholeheartedly supports our little effort, providing us with electricity from various empty apartments adjacent to the one in which we're shooting. Our moody d.o.p, James, who is very quiet and vaguely absent until he is brought his first of several lattes of the day, has got more than he bargained for on this movie: he has to do virtually all the lighting himself, not to mention cope with the electrical problems, the grim reality of a maximum of two takes per set-up, and an inexperienced (if enthusiastic) crew. (It frightens me to think that besides him, I have the most on-set experience, which isn't saying much.) Only last evening he chastised me for putting him in the worst possible situation, what with not having either someone to do the lighting or a trained assistant cameraman to do all the loading and down-loading and change the mags and whatnot. "Sorry," I say demurely, then, under my breath, "Deal with it, dude."

Overall, however, despite numerous frustrations and the use of poor Wash–the first a.c., grip, and best boy–as the designated whipping boy, James, an avant-gardist of the first order, is pretty much game for anything. Tonight we are transforming the filthy empty apartment into a hotel room, helpfully provided with furnishings by Paul, the superhustler superintendent, who wears tight white leather shorts laced up the sides and very little else. In this scene, Monti gets fucked by an old hippy john named Peter Festus, played by Miles H. Wildecock II (oddly, not his real name), a bartender at the infamous gay dive, The Blacklite, on Western between Santa Monica and Fountain, the future sight of the wrap party, which, at this point, is not even a glimmer at the end of the tunnel and, as far as I'm concerned, is not even a historical inevitability at this point.

Before the sex scene, though, we have scheduled in a scene with Tony and Rocko–his live-in girlfriend's toddler–both naked in the bathtub. They play adorably together until Monti's beeper goes off and he has to leave. A direct homage to/rip-off of *Flesh*–very Joe Dallesandro of the nineties, n'est-ce pas? Whatever. Ricardo is already starting to work my nerves, but I suppose this is to be expected. I told him before we started that on a film shoot of this kind everybody always thinks they're working harder than everyone else, because you're working so hard that you can't believe that anyone else could possibly be working as hard as you, but he wouldn't believe me, so now I'm going to have to work twice as hard as him just to give the appearance of doing the same amount. Also, almost everyone on the crew is coming to me complaining about Ricardo yelling at them and being mean, so I have to pull him aside and politely request that he chill a little. He tells me that everyone is saying the same thing about me to him, but I don't believe him. That's textbook Ricardo strategy. I'm a tad livid, but I do have to take into consideration that it is, after all, his first movie. I knew co-directing would be disastrous, but actually it's only minorly catastrophic. I don't think I'd ever do it again, however.

So Dede leaves with Rocko and we go on to the opening fuck scene, which contains full frontal nudity but is a simulated sex act with the john, Festus, doing the hustler, Monti, doggy-style. At one point I think I see a tarantula, but it turns out only to be the biggest cockroach I have ever seen, so I take a picture of it with someone's finger in the frame in order to give it scale. Tension mounts as we close the set to the bare minimum crew in order to shoot Monti's unsimulated jerk-off scene. It goes swimmingly, although I must say I am finding that the process of putting sex on film is really

135

starting to make me lose interest in the dirty deed altogether. The shoot finishes around midnight and the crew is disgruntled and exhausted, so I feel compelled to help load the equipment. I even learn how to wrap cables and disassemble grip stands. I even learn what a grip stand is.

DAY THREE

Another early morning call-time in order to take advantage of the more diffused light and to avoid scary LA cops, since we are shooting entirely without permits, as you may recall. A hustler acquaintance of Ricardo's was recently arrested for littering when he was observed throwing a cigarette butt on the ground, so we must be prepared for harassment, considering the nature of the beast.

The scene this morning takes place at Plummer Park, where our hero stops to wipe the blood off his (actually Ricardo's in real life) 1967 black-topped white Cougar. After several takes a cop actually does show up, having received a call from Park security, but he's a queen and only half-heartedly reprimands us for not having a permit. In fact, he seems to be rather star struck by Tony—as are, we will discover, a lot of people. A mulatto hustler whom we will later interview on Hi 8 informs me that another movie about hustlers is currently being made and that they are also using Plummer Park as a location. After a little digging (friends at ICM, darling) I discover that the project in question is a cheap (a mill or so—we should have it so cheap) feature called *johns* (what is it, a fucking e.e. cummings poem?) starring David Arquette as a hustler whose money gets stolen from his shoe as he's sleeping in Plummer Park, and co-starring Barbra's ex, Elliott Gould, as a shopping-cart hobo. I have a feeling there is about to be a glut of films about hustlers, so we'd better get busy, since ours will be the definitive one, right?

A tense moment on the set as we discover that our amputee actor, Kevin, has called in sick, forcing us to reschedule his big unlove scene with Piglet. Apparently all those special effects and stunt falls yesterday banged him up a little. He is also going through a lot of turmoil in his personal life, has to move tomorrow, and, as we will soon discover, just got beaten up by his roommate slash whatever who was to play Billy Ray Jaded in *Hustler White* and has already been in a scene but has now disappeared and must be recast. Kevin is also having second thoughts about the stumping scene—in which he fucks Billy Ray Jaded with his leg stump—because he says everybody already treats him like a freak fetish and this scene will only exacerbate things.

Poor Kevin. He also recently lost his rich West Hollywood veterinarian boyfriend of seven years to AIDS and was left penniless, etc., etc. A little rain cloud follows him wherever he goes, but I must say I find him incredibly funny and sexy and cute and nice, even though he is an incorrigible polemicist slash shit disturber who likes to fuck with people's heads including that of Matt, our cute little politically correct scientologist-raised Prince Albert, who bristles when Kevin goes on one of his anti-women tirades. So anyway, we have to find a new stumpee, and what's worse, we aren't at all convinced that Kevin P. Scott will be back, and he no longer has a phone.

It's back to Ricardo's bungalow for the evening shoot, in which Bud Cockram (almost his real name—actually, it's Cockerham, and he works at the Tom of Finland Foundation) entertains a john, Ambrose Sapperstein (Graham David Smith), by putting cigarettes out all over his body and slicing him up with a razor and generally treating him like a human Veg-O-Matic, all unsimulated, of course. You see, it's Graham's real-life fetish. Graham is an Englishman of the Quentin Crisp era, a remarkable chap who not only writes children's books under a pseudonym and paints extraordinary images of S & M and sexual torture inspired by his own personal experiences, but was also the longtime companion of Eric Hebborn, one of the world's foremost art forgers, never apprehended, whose work has hung in the Louvre and the Metropolitan Museum.

If I'm not very much mistaken, and I know I'm not, the last film Graham appeared in was Fellini's *Giulietta of the Spirits*, so of course we're honoured. Of that experience, he tells a highly entertaining, if implausible, story (the best kind). One day on the set it somehow transpired that the cinematographer of *Giulietta*... handed the camera to Graham, who proceeded to drop it. Fellini calmly walked over to the horrified youth and dead-panned, "I'll never forget you, my boy." Graham is currently writing his memoirs, which are eagerly anticipated by the likes of *Vanity Fair*, so I'm sure he'll tell that story in more detail, and better. Ricardo met him when they were in the same group art show in San Diego, where Graham resides. He is currently writing a little diary of his adventures working on *Hustler White* which he will publish somewhere smashing; similarly, Ron Athey will be visiting the set to do a piece on the making of our modest movie for the *LA Weekly*, including his own role as the macabre john, Seymour Kasabian.

The shoot tonight is extremely difficult because electricity and morale are currently scarce. We are trying out a new a.c. (assistant cameraman) whom everyone, but everyone, hates—a dreary drip who makes all sorts of inappropriate and unfunny jokes, someone who has been working in "the industry" for a long time and thinks our little endeavor is a fiasco unworthy of his technical prowess. Our d.o.p. also dislikes him, but he is making things easier for James in the lighting department. We use ass. cameraman to set up for the scene between Bud and Monti, but the following scene, wherein Bud uses Ambrose as, variously, an ashtray and a side of beef on a meat hook at your local butcher's, will obviously have to be a closed set; even Ricardo is not certain he will be able to withstand the carnage.

As someone who has had his mouth sewn shut for the camera on two separate occasions, I remain unmoved. It's all show business to me. For the scene with Monti and Bud, we have a nude bondage model in an antique wheelchair (our very own art director, Steve, who still, even naked, doesn't strike me as particularly sexy yet), plus another bound boy hung upside down from the rafter. The new a.c. is nonplussed but trying to act casual by saying really insipid things; eventually I am forced to take him aside, calm him down, and inform him that the upcoming scene is very sensitive, so he will be free to leave when we are ready to shoot. He thanks me for my "professionalism" and for keeping him abreast of things.

So it's aloha with a steel guitar for the new a.c., cousin. Ambrose's pin-cushion act goes well; as the razor slices across his back and buttocks at the hands of a nude, tattooed and heavily genitally-pierced Bud, he exclaims ecstatically, "Thank-you my dear boy. Delicious, delicious dear boy," etc. Oh, the pain, the pain. It's not really my cup of hemlock, but Ricardo and James are really into it, both taking lots of snaps for their respective family photo albums.

DAY FOUR

For the first time we have a more reasonable call time, like eight a.m. or something, so I'm hoping this will help crew morale which at this point, to be frank, is a tad lower than a snake's belly, as my mother would say. In fact, Steve is on the verge of quitting but sticks it out, I discover later, because he likes me, he really likes me. In the morning we pick up some stuff we missed of Tony on the

Boulevard, and on our return to the production office we're informed that there is a problem at the lab with fogging on one of the rolls we shot. Owing to Murphy's Law, more reliable than that of Gravity when it comes to movie-making, I'm convinced the damaged footage includes some of our money shots, like Tony and Rocko in the tub, or Tony's solo, and they're ruined and we'll never find that recipe again.

Meanwhile, Annie tells me that in order to get the dolly I need for the Rusty video shoot on Sunday—which is necessary if I want to supply a transfusion of liquid capital into this pallid production—we need a million dollar insurance policy. Oh sorry, mine has just expired. Oh well, I'll deal with it later by forging one from a friend back in Toronto because as you know, the laws of mortal man do not apply to independent film-makers. Emily, our cute seventeen year old militant lesbian Princess Albert who went to Scientology school, drives me and James to the lab to assess the damage in case there's a problem with the camera or one of the mags or something.

Oh yeah, and it begins to rain cats and dogs. In LA. In June. Like, when are the locusts scheduled to arrive? This is definitely not turning out to be my day, although at the lab we do discover that the problem is far less severe than I had expected—virtually unnoticeable, even—and it's not a scene that would be impossible to reshoot, so my stomach loosens up a little, and my ulcers call a temporary truce. We speed back to the production bungalow so I can change into my costume and slap on the make-up for the afternoon shoot on the patio of the Yukon Mining Co. Restaurant on Santa Monica, one of Ricardo's real life "offices" (the other, of course, being Astro Burger, where we will be conducting some of our hustler interviews).

Although we did get permission to shoot here, for a change, the ownership is a bit disgruntled that we are pretty much taking over the patio, but they are gay and therefore mindlessly supportive of our little gay movie, especially considering we're not paying them. (Other gay establishments, like The French Market, are donating free sandwiches and such, which is good, since our catering budget is about as meager as the menu at the Fashion Café.) The shoot seems to go well, although it's suddenly raining, which might cause some continuity problems. But as we have no continuity person anyway, I doubt that it's going to be one of the movie's strong suits. And as you know, I don't give a damn about continuity, anyway. I sit at a table by the street with my little laptop, in character as Jürgen, looking over a list of the hustlers I have encountered since coming to LA and rating them on a scale of one to ten under the categories "Mind", "Face", "Body", "Soul", and "Teeth"–a system, incidentally, that I and Ricardo actually used during our auditions, but don't tell anybody, otherwise we might be perceived as demented.

It was kind of a joke, in a way, but of course I know from experience that there really is no such thing. The only one who scored tens across the board, of course, was Tony/Monti–who, in his pale blue, skin-tight t-shirt pulled up under his armpits to display his

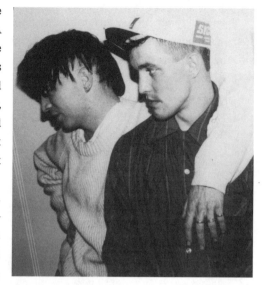

Me and Joe the Ho, my first hustler boyfriend and also my last. I would later drive Joe into becoming a Nazi skinhead. Photo by Parker.

ample nipples, looks particularly radiant today, as does Ambrose, basking in the afterglow of his bloody valentine to us the previous evening. After the rain lets up a little we do a great extreme telephoto shot of Monti's ass as he walks down the street, stuffing his bloody wife-beater into his back pocket. (Wife-beater: that's Tony's expression for tank-top. Isn't he adorable?) I just know it's going to be my favourite shot.

Speaking of wife-beating, have I mentioned that by the end of the making of *Hustler White*, three of our actors will have been beaten up and robbed by their respective live-in hustler boyfriends, each of whom auditioned for our movie? Well it's true. First off, during pre-production the original Monti, whose sparkling track record I told you about earlier, slapped around one of our actor johns before relieving him of his art collection. Secondly, during production, Kevin, our amputee, was sucker-punched by his roomie, the original Billy Ray Jaded, who absconded with some of his valuable gardening tools (Kevin is an expert horti-culturist who has won many prizes for his succulents and orchids and such). And

last but not least, shortly after the movie was in the can, Miles H. Wildecock II, another of our johns, was rolled by a hustler by the name of Ed Campbell whom he took into his home and who high-tailed it to Seattle with a significant chunk of Miles' wardrobe and jewelry collection. I remember auditioning Ed; he was, as I recall, as thick as two short planks, so I'm not surprised. It's undeniably another case of life imitating art as Festus, the character Miles plays in *Hustler White*, has his wallet stolen by a hustler named Monti. Anyway, I can kind of relate, because my hustler ex-boyfriend, Joe the Ho, beat me up a couple of times. He never ripped me off, though. I guess he must have really loved me.

Meanwhile, back on the set of *Hustler White*, we're shooting Ambrose at a pay phone at Plummer Park, and Ricardo and James are having some big argument about whether or not to include a flower in the frame. Those two are starting to wreck

139

each other's nerves. Ricardo thinks that James listens to me but not him, and he thinks that James and I work together but we expect Ricardo to work for us, not with us. I kind of really don't want to get involved, but I am involved, we are all involved. So I'll just wait until it all comes to a head on Day Six and deal with it then, badly.

Ricky and I have a strange relationship. I–I don't even want to talk about it. Let's just say he's a "Black Magic Woman"–as I keep singing to annoy him–and well, he hasn't called me anything but Judy for at least two years, except now during the shoot he's taken to calling me Bruce-Judy, so what can I say? It's the kind of gay relationship that really doesn't exist anymore, and probably for good reason. And you know me. My emotional range extends from about vaguely depressed to neutral. It's not that I don't care; it's that I can't afford to.

140

DAY FIVE

More early morning exteriors on the Boulevard, this time with international gay porn star Kevin Kramer, probably the top bottom currently working in the business, replacing the hole left by the late Joey Stefano. It ain't easy, as Kevin will tell you, to become famous as an exclusive bottom, but the very business-like yet personable Mr. Kramer has managed it, having just come off a porno co-starring with Jeff Stryker (it's even bigger in real life than it looks on video, Kevin confesses, wide-eyed) and having recently appeared as coverboy of the Advocate's *Freshmen* magazine. Ryan Block, who will appear in the "Black" scene in *Hustler White*, also worked on the Stryker film, but it was a solo jerk-off. Although he has given up his booty in videos on rare occasions, Ryan is, if I'm not very much mistaken, a natural born top. More on the Marky Mark of gay porn later. Meanwhile, we are shooting Kevin on the street, in a pair of denim cut-offs designed specifically to accentuate what could only by described, in Kevin's case, as the male pussy. We also shoot him at the exterior of the Black House–the famous fortress-like house painted entirely black, owned by Susan, the eccentric heir to the Levi-Strauss fortune–in the midst of an unassuming residential neighborhood in Hollywood. James and Ricardo are quarreling again, but apparently they have this love-hate thing going on. Ricardo will later admit that he wouldn't kick James out of bed for failing to remove the daylight filter on an indoor shoot.

The interior location for the rest of the day–the porno shoot scene–is a dingy, black, rat-infested hole in the wall storefront on Addams, a brick's throw away from South Central, with an abundance of night-of-the-living-crack-people milling about. On Saturdays it's a gay black after hours sex club, apparently packed to the rafters. The bathroom walls are papered with porn people sporting huge hard-ons, including, as it turns out, one of our very own porn stars for this scene–Alex Austin–who appears in the top corner of the crapper. He is very proud that his picture has been included in the pantheon.

The club, aptly called The Movement, is run by a demure friend of a friend and his friend, named Artist, who looks like Seal and has a black past in more ways than one which is why he is reluctant to appear in our movie as a sexual icon in the "Black" scene, particularly since Ryan Block, a famous black porn star with whom he is somehow mysteriously acquainted, will be there, but I can't go into details. Draw your own conclusions.

Apparently, the two friends who run the club are no longer friends owing to some dispute over our use of the space, but I don't want to know. As a location, it's touch and go right up to the last minute, but finally we are given the green light, which, as you know, doesn't get any greener.

Anyway, we're on the way to the Addams Street location, which is just around the corner from the Church of the Harvest, but we're still only about a block away from Ricardo's, and we stop to get some popsicles. Ricardo is driving the Lincoln Town Car that belongs to Annie, our production manager; on the passenger side is Kevin, our sweet amputee, bald as a proverbial billiard ball and wearing only his prosthetic and a teeny-tiny pair of cut-off jeans with the fly open and revealing red bikini underwear (and he's sexy as hell, I might add, with his little washboard stomach and pierced nipples); in the back seat is me dressed as Jürgen in a white shirt and black suit and tie and lots of make-up, and Søren, our Berliner sound guy with short bleached hair who just turned twenty-seven yesterday, incidentally, making him one of the elder members of the crew, mind you.

So as we pull into the parking lot in our ingenuous pursuit of popsicles, two muscle-y cops on bicycles catch the eye of Kevin, who looks away immediately, having had more than his fair share of run-ins with, and beat-ups by, the charming Los Angeles police department. Espying a long-haired Mexican in a Lincoln, with a "skinhead" in the suicide seat and a couple of suspicious-looking Euro-trash types in the back, the cops swiftly dismount their mountain bikes in unison and, likewise, adjust their billy clubs and holsters and whatnot. As Ricardo emerges from the 7-11 with his hands full of a quartet of dripping popsicles, one of the men in blue shorts starts to yell, "Excuse me, Miss. Halt, Miss," et cetera.

Not being a woman, Ricardo keeps walking, obliviously, a cartoon bubble containing a nice refreshing fudgesicle floating above his head. (Later Kevin pointed out that the cops must have been addressing one butt-ugly woman from behind if they thought Ricardo was a female, and we all laughed and laughed. But we weren't laughing then.) The twin beefy policemen commence to interrogate us for an hour and a half. They make each of us get out of the car—which they are convinced is stolen because they seem to think we don't look like we belong with it—one by one, and frisk us each a bit too thoroughly.

One cop seems suspiciously eager to pat down Kevin's crotch because, he claims, people often carry concealed weapons there. Trust me, in this case there is no "there" there to conceal anything, there is barely enough room in those shorts to house Kevin's own, apparently not inconsiderable, God-given "weapon". Even thought we try to explain that Kevin and I are in costume because we're making a student film, our standard lie, the cop still can't contain himself from making a snide comment about Kevin's underwear. Kevin, ever the provocateur, observes, "You're paying a lot of attention to my crotch, aren't you." The cop replies mysteriously, "Yeah, I always check out dick on the street," apparently attempting to establish his West Hollywood beat street credentials. "Takes one to know one, I guess," fires back cute Kevin, although Ricardo and I are at this point rolling our eyes and muttering "Kevin, shut up," under our breath through gritted also almost adventurous somehow (or is that adventuress?) and remain outwardly calm, as does Ricardo. At this point in the shoot, it is just another little major catastrophe, one of too many to keep track of, even.

Fortunately, providence or, rather, Kevin P. Scott, intervenes, by going post office. He starts to go off on what can only be described as a good old-fashioned, anarchist rant about how we have been detained for absolutely no reason, how we are being discriminated against on the grounds of ethnic origin and sexual orientation, how we have been presumed guilty and are now being expected to prove our innocence, and by the way, why is it that the police recruit insecure men with small penises? So that they can brainwash them into robotic, fascistic tools of the patriarchy, et cetera.

It's really quite impressive. For such a sweet guy, Kevin is really bitter, and now he is in his element, demanding that the two goons call in a supervisor so that he may lodge a formal complaint of police harassment and violation of his civil liberties, which Americans are really big on. The cops call in a sergeant to mediate, shifting the emphasis of the ordeal from potential car theft to potential law suit against the already beleaguered police force, owing to the Rodney King incident and the Simpson trial and all. The supervisor is also an asshole, but not quite as obvious a one as his underlings; he watches Kevin and the bicycle cop—with their faces literally one inch away from each other—get into an even more heated, name-calling exchange, hoping, no doubt, that Kevin will really lose his temper and strike the cop, landing us all in jail tout de suite. Kevin has a few more good lines, like when he lies, "I'm a property owner. My property taxes pay your salary. You work for me." The cop responds, "Then why don't you try to fire me?" "All right," shoots back Kevin, "I'm firing you. You're fired." Me and Ricardo manage to cool Kevin down and miraculously, the cops, who in LA, are very concerned about self-image these days, for obvious reasons, let us go. Of course by this point, we are at least two hours late for our shoot, but like I always say sometimes, better late than jailbait.

After our traumatic ordeal, the "Porn" shoot, wherein Jürgen visits the set of a Hollywood porno set at the invitation of his friend Roger V. Deem, goes remarkably smoothly. Ricardo records a sex scene between our two real life porn stars, Kevin Kramer and Alex Austin—the latter of whom, incidentally, has a new girlfriend that he will bring over to Ricardo's later to meet us. It's an elaborate shoot, but a fun one.

teeth. It goes downhill from there. To make a long story short, the cops, after waiting for a squad car to arrive, run the license plates and discover that the name on the registration doesn't correspond with the owner's name we've provided, plus they run my name and Ricardo's through the computer and inform us that we both have warrants out for our arrests—mine for the not unimpressive sum of eight thousand dollars.

I am convinced in that moment that I will be spending a minimum of one night in the gay jail, and then will be deported, and that I will have to be replaced by a Bela Lugosi-style body-double for the rest of the shoot. ("Let me hear you call Greg Araki a cocksucker," I can hear them say as they audition my replacement.) I feel slightly panicked inside, but

142

Paul Bellini, a writer for "Kids in the Hall," visits the set from Toronto and is instantly given a cameo: next week he will act as caterer for the "Black" scene, philanthropically cooking an incredible Italian meal for twenty. (Josh, our assistant director, goes out with "Kid in the Hall" and current Larry Sanders regular Scott Thompson, who also had a cameo in my last feature, *Super 8 1/2*, incestuous faggots that we are.) Ricardo is playing the camera operator of the porn shoot (his little cameo) and actually shooting on Hi-8. Alex can't seem to get it up, but that's okay because we don't want to go beyond NC-17 anyway, if possible.

One of the extras for the scene is Billy, a hustler who Ricardo recruited off the street earlier today when we were shooting Kevin's exteriors. (Ricardo has a real flair for casting, I must say.) Billy is a displaced New Yorker who still speaks Brooklynese, looks a little bit like John John Kennedy, and plays the Fool in the Shakespearean sense, repeating lines over and over again like "It's all coming back to me now," and "Time to spank the monkey," apparently a reference to his crack habit. He tells stories about how he recently gave himself up to the police over some outstanding warrants because he needed a place to crash for a few days. They wouldn't arrest him, though, so he pitched a fit, but all they did was throw him out, so he went to the supermarket and boosted a jar of peanut butter, then sauntered into a nearby restaurant and borrowed a spoon and had a "hustler lunch" (Jiffy peanut butter straight from the jar, very high in protein), so that he might be arrested. Other bon mots attributable to our friend Billy include the by now famous line, "My nipples have been hard ever since I moved to Los Angeles." Also, for some reason he has a tractor tattooed on his stomach. I was afraid to ask.

Ambrose, our English masochist who is visiting the set as a journalist and extra today, ends up hiring Billy for the evening; you see they are both members of the human ashtray school, Billy also sporting alarmingly deep cigarette burns on the tattoo of a cross on his inner arm. It's so nice when like-minded individuals hook up on a film set, especially a set as friendly and sincere as ours. Even our porn stars have commented on how different the atmosphere is from a real porn set; why, you can even relax, make jokes, and be yourself.

DAY SIX

Today starts out smoothly enough, although there is something brewing between James and Ricardo that has got to give. I keep telling Ricardo that he has to work it out by talking to James, but he hasn't done it yet. I'm kind of mad at Ricardo too because we had a fight the other day in which I said to him, about some decision I had made concerning something crucial, "Don't you trust me?" and he replied, "No," and I said, "Well that just about says it all, doesn't it." It wasn't pretty. So today we start out innocently shooting an exterior at Hunters, the hustler bar on Santa Monica, with Alex Austin and Glen Meadmore in his cute little Mustang. Alex is wearing black leather chaps with nothing underneath, so Ricardo has to keep him covered up with a shirt until we are ready for each take. Ricky seems curiously absent, sometimes literally so, as he keeps on disappearing.

143

Later I find out that he had a big fight with his ex-boyfriend again and is also stressed out by the shoot, so he escaped inside Hunters and had himself a few drinks without telling anyone. The rest of the morning is a bit of a shambles, I'm afraid. First of all we lose two of our Prince Alberts—Matt and Emily (Ricardo calls them brothers, even though Emily is a hot bull-dagger—come to think of it, they are kind of like Alf and Ralph Monroe on Green Acres)—who have to go to the space we're shooting the video in tomorrow to clear it out and prepare it, a condition of the rental. Meanwhile, our production manager has to take away our a.d. to pick up the dolly, a task which they think will take a few minutes but which ends up being a three or four hour job, seeing as said dolly weighs five hundred pounds and takes six people to get in and out of the van.

144

Also, if it's dropped or damaged, the fake, million dollar insurance policy we had to forge won't cover it and we'll really be in trouble. So, with a third of our crew missing and no one in the office to co-ordinate everything—not to mention our slate and a reflector missing and Ricardo in a foul mood—we only get a few exteriors done before throwing in the towel for the morning.

Back at headquarters, Ricardo and James and I finally have it out, which is good because it clears the air a little, and by the end of the shoot Ricardo will even have a little crush on James, especially after James serenades him with some a cappella Cat Stevens songs one afternoon in a car on the way to a location. It's actually quite moving. One of the first questions Ricardo asked James after he met him was, "Have you ever slept with a man?" and James replied, "Of course, several times," with that European hauteur of his standing out in stark relief against his Texas background. But I don't think they're going to end up in bed together, frankly. I mean, I just can't feature it.

The afternoon shoot is back at the Addams Street location. Everyone is pretty burnt out and grumbling about having to do the video shoot tomorrow. We're taking advantage of the dolly but no one knows how to use it and it squeaks. We shoot Billy Ray Jaded, as played by Superhustler, jerking off to the *Amputee Times*, an actual magazine, but he can't get it up so we tear some of the dirty pictures off the bathroom wall and put them inside the magazine for him. He is still soft so I offer to fluff, which is strictly another job for me because although I do find him kind of hot, I'm still feeling asexual—but even though I give him the works he's still not hard. For some reason no one seems to be able to get it up on the set of *Hustler White*, so at this rate we may just get that NC-17 I've always wanted (as opposed to XXX, i.e.).

Between takes I leaf casually through some of the porno lying around and before I realize what's happening, I get excited for the first time in I don't know how long—sexually, i.e. Ricardo notices and laughs at me with gusto so I soon lose it, but at least I know it's still there.

During a break in the shoot, we all take turns feeling the bullet that is lodged in the Superhustler's bum that he never bothered to have removed after he got shot once, walking down the street in Hollywood. Interesting. The next set-up is the stumping of Billy Ray Jaded, which I pretty much have to leave up to Ricardo because I find out that we might not be able to get the dolly into the space for the video shoot tomorrow, which means we may need to find a last minute replacement space. Annie drives me all the way to Silverlake to meet with the owner of We've Got Bad Taste, Exene Cervenka's new store, which has an adjacent empty storefront we might be able to use. The space is full of junk, and Exene is reluctant to let us use the store because she hasn't heard the band and she would rather a band that she knows and likes use it.

As it turns out, the original space works out after all, so it's all academic anyway. But it was nice to finally meet the woman who sang "I Must Not Think Bad Thoughts" and "White Girl". I'm under a lot of pressure to pull off the video shoot tomorrow because our British money for production still has not come through and if not for the video there would be no movie at all at this point. But I'm sure I can probably pull it off. As Paul Morrisey once said, as you may recall, when I was introduced to him as Bruce LaBruce, "Why not?"

DAY SEVEN

The Rusty video shoot is today, and I'm a bit concerned, as the name of the song is "Misogyny" but there are no women in the film, images from which will be used exclusively for the video along with wrap-around footage of the band which we're shooting today. Actually, I'm not really that concerned. I mean, the budget for the video is coming from Atlantic, a major label, so I'm sure if they don't like it they'll just pay for another one. I think. Before I leave for the location, Ricardo and I have another fight, this time over points. I tell him he's being greedy. I'm extremely upset that he would bring up a money issue when I am spending my day off directing a music video partly to get more cash for the movie. Later, he will apologize (sort of) and tell me I am right, which must be a first, but it doesn't matter anyway because the video goes smoothly and I can finally see a light at the end of the tunnel on this hellish and impossible, yet somehow perversely enjoyable, shoot.

Tony, ever the professional, shows up in good spirits for the video–which he isn't getting paid for either but is again doing for the good of the film–but half way through, his girlfriend Dede becomes "ill" (time to spank the monkey, je presume) and I have to wrap him as quickly as I can. Me and James, whom I have to offer a small sum to shoot the video, have lots of fun playing with our expensive dolly and all and it takes us a lot less time than I had anticipated, which appeas-es the crew somewhat. Jeff Rogers, the manager of Rusty who has also generously put some money into *Hustler White*, becoming an executive producer–gives me an expensive pair of designer sunglasses that are very Lina Wertmueller, so I have a new image now, which always gives me hope.

DAY EIGHT

We've had to reschedule the final scenes of the movie–the climactic *Whatever Happened To Baby Jane?* beach sequence–for today, to accommodate Tony's European schedule, which starts on Wednesday; later, between commercials and runway shows he will be flown to New York to audition for a Demi Moore movie no less. (*Striptease*, as it turns out–good thing he lost the part, to nevertheless sexy Robert "T2" Patrick.) But first we shoot the very very final scene of the movie, the one which the final credits are to crawl over, and a still from which may grace the poster. (As it turns out, not–in a

145

stunning failure of the imagination, my distributor decided to opt strictly for beefcake on the poster, despite my vociferous objections.)

In it, Zoltan, our very handsome and butch Hungarian hustler, must sit in a chair in a pair of white jeans and pee in his pants. Zoltan is extremely charming and sexy and a great raconteur; some time you must have him tell you the grueling tale of his escape from behind the Iron Curtain in the early eighties, a story somewhat akin in certain atmospheric details to *Midnight Express*. Although Zoltan has endured many life-threatening situations in his life that might have induced anyone in the same position to pee his pants, when asked to do so on cue in front of a camera crew for a little romantic comedy about hustlers on Santa Monica Boulevard, it's a different story altogether. It's hard to pee in your pants on command–an idea I stole, by the by, from a scene in the British novel *The Swimming Pool Library* by Allan Hollinghurst–because we are so scrupulously conditioned from birth not to commit this little sin.

A half an hour and three beers later, Zoltan gets it on the second take, and how–a veritable Niagara Falls, which somehow turns me on, in the same way that hearing a guy standing at a toilet pee a particularly strong, loud stream of piss turns me on. Too bad Zoltan is married, apparently to a hot piece of rice, because he is definitely husband material. When we're through, Zoltan accompanies us to the beach to help with the next shoot, which he doesn't have to do but he does anyway because he's a nice guy, lugging heavy equipment and everything.

The location is El Matador Beach, where, apparently, Aldrich shot the final scene of *Baby Jane* or something. That's Robert Aldrich, one of the great ones, who directed *Autumn Leaves* with Joan Crawford and Cliff Robertson, who I recently saw at Trattoria (an expensive restaurant on Beverly near San Vincente) while I was dining with Gus Van Sant, who was in town shooting a commercial for the Levis company, who were paying for the dinner, which is why I was there in the first place. Gus leaned over and said "There's Cliff Robertson," in that charmingly star-struck way that he has, and I looked, and it was.

In a weird way *Hustler White* is kind of a remake of *Autumn Leaves*, or anyway it's like all great Aldrich movies, like *Baby Jane* and *Sister George*; i.e., chock full o' grotesque, deluded characters in obsessive relationships. So anyway, El Matador beach is well on the way to Ventura up the PCH (as, I discovered in San Francisco recently, only Los Angelinos call it) and in order to access it one has to essay a dirt trail and several sets of stairways down which we must now carry all the equipment. It's a race against time, as we want to take full advantage of the magic light that occurs just before and after sundown. There are about three photo shoots already in progress on the beach, but we must obviously look like we mean business, because they allow us to play through. The scene calls for my character, Jürgen, and Tony's character, Monti, to make out on the beach, only going as far as heavy petting, mind you. Tony is a great kisser, as I said, and I have to admit I get sexually excited again, even though he's not really my type, which drives Ricardo crazy whenever I say it because he says Tony is the world's type.

146

That's twice in three days, so I guess maybe I'm beginning to relax a little bit.

It's been a long day, but when we finish at the beach can we go home and relax? Of course not. We've had to reschedule the autoerotic asphyxiation scene between Eigil and Piglet for this evening. Piglet is played by Ivar Johnson, a very passive young man with a shaved head and a pierced septum. If you think my emotional range is limited, you should get a load of Ivar's. He makes me look like Sally Field as *Sybill* by comparison, or even Sally Field accepting her second Oscar. In this little episode, Eigil, flat on his back, is having sex with Piglet, who sits on top of him with a belt wrapped around his neck in order to increase the pleasure. The belt is too tight, however, and Piglet, unbeknownst to Eigil, begins to choke.

After several rehearsals and a rare second or third take, Ivar/Piglet's neck is raw and close to bleeding, but he doesn't complain in the least. He just laughs his blank little laugh and asks for another cigarette. Up until a few years ago, Ivar was in the closet and working at a bank in the suburbs, until one day he chucked it all to move into the city and become a modern primitive. Now he works at a sex club called Basic Plumbing, performs with Ron Athey, as well as occasionally doing his housework for sexual pleasure, and has a starring role in *Hustler White*. A success story for the nineties.

By the time we got started it was already ten o'clock, so we didn't end up finishing until two in the morning. The scene had been shot in Ricardo's office slash dungeon—my current bedroom—so I put on my eye mask and insert my earplugs and try to get some sleep as the crew packs up all the lights and grip stands around me, literally stepping over me as visions of Judy crying on Mason Rose's couch dance in my head.

DAY NINE

Day nine is the day we pick up a scene we missed earlier: I am in the Lincoln chasing Tony, who is on foot, up Lillian Way until he jumps over the wall at the Rock 'n' Roll hotel and I exit the car and try to follow him but fail. I do my Jerry Lewis routine and fall flat on my ass and I'm sure I've torn my only suit but miraculously I haven't. We're supposed to shoot another exterior this morning from the roof of the bank building at Santa Monica and Mansfield that our production lawyer used to work in when he was employed by Roger Corman, but when we try to sneak up there like we did in pre-production, somebody tips off the building manager and he kicks us out.

So we have to shoot the hustler group scene from the roof of the van, which works for me. Included in the group are our hustler twins, dressed in matching acid wash and looking kind of look like Nelson rent boys; Divinity Fudge's boyfriend, who has "Daddy's Boy" tattooed in large letters across his lower back; Billy, the human ashtray, Kennedy lookalike; and a few others whom we've picked up along the way. Previously, we had told Billy to be at this location at seven in the morning on this particular day, if he wanted to be in the scene, but the time was changed to eleven and we had no way of notifying him, as he lives on the street, so he has been here for four hours, sleeping on the grass in front of the bank, taking a little hustler nap.

A couple of hustler acquaintances of Billy's show up, a heavy metal fellow and his cute friend who has "Hollywood" tattooed on his stomach, but who only sticks around long enough for me to take a couple of snapshots of it. The heavy metal one starts talking lovingly about his hot girlfriend who, as it turns out, has only one flaw, as he refers to it, as once did Candy Darling: her penis. They can't afford the operation for her, so Billy helpfully suggests that she tie some dental floss around it until it turns brown and falls off, like they do with Rottweiller's tails. The heavy metal guy says they

should just tie dental floss around it and then tie it to a door and slam it like they used to do to remove a rotten tooth. After this charming exchange, he agrees to be in the scene we're shooting, in which Piglet approaches a group of hustlers who are gossiping about the mysterious disappearance of an amputee hustler, Eigil, with whom Piglet is infatuated. As we prepare for the shot, a limousine pulls up to the corner. The heavy metal hustler leans in through the open window and asks if he can borrow their cellular phone so he can return a page he just received. He makes a hustler date right on the spot. So hot.

This is Tony's last day, which is kind of sad because he's been so great, and our final car interiors don't go so well because everyone is exhausted from the long day yesterday and it's hot and the car is crowded with too many crew members and Tony's having trouble with his unreasonably long monologue and there seems to be a problem with one of the mags and the film jams in the gate for the first time during the shoot and I don't know. It's so difficult. Let's skip to the next day. Oh, except I forgot to tell you about the crazy deposed Russian Princess.

As we are shooting a car scene on the Boulevard between me and Tony—I'm in full make-up and my Jean-Luc Godard suit—a woman with a semi-bee-hive hairdo, oatmealy skin with what looks likes hives on her face and arms, a tattered, fairy tale dress, and a thick Slavic accent approaches me. "Are you a director?" she asks, then, stepping back and evaluating me more closely, "Do you have AIDS?" "Yes, and no," I reply distractedly. Clearly insane, she goes off on a tirade about how she is a superstar from Moscow and that she's looking for her Svengali to make her a star in America and I'm the anointed one.

I listen politely for a second and then bark to an assistant, "Someone give her a phone number," not expecting them to give her a real one. Unhappily, they did, and I can now add yet another stalker to the growing list. The last time she called, I gave the phone to Ricardo and he explained very slowly and very carefully how if she didn't stop harassing us he was going to call the police and have her arrested and the entire time she just laughed maniacally, saying, "Oh, Bruce, Oh Bruce," and when Ricardo said "I mean it. I'm not kidding," she said "Oh Bruce, you make me so happy," and hung up. I would say "only in LA, kids," but I have a couple of stalkers back in Toronto, so I know they're everywhere.

It's the day of the interior of the "Black" scene, in which Kevin Kramer, as a confused hustler, applies in person for a position with an escort agency, only to be gang-raped by the all-black group of hustlers presided over by a black male Madame, played by the illustrious Mrs. Glass. We are shooting at the house of Miss Vaginal Davis, who is appearing in male drag as her street character Buster Booté. Miss Davis is a bit taken aback when we arrive with a crew of ten, a cast of eight, a five hundred pound dolly, and all the lighting and grip equipment, and he's shocked by our moxy as we plug into all the neighbors electricity in our by this point automatic, we're-making-a-movie-get-out-of-our-way mode. Coincidentally, Billy, a good friend of our star Tony Ward, lives next door with his best friend, a parrot whom he found abandoned and nursed back to health, and he gladly donates his electricity to us. Miss Davis' pad is in a rather obscure location near Koreatown, so a few of the actors, like our porn star Ryan Block, have trouble finding the place. Ryan, who finally arrives two hours late, is managed by Gino Colbert, aka Sam Schad, former porn star and current producer and director thereof; it is he who convinced Ryan to appear in *Hustler White* on the basis of my reputation, and will later take me and Ricardo out with Ryan for a porno power dinner.

We have had a lot of trouble casting the black scene, even though the rape is simulated and only full nudity is required. Our other porn star, Tony Powers, shows up, as does Ron Athey acolyte Divinity Fudge, but we are a couple short of a gang-bang, so Ricardo and Mrs. Glass head over to the Boulevard for a little ad hoc casting. They return with two large black hustlers who seem to be a little anaesthetized (might as well face it you're addicted to crack) but otherwise up for pretty much anything. One of them is inordinately enamored of Josh, our a.d., and begins a continuous ten hour rant about how he wants to plough his little white booty, much to Josh's cute embarrassment.

Because it is the second-last-day of 16mm shooting with the Aaton, spirits are high and the shoot is relatively fun, except when the landlord arrives and we have to go all Anne Frank until Miss Davis, who says she's just shooting one of her little art videos, gets rid of her without letting her past the front door. Also the catering, an Italian feast generously prepared by Paul Bellini, is taking its time getting to the location, which is causing a little unrest. Bellini seems to have recovered from his ordeal of a few days ago: while driving Scott Thompson's rental car without insurance on Santa Monica Boulevard, he got distracted by some hustler white and got into an accident in front of the Formosa Café. (Incidentally, during pre-production, a hustler we were interviewing told us we should go down to the Formosa Café because Puck, from the "Real World," was eating there. He was really excited.)

Mrs. Glass looks spectacular in her caftan, which she purchased especially for the shoot from By George on Hollywood Boulevard; it looked particularly good sticking out of the bottom of the door of our rich friend Heidi Richman's bronze Mercedes convertible a la Shelley Duvall in *3 Women* on a shoot last week. Ryan Block, whose real name is Joaquin, is really getting me over my asexual mode as he walks around the set in his little leopard skin briefs. Near the end of the shoot we bring out two birthday cakes with candles and everything; one for Søren the soundmensch and one for Annie the production manager. They are suitably touched by our disarming sentimentality, as naked black men with giant schlongs eat birthday cake from paper plates all around them.

DAY ELEVEN

The final day with the Aaton has come at last. It seems like we've been shooting for months, but I suppose that's natural. The ordeal has definitely bonded the crew in the cutest way, but I won't bore you. Let's just say the Manson Family was never this tight (except maybe when they had been drinking), although at this point I must

150

say I feel equal parts Susan Atkins and Sharon Tate. Today we are shooting Ron Athey's role as Seymour Kasabian, the mortician john inspired by the Andrew Crispo story. (Yes, the Kasabian is a gratuitous Manson reference, but don't worry, it's a non sequitur, like everything else this summer.) Having already been warned by the stern woman at the Hollywood Cemetery of the steep rental price for the location, we realize we will have to shoot the cemetery scenes guerrilla-style.

As there is only room for one director, Ricardo volunteers to go off with his now best buddy James, Søren the soundman, and our two characters, Seymour and Piglet, in Ron's '65 Barracuda to shoot the scene surreptitiously. Apparently all goes well except at the very end when the middle-aged woman in the yellow pencil skirt gets wise to our scam and comes running out of her office pulling a *Cagney and Lacey* and yelling, "Freeze! You need a permit to shoot here! Freeze!" trying to catch the Atheymobile as it squeals away. This seems to amuse Ricardo to no end, as he laughs and laughs. After shooting the rest of the exteriors in a nearby mortuary parking lot, it's off to Ron Athey's Silverlake digs to finish off the interiors in which Piglet is to be mummified with gaffer tape. Scott Thompson visits the set, and seems somewhat agog, fascinated, and a little concerned by the mummification process.

I'm not really worried about a John Landis-style manslaughter suit with Piglet becoming our very own Vic Morrow, i.e., because Ron is obviously very experienced and a true professional in every sense of the word, et cetera. The mood of the crew is buoyant; the bonding, palpable. It's kind of like the Stockholm syndrome, the phenomenon of kidnap victims or hostages becoming inordinately attached not only to each other, but to their captors (that would be me and Ricardo) as well. Anyway, Ron is a self-admitted bad actor, which is precisely the style of acting we're looking for in *Hustler White*, and his turn as Wynona is truly frightening. Wait until you see it. What am I saying, wait until I see it. No dailies, remember?

WRAP

Aside from the annoying pick-ups we have to shoot with James' trusty Bolex on the twelfth day, and a couple of afternoons of Hi-8 hustler interviews, the shoot, for all intents and purposes, is over, and not a minute too soon. The wrap party, held at the historic Blacklite, an ex-brothel on Western between Santa Monica and Fairfax, is an intimate affair with Miles, one of our actors, tending bar. The post-party, at Dede's (Tony's girlfriend) is even more intimate. I can't go into details. Let's just say certain members of the crew are still playing musical beds, and as for me, my asexual streak is briskly terminated when I end up going all the way out to San Pedro with sexy Ryan Block, our straight gay porn star, so that he can, ahem, show me his portfolio. And quel portfolio.

Not That It's Any of Your Business

I suppose you want to know what happens next, all the Edward Gorey details and all, not that it's any of your business. Well I'm going to tell you anyway, as punishment. After the *Hustler White* shoot I'm exhausted, both morally and financially, so I head to San Francisco where, to steal a line from Vaginal Davis, young people go to retire. "Spring chicken" not being exactly the expression I would use to describe myself, I don't quite know what I'm doing here except murdering time, one of my favourite occupations. Oh yeah, I almost forgot, my previous feature *Super 8 1/2* is opening for a two week run at the Red Vic on Upper Hate (somehow the homonym always seems more appropriate) so I guess I'm on a publicity junket, which is good because as a Capricorn, I find I can't travel anywhere on an actual vacation; I always have to be working.

Actually, to make things easier for myself I usually choose to be on a publicity junket at all times, in case you see me on the street and wonder why I'm acting so grand. I'm staying on Lower Haight (enough with the homonyms) with gay husband and wife team MarcandKevin, my San Francisco treats who always most generously give me unlimited access to their Jacuzzi, their wet bar, their dueling modems, and any one of their five bathrooms. Marc also happens to be a famous fag photog, which is very convenient for photo shoots.

Take my advice: always befriend the journalists and shutterbugs when you're travelling, and try to be their house guest if you can swing it. Nobody's going to give you a bad review or take an ugly picture of you if they have to wake up and face you in the morning over a cup of coffee. Kevin also happens to work at *Wired*, so it's all very infotainment highway, I assure you. Anyway, now that the scene is set, I'll go through my San Francisco ordeal day by day just to show you what I have to put up with in this life.

DAY ONE

Interviews with *The Bay Area Reporter*, *The Guardian*, *The San Francisco Weekly*, and *The Sentinel* at the Red Vic, whose staff is extremely nice and supportive of me and my work, by the way, as opposed to that harridan who refused to program *Super 8 1/2* at the Castro, despite the fact that it sold out that 1500 seat theatre during the film festival. Later, I watch *Romper Stomper*—one of my favourite movies—with Marc and Miss Joan Jett Blakk, the infamous Afro-

151

DAY TWO

Photo shoot in Marc's Jacuzzi with a bevy of beautiful boys in the b.g.: local scenester and go-go dancer Santiago, local up-and-often-coming photogs Brook and his ex-wife, Donal. They are all naked; I am in a red swimsuit by Raymond Dragon (you know, the ex-porn star turned designer) and red windbreaker, seated in front of my little laptop.

It's all very Annie Leibowitz, only good. High concept even, gazing, as I am, into a cracked mirror. (No, it was cracked before I looked into it, you cad.) Then we all rush to the Roxie to catch a press screening of the great and scary Nico bio-pic, the director of which I will later meet at the Berlin Film Festival where she will inform me that she next plans to tackle Romy Schneider. I guess she has a thing for dead German blondes, but then again, who doesn't? (Or was Romy a redhead? No matter. Dead redheads are even better.) We run into Miss Block there (Adam, the journalist, not Ryan, the porn star), who takes us to that biker bar under the freeway overpass—you know the one—where we sit out back in the G.J. Ballardesque cityscape with Bambi Lake, the famous non-famous pre-op transsexual ex-Stranglers groupie bitch who recently published her mammoirs. I met her in LA at the opening of the Silverlake store of a legendary female SoCal punk where I almost shot a music video but decided not to at the last minute because the legend scared me.

Incidentally, the "art director" of *Hustler White*, a surfer from San Diego with whom I had a triste tryst after the shoot, would later have a torrid affair with the legendary punk's gay partner in the store (you know, the one with the plugs—the partner, that is, not the store, i.e., hair, not electrical) while I am away at a film festival in Helsinki, and then, purely by coincidence, would be given an exhibition of his paintings in that same space.

Then my *Hustler White* collaborator will have an affair with an ambitious young San Francisco artist who also once happened to have a fling with the legendary punk's gay partner, and also coincidentally had an art opening at the store. Then my collaborator will arrange an art exhibit for this same youngster in San Diego, after which the youngster will summarily dump my collaborator. I

American San Francisco drag queen by-way-of-Chicago by-way-of-Haglanta by-way-of-Detroit where she was raised, who once had the temerity to run for President à la Pat Paulsen. Miss Jett Blakk and I respect each other despite her orthodox fag politics and my anti-gay tendencies, like when Democrats and Republicans marry.

Marc, who is Jewish, is not amused by *Romper Stomper*, and I suppose my swooning over the sexy Nazi skinhead boyfriends isn't helping any. Incidentally, one of them—Daniel Pollock—was tragically killed in a car accident days after the picture wrapped, which makes it all the more poignant for me.

152

mention this only to provide some insight into the not always pretty underbelly of the gay world: all the poor old Margos, all the fine young Eves. Anyway, Bambi (remember her?—don't worry, neither does she) keeps bugging me to put her in a movie with Hank Rollins. As if.

DAY THREE
Or something. I have no recollection of this day.

DAY FOUR
I accompany Joan Jett Blakk—strictly as a favour, mind you—to the Castro as her date for the Betty Boop look-a-like contest for which she is a judge. She is stunning in Angela Davis drag, replete with Afro wig, black jeans and turtleneck, and black leather *Avengers* boots. You know I love her even though she is a gay politico. She happens to be very smart and very funny and, like all drag queens, very tragic.

Afterwards we make a pit stop at the Detour where Woody tends bar. Woody, of course, is the ex of Mark Goldstein, a former senior piercer at the Gauntlet with whom I once drove from San Francisco to New York in a beat up old Datsun painted black, along with Michael Blue, the infamous DJ and porn star with whom I was at the time having a rather high profile summer affair. Not being able to go back to Michael's place on account of his boyfriend being there, our initial encounter took place, literally and metaphorically, in the sewer. But that's another story.

Anyway, Woody is just getting off work, so he smokes us up with some murdering weed and I'm really very stoned and Miss Blakk drags me to this terrible "dragapella" group called the Kinsey Sicks (it's all very AIDS-y, of course) who are famous for their a cappella cover of "Macho Man" by the Village People and the audience is just full of these. It's lousy with these San Francisco gay politico types who smell of liberalism, reek of liberalism, and of course my date knows them all, knows everybody in town, and she keeps introducing me but I remain pretty demure because I'm so stoned; like this stuff must have been laced with something, I've got to tell you.

The guy behind us in line who is talking to Miss Blakk—some big-wig AIDS activist who lobbies in Washington—is cracking jokes about Log Cabin conservatives, the gay Republican organization; meanwhile, he looks about as Log Cabin-y as you can get without wearing a stove-pipe hat, with his high-riding, carefully pressed jeans, long-sleeved, tucked-in, straight-as-an-Arrow shirt and tasseled loafers.

My host Marc has come, I suspect, just to watch me squirm through this horrible spectacle: these hideous drag queens telling quasi-political jokes and just, like, not even aspiring to the standards of old school queenery, not even close, mind you. Just retarded, infantile schtick. Overdone, over-produced, tacky, crass, ugly, stupid drag. Hated it. When they come off the stage for audience participa-

153

tion I start to panic and almost bolt several times. Not to mention that my stocks are plummeting. If I'm sighted here, my reputation will be ruined. Anyway, I suffer through that ordeal and then we go back to Marc's Jacuzzi and get stoned again and then go to this silly club called Hellbound which has good music and tired club kids and a performance involving Godzilla and Mothra and a lot of papier-mâché and open flame which is cute but dumb, not to mention a fire hazard.

DAY FIVE

At the Red Vic I see *Willy Wonka and the Chocolate Factory* for the first time ever; unbelievable but true. Intense identification with Veruca Salt. The marquee reads,

from left to right, "Next: Bruce LaBruce's Super 8 1/2", "Willy Wonka and the Chocolate Factory", and "Coming Soon: Last Tango in Paris." Loving it. Then at Marc's I watch *The Lucy Show* stoned, getting off on all those primary colours in the credits, and then take a Jacuzzi with a friend I'm supposed to go out with, but he takes too much synthetic heroin and almost ODs or something, so Marc and I go to the Hole in the Wall, the gay biker bar that has gotten just a little too trendy, where we hook up with Don Baird, who spins there on Mondays, and his new boyfriend who has a sexy hairlip.

Some grizzled leather granny comes up to ask me if I would be so kind as to pee into a beer bottle for him so that he might drink it. I decline graciously. Miss Blakk is also very much present, and gets into a good old-fashioned, bull-daggery fight, smashing a beer bottle on the bar and brandishing it at someone for accidentally almost hitting her upside the head with a pool cue and not being sorry enough about it. Isn't she the hot-tempered one. Then we go to Don's briefly. He's nice as pie—no ugly psychodrama like last time, but we won't go into that. (At any rate, I support spousal abuse amongst homosexuals.) We tricked once, and he did a nude photo-spread for *J.D.s*, my ex-fanzine. He looks like a better looking Jack Cassidy. He just better stay away from open flame, that's all I have to say.

DAY SIX
Um.

DAY SEVEN
The thing about San Francisco, I ruminate as I fly back to LA is that everybody is a drug mess. All they ever do is talk gay politics, go to funerals, complain about not having any boyfriend prospects because they've already all slept with each other a million times, and take designer drugs. A couple of old friends who used to be quite stunning really look the worse the wear for it, too. I, on the other hand, who have never really been considered a classic beauty, was told by more than one person last night that I looked "do-able" in my new tight little burnt orange crushed

velvet shirt and orange Lina Wertmüller sunglasses. I have been receiving some rather special compliments lately. I'm sure I don't have to remind you that in the gay world, one must never underestimate the importance of outer beauty.

Like An Inferior Tennessee Williams Novella

Meanwhile, back at the Spahn Ranch (as I am wont to call my LA digs–and for good reason), most days I find myself involuntarily lying in the sun outside of my little bungalow reading fashion magazines. People say I'm going to get melanoma, but I counter by laboriously explaining that when I was growing up on the farm I used to spend eight hours a day roofing houses or ploughing fields shirtless in the sun, so I'm sure I already have skin cancer to look forward to. (Being a natural redhead doesn't help, either. Look what happened to Romy Schneider. Or did we establish that she was a blond?) It's kind of like when people tell me that I sit too close to my twenty-six inch colour-console tv, that I'll get radiation poisoning, and I reply testily that I worked at a nuclear power plant for six gruelling months to put myself through university, learning only too well the definition of a half-life, and if I were meant to be contaminated, it would have happened then. In fact, you might not want to sit too close to me. You may think I'm kidding, but I'm not. And yes, it was exactly like *Silkwood*, I, of course, cast in the Dolly Pelliker role. People. What do they know?

LaBruce lounging in LA without a cent to his name. Photo by someone whose name I can't remember.

The rest of the summer plays itself out like an inferior Tennessee Williams novella. I spend most of my weekends trashing around with the gay Trinity–Mrs. G., Miss G., and Babyface–who, like virtually every queen in LA, all have jobs in the Industry. (And all fellow Capricorns, I might add, just like my friends Glenn and Hunter in New York. Something about gay Capricorns....) That is but exactly what makes it all so glamorous to a country cousin like me, but of course they are all oh so blasé about the minutiae of the biz that they can barely conceal their ennui when I ask, wide-eyed, for insider gossip.

We have our little barbecues and play movie star gin while drinking gin martinis and watching Bette Davis drink much gin in John Huston's second film, *In This Our Life*, for about the forty-seventh time. Miss G., the wanton, is wont to watch Bette Davis movies until the invited guests are crying for mercy, something you could only get away with in LA. I mean, you could do it in New York, Hunter, but everyone would think you were nuts. I also make a point of going to Zuma Beach every weekend, usually with Yves Montand (well, that's what we call her), just to give my embryonic cancer cells a more picturesque setting in which to multiply.

We lay together on a Navajo blanket waxing philosophical about my Eves and Yves' Eves and everybody's Eves. Yves has an epiphany: Eves only exist as long as there are Margos. In other words, and it's a radical hypothesis, Margos create Eves. Suddenly it all becomes clear to me—it's my identity as a desperate, insecure, aging, paranoid yet brilliant quasi-star that forces young ambitious film-makers to butter me up, steal my ideas, copy my life, and leave me in the dust. Now I get it. (For those of you who came late—and there's always a few—the Eve in question is a reference to the classic Bette Davis vehicle *All About Eve*, in which Davis—as Margo Channing, Broadway legend—takes under her wing a starving young actress named Eve—played by Anne Baxter—only to discover that it has been Eve's plan all along to usurp her position as the grand dame of the Great White Way.)

156

In gay parlance, or at least in my parlance, anyone who is younger than you—or who at least looks younger than you—and will stop at nothing short of mass murder to get where you are, including sleeping with anything that exists outside of an oxygen tent (and even then, exceptions have been made), is an Eve. It can also be used as a verb, as in the sentence, "He Eved his way up the ladder at ICM," or "Stop Eve-ing me, I've had a hard day." Yves, who is not an Eve, but a Margo, lives in those Hollywood Hills, an exotic woman of Peruvian extraction who one day after the beach forces me to watch him feed two live rats to a large boa constrictor whose name escapes me. I sit in horror as the beast moves imperceptibly towards his prey, like an Eve. I guess I've got Eves on the brain, and in fact, if truth be told, I am SuperMargo. Did I mention that Yves decorated Slash's house?

Relations with Charlie—I mean Raoul—my West Hollywood host, are uneven at best. We did manage to shoot a feature film together without putting out contracts on each other's lives, but the on-going partnership which we once discussed is out of the question. Too many nasty, incriminatory little scenes were played out behind the camera; the play, as usual, was off-stage. Fissures in our intense, almost unnaturally close relationship began to appear early on, and now the proverbial finger is in the dike. He can be so cheering at times. A couple of weeks ago he walks into my bungalow where I am sick and weak in bed with the flu, and announces, in his sinister dead-pan, "It smells like death in here." Flowers would have sufficed. I'm actually starting to like him again, in that way I have. He's like the cartoon Charles Addams forgot to draw, updated for the nineties.

Raoul has already said he gets the feeling that we won't be friends after *Hustler White* is finished, and he may be right. I know it won't be the same, it never is, but it might be better in other ways, who knows? Sometimes I feel like the eternal optimist in a Mike Leigh film, but you know they always turn out to be the most tragic characters of all. I do feel, however, that there have been too many barbs caught in my skin, too many hooks to forget convincingly.

My Sylvia Plath training is really paying off now. Case in point: Raoul wants my blue PONY t-shirt to give to his friend Pony, and when I tell him "no" because it's my favourite and I have so few clothes in LA, because he wants it too much and, worse, feels he's entitled to it, he replies, " It doesn't suit you." Little things. I can laugh about them now (well, maybe not the time he told me

I was the type of person who probably wouldn't go to his own mother's funeral), but only when I make him into a character, like Ted Hughes.

His recent attempt to get an original idea credit for the movie was a little bit of a disappointment, I must say, considering how closely we developed the project together from its very inception, but that's what usually happens when you spend a lot of time with someone: you get disappointed.

Not everyone has the constitution for heresy and exile, nor should they be expected to. That's my job. But lately the question that burns like brown liquor is, can one be a well-adjusted exile, a happy, healthy heretic? You know, the great-art-is-produced-by-mutilated-egos theory, which I seem to subscribe to more and more, along with Xanax. I just had a weekend of debauchery, and this evening I'll go to the boxing gym with my sweet little seventeen year old dyke friend Emily—or Embryo, as I like to call her—and run three miles and work out and I'll do it again on Thursday and then go back to the debauchery on the weekend. I want it both ways, and I just don't think it works like that. Look at Dame Lewis Reed, His Louness. I suppose drugs and debauchery aren't the only way to fuck up the tyranny of everyday life—maybe just the most convenient. But the point is, any extreme of experience is going to cost you something.

Speaking of which, it's a couple of weeks later on a Friday night and I go to Cuffs—after Hai Karate—with Mrs. G. and dear Mr. Peter Christopherson, the ex-Throbbing Gristle, ex-Psychic TV, current Coil member who also directs music videos by the likes of Van Halen, NIN, Rage Against the Machine, and Silverchair, and I'm drunk and almost hook up with a couple of different guys but don't for various reasons. Mrs. has taken Peter home, so I'm out on the street alone in Silverlake at about four in the morning, damn it, and there are no cabs—obviously, it's LA—so I go to Basic Plumbing, the sex club, to see if Piglet is working, but he isn't, probably because, as I discover later, I'm at the wrong sex club, I'm at the King of Hearts which is a few hundred yards down. So I cross the street to a pay-phone and call Mrs. and ask her if she'll come and pick me up and she says yes because she worries about me, so I sit on an abandoned tow truck and wait for him, not realizing I've told him I'm sitting in front of the wrong sex club.

So this car pulls up and without even looking or thinking, whichever applies, I just jump right in and slam the door shut assuming that it's Mrs. Glass but it isn't, it's this guy who was bugging me at Cuffs. So I'm in the car and the door's shut and I say, "Thank-you, you're a dear," and turn my head and see that it's this creepy, snaggle-toothed guy, and I say "Yikes," and scramble out of the car. I go back and sit on the tow truck but Mrs. doesn't show up after an hour (because she's gone to the wrong place, or rather, the right place) and other cars are cruising me like mad (probably because I'm wearing my PONY t-shirt, which, besides being a rare vintage sportswear logo, is an acronym for Prostitutes of New York), and so I approach a pick-up truck that has stopped and behind the wheel is a handsome, strapping young six-foot-four-inch black guy of about twenty, in overalls with dreads and no shirt, and we shoot the breeze for a while and then he offers to drive me back home to West Hollywood.

When we get there I invite him in and we have amazing sex but then he leaves at 8 a.m. although we do exchange numbers, but when I call him on Sunday he doesn't seem too enthusiastic, big surprise. He was kind of butch, a guitar player. Long legs, big thicker. Came in buckets. Lots of kissing. Sunday afternoon I end up at Sucker again, the good old-fashioned tea dance slash hardcore punk club that always rips my head off. The thing about Sucker is you go in one end and come out the other, somewhere light years away, usually in hyper-drunk. It's not just that it's daylight when you enter the place—with its Calvin Kleinesque wood panelling and the smell of cheap draught beer—and dark when you emerge. It's more a collapse of time and space, a flattening of dimensions. Or is that dementias?

A fascinating woman at the bar is telling me that AIDS-related dementia does not exist–il n'existe pas, baby–that it is merely the normal way the mind has of coping with such an ordeal. R.D. Laing devotee that I am, I concur enthusiastically while picking up the three double Stolies I've ordered for me and the girls. I ask Mrs. Glass if we can go to Cuffs, to which she replies, "Access denied," but somehow I later find myself at the old Snake Pit anyway. On weekends this dingy little bar is so congested with cruisers that it is not uncommon to be caught in gridlock. This time, I end up going home with two guys. The one I'm into is this hustler type who, when I first met him at a party in Beachwood, seemed like a respectable citizen. As it turns, he's strictly leasable, with the biggest set of balls I have ever seen, but he has taken too many downers, so he bails, and leaves me with the kind of older, trolly one– the john, as it were. I stay though, because he has poppers and a big dick. Yes, it was a poppers slippage. Happens to the best of them.

Nothing Left But to Lead a Life of Dissolution

I'm only telling you all this to give you an idea of how gay film-makers spend their time when they have a movie in the can but all the money has dried up and they have nothing left to do but lead a life of dissolution. After the *Hustler White* shoot we are so sans funds that for six weeks we can't even afford to get the film processed. We finally get to see the "dailies," as I some day hope to be able to call them in earnest, in mid-August, and thank God almost everything has turned out okay. I have just enough time to complete the tie-in music video for Rusty before returning to Toronto and then jetting off to Helsinki for a film festival.

The obvious problem with Helsinki for me is that it is the capital of a country of professional drinkers, and I am definitely a "when in Rome" kind of guy. Just how heavily they drink in this scandalous Scandinavian country—which actually seems to have more in common with Russia than Sweden, Denmark, or Norway, and whose citizens seem to speak English with Transylvanian accents—becomes apparent to me at the opening night party for the festival. I am having a drink with the chief programmer—a not unhandsome fellow in his middle thirties with a red cell-phone habitually crammed to his ear—when a group of burly boys pass by carrying the body of a young man, depositing him, as it turns out, ceremoniously on the street outside the club.

When I enquire after the health of the gentleman, my host assures me that he is merely being allowed to sleep it off where no one will trip over him, implying that it is a daily, if not hourly, occurrence. "Do you know him?" I ask ingenuously. "Of course, he's my brother," he replies, with affection. In Helsinki, you may be sitting around a large table at a bar with a group of people, talking intensely about international cinema or the French nuclear testing off the coast of New Zealand or the emerging Russian mafia when suddenly, a Finn, maybe even the school teacher girlfriend of the festival organizer, will pass out sitting up, tilting slightly, and no-one, certainly no other Finn, will bat a bloodshot eye. An hour later she may come to, and, miraculously, continue the train of thought in the middle of which she previously derailed, seamlessly re-entering the conversation. These, I think to myself, are my people.

So, as far as I can recall—which isn't very far at all—it was an agreeable festival. Included was an extensive Warhol retrospective, with films such as *Nude Restaurant, Beauty #2, Haircut, Empire,* and *Poor Little Rich Girl,* allowing me to approach the completion of my Warholian indoctrination. Taylor Mead was also a guest of the festival, and although he remembered neither me nor my movie from New York a few years back, we did a glamorous little press conference together, replete with flashing cameras and autograph hounds, which posited me once again in that neo-Warholian role that I both adore and abhor. Otherwise, I have plenty of time to meander in dark windy cemeteries or along the waterfront under dramatic Northern skies, brooding about my insignificance, one of my favourite pastimes.

The Long and Arduous Adventure of Post-Production

I'm back in LA and, although it is October, the sun still cooks my freckled flesh as I flounce fruitily down Santa Monica Boulevard toward Apricot Entertainment on Orange Street, the location of our little office. Things, it seems, have gone sour in the editing suite since I went away: our post-production manager slash assistant editor, who booked us into this glorified broom closet in the first place, has been fired for Eve-ing above and beyond the call of duty, and my editor

159

and co-director are not exactly seeing eye-to-eye. Thus begins the long and arduous adventure that is post production. I won't bore you with the quotidian details; suffice it to say that slowly, imperceptibly, my life will turn, with all its paranoiac and murderous implications intact, into a Dario Argento movie.

After a month of working closely with my sweet editor Rider, who has done everything short of turn tricks to help us finish this film—calling in favours, fielding industry stalkers like a seasoned pro—the money runs out yet again. Another month of begging for funds during the week and sliding into a general Sodom and Gomorrah-ish routine on the weekend ensues until finally I have managed to scrape up enough dinero to rent a decent editing facility,

this time at Midtown, directly across from the Beverly Center, the heart of the Creative City. Working on computer, and particularly on the D/Vision—a relatively low-rent non-linear computer system which is not designed for feature film editing—presents a whole new spectrum of headaches, such as the great crash of '95, as it will soon come to be known.

Rider, who I met in Chicago while I was working on a music video which was eventually shelved by a cowardly alternative label, is definitely in for the long haul, although relations between her and my collaborator, not to mention between my collaborator and me, have deteriorated to the point where as the producer I feel I have no choice but to exclude him from much of the latter stages of post. "Whatever it takes"—that hackneyed, casually fascist independent film cliché—becomes the mantra of me and my editor as we plow through EDL's and DAT's and D88's and God knows what else.

Thankfully, Rider just happens to be a prodigy, and the down-to-earth, workaholic Gene Shallit look-a-like Jewish man who runs the place, (and who, incidentally, is related to either Leopold or Loeb—I can't remember which—and, through marriage, to the guy they thrill-killed; as is always the case in the Jewish and homosexual world, it's three degrees of separation) is providing us with plenty of tech, not to mention moral, support. We have learned that on the basis of a rough cut, our modest little movie has been accepted for a single midnight screening at Sundance on January twentieth, a deadline which, if we work fourteen-hour days for the next four to six weeks without a coffee break, should be a breeze to meet, despite the fact that more money will have to be procured and we are both edging dangerously close to nervous exhaustion.

Plus I think I may be coming down with a slight case of AIDS. Just kidding. Anyway, I sincerely hope not. It could ruin my career. (I pilfered that joke—from Glennda O.)

Sometimes, in the wee small hours of the morning in the editing room—where we have been confined for so long we've started decorating it, like a prison cell, with pictures of Carla Bruni and my new husband Jason Gedrick and such—we'll be eating our obsessively favourite chocolate bar (Nestle's Crunch) and drinking our umpteenth coffee, and one of us will start to get a little giddy and we'll start to laugh, and we'll laugh and laugh until tears are running down our faces, and then, suddenly, we'll get really depressed and almost start to cry. It's kind of terrifying.

We're desperately short of money now. One day I've had enough, I just can't cope anymore, so I disappear in the afternoon to see a matinee of *Heat* (mostly because of Ashley Judd, and because Michael Mann is an existentialist), forgetting that I've left Rider in the editing room with no money to buy lunch. When I get there, close to dinner time, she is almost delirious with hunger and exhaustion and anger. My collaborator, now cast as Iago to my Othello—putting Rider smack dab in the Desdemona role—has also shown up at the worst possible time, attempting to convince her of my innate evil. The ensuing messy, ugly little scene will constitute one of the lowest points of the entire process; yes, we will finish the film two days before the deadline but, as I point out to Rider, it will be a Pyrrhic victory, or, as she puts it, we will cross the finish line, but not before someone lops off several of our limbs. Pardon our mangled metaphors.

Christmas is a joke. Aside from having a charming lunch at Ben Frank's with Gus Van Sant and Chris Monolux—manager of the Dandy Warhol's, one of whose songs we're using on the *Hustler White* soundtrack—I and Rider work ten hours straight the day before the jolly holiday, and twelve hours the day before that, only stopping long enough to watch *Bell, Book, and Candle*, my favourite seasonalish movie.

I also read aloud to Rider, as she works at some mundane yet necessary task, from an article about Rwanda in the *New Yorker* which documents how the Hutus, an historically agrarian tribe, rose up against and slaughtered with machetes a million Tutsis, traditionally herdsmen, just like Cain killed his brother Abel when God favoured Abel's offering of meat over Cain's crops. I orate this terrifying story to her just to keep our little independent film problems in perspective. Afterwards we try to find an open restaurant so that we might have our Christmas pudding, but everything is closed and deserted and desolate as only LA can be at this time of year. Rider drops me off and I fall into a deep sleep as visions of sugar daddies watusi in my head.

On the loneliest day of the year I attend an oxymoronic Christmas barbecue, then go to see the latest Jean Claude Van Damme movie with Jeffrey and Mrs. G. and one of two Finnish ballet dancers I met in San Francisco last year who's in town with the Joffrey, dancing *The Nutcracker*. Afterwards, we go to the most sordid gay bars we can think of—always at their glamorous best on major holidays—one of them even offering a buffet featuring Roast Beast. I decline, not wishing to contract a case of Christmas hepatitis. The cute and sweet, not to mention stacked, ballet dancer and I end up in bed together; Santa, je suppose, has been good to Bruce this year after all.

It's work, work, and more work, not to mention work, between Christmas and the end of the year. New Year's Eve is spent quietly at the House of Athey with Miss Davis, Miss Meadmore, and Mr. and Mrs. Athey himself, the four of us indulging in a nice non-alcoholic fruit punch (Miss Meadmore and Mr.andMrs.Athey are non-drinkers) and watching some pretty rank porno from south of the border. What better way to bring in the new year than a healthy dose (if you'll pardon the expression) of *Tijuana Toilet Tramps*? Mr.andMrs.Athey—who, incidentally, used to fuck his retarded brother—is an affable host: an affectionate woman who always makes you feel special.

Miss Meadmore is one of the nicest gay born-again Christian country-and-western singers you would ever want to meet. And Miss Davis, well, Miss Davis can recite by heart the lines of every character in *Suddenly, Last Summer*, and doesn't wear any underwear when she does drag. As Baby New Year gazes luridly into my eyes, I feel blessed to be in the company of such gay royalty.

Thanks to yet another favour called in by Miss Rider, she and I spend the first weekend of the new year at a very posh sound facility in Santa Monica called Pacific Ocean Post, working slavishly, as per ushe, on our free gratis ten thousand dollar sound mix. This place is so high end, in fact, that there is an in-house chef—but not, alas, for beggars like us. We

only have twenty-two hours to mix a feature—which is a bad joke—but it's better than mixing it on a high speed dubbing dual-cassette ghetto blaster, which was my back-up plan. Finally, we're ready for the lab, but the only one that can promise to complete the film by our deadline is in San Francisco, so it looks like another ten days in Sodom, the title of a Harold Robbins novel if I ever heard one.

Sundance, Bloodier Sundance

Despite a few more major catastrophes—someone fucks up the credits, the rushed sound mix is a minor disappointment—we receive our first answer print on January eighteenth, two days before the Sundance deadline. By this time, however, the excitement for me is long since spent. Oh, I'll celebrate, all right, at some bright point in the future, but you won't be around to see it. At this stage of the game, however, I am as emotionally wooden as my Hollywood look-a-like cousin, Howdy Doody. My collaborator having made his own travel arrangements, I and Rider jet up to Park City, Utah together for what should be our triumphant moment, the premiere we've almost killed ourselves to pull off, and yet I can't feel anything, only a vague apprehension at unveiling our Frankenstein's monster for the first time to three hundred jaded industry faggots. I shouldn't even be telling you this.

Actually, I just decided I'm not even going to get into exactly what happened during the forty-seven hours of my second appearance at Sundance, bloody Sundance. Suffice it to say, I stayed in a dim condominium with my co-director, my editor, and my star; an ugly psychodrama worthy of Ibsen ensued; and I almost, almost, managed to escape with my dignity intact. Oh, there were moments of triumph—like brazenly walking into a GLAAD-sponsored brunch the morning after the *Hustler White* screening knowing full well that I represent but exactly what many of these forlorn fairies spend their beleaguered lives trying to eradicate—but they did little to ameliorate my general malaise.

The point, if there is one, is that Sundance is no longer about the appreciation of independent film-making, but about its cynical co-option by Hollywood in pursuit of the almighty dollar. Several people who saw *Hustler White* at Sundance commented that they'd never seen a screening where the audience members spent more time looking at each other, to see how they were supposed to react, than at the picture itself. "Should I be taking this seriously?" they seemed to say with their furtive sideways glances. "Is there any commercial potential here at all?" "Should I be laughing?" It's kind of like that made-for-tv movie I saw once with Pepper, in which Jill Clayburgh played a prostitute and Lee Remick a social worker, or journalist, or something. Jill, as usual, was giving it her all, clearly doing it for the sake of art, whereas it seemed that Lee was just doing it for the paycheck. Oh well, Lee had a hard life, she probably had something else on her mind.

After a brief return to LA to tie up some loose ends and say my teary good-byes, it's back to Toronto for a brief respite before continuing the gruelling *Hustler White* tour. My landlords have jacked up the rent in my spacious studio, so after four years, I am forced to relocate. I have mixed emotions about leaving the site of my first really serious nervous breakdown, but I suppose we must not be too sentimental about such things.

I first moved into the studio with two other idealistic film-makers, in order to shoot *Super 8 1/2*. In the interim, the movie got made at the expense of the only real relationship I've ever had; one of the film-makers—my original d.o.p.—was institutionalized; the other got married and pregnant, in that order, and moved to Vancouver; a variety of strippers and stalkers moved through the space; and I retreated into a kind of emotional plastic bubble. In LA I had a brief affair with a handsome lad who worked for Lufthansa—total husband material—with whom I actually really did want to have a relationship, but I talked myself out of it. I guess I'm still not convinced that the crazy glue they used to patch me up is going to hold.

Anyway, I end up moving to beautiful downtown Parkdale, Toronto, which one cultural critic has called the New Gay Village although, thankfully, there are still plenty of crack dealers, hookers, hoodlums, and assorted crazy people milling about. It's an actual house, so maybe I'll get domesticated and even someday approximate some sort of semi-convincing imitation of a real life, like Lana Turner, who knows? Somehow I doubt it, though.

Ah, All the Young Eves

So I'm sitting in an Irish Pub called the Royal Oak in Vauxhall, London with my beatific host, Alastair; his close friend, Big Mac, an Irishman; and Fergus, a budding young Scottish film-maker studying in Manchester who I met at my dear friend Glennda Orgasm's quasi-glam photo shoot the other day in front of Buckingham Palace. Fergus, it seems, wants to make a movie inspired by yours truly. He is not alone. I run into a lot of aspiring film-makers who claim to be inspired by my work, which is less flattering than it sounds—they usually add, in a sidebar, that I motivate them because if I can do it, naturally it's a cinch that anyone can. Ah,

all the fine young Eves. Fergus' father smokes for a living–produces smoked meat, fish, and cheese, i.e.–and sells it to the likes of Harvey Nicks.

Once, Fergus tells us, his père was hired to cater a party of fox hunters, so he smoked some fox and served it to the snooty sportsmen without deigning to inform them what it was they were spreading on their crumpets. After announcing that it wasn't precisely smoked salmon they were munching on, half of them started to vomit, while the other half asked for more. Fergus is like a good novel.

He tells another story about a second cousin of his who used to be a cop in Hong Kong, then a secret agent for a radical Protestant anti-IRA organization, and is now in a witness protection program, farming oysters on the Hebrides Islands off the coast of Scotland. When he visited her, she sat in a shack with her oysters, a stack of *Playgirls* and a male sex slave at her feet. It makes me feel a little inadequate whenever I hear that such people exist, but then again, maybe they don't: Fergus could be a compulsive liar–but that's okay, because I like them too, even though they also make me feel inadequate.

I have a feeling that Big Mac–a sexy, swaggering Irishman, six-foot-four-inches tall with a broad, handsome face slightly softened by the booze, dark hair, big hands, and a romantic brogue that could melt your heart–does not feel inadequate and, in fact, has taken an immediate and inexplicable dislike to the boyish, impish Fergus who, while somewhat fey, is probably more butch than me.

As we sit swilling Guinness on hard wooden benches, Big Mac, who is as straight as they come, glares at Fergus as he tells his stories, interrupting him from time to time without averting his eyes from the poor boy's face, to ask Alastair and I out of the side of his mouth, "Where'd ya pick up the fruit?" Fergus, who is drinking a half pint for every three full pints of Big Mac's, squirms nervously as Alastair and I exchange amused smirks. Strangely enough, Big Mac and Alastair have had an affair on and off over the past year and a half, even though Big Mac, as I mentioned, is straight, has fathered a child on whom he dotes, and is a sound engineer and sometimes-bouncer for the likes of Goldie. Alastair is a dreamboat, also handsome and sexy with his Northern Uproar accent and, up until recently, decidedly Rockabilly. He reads virtually straight and, in fact, has mostly heterosexual friends–like Big Mac and Chainsaw, who you'll meet in a minute.

I met Alastair via a correspondence through my ex-fanzine *J.D.s* with his late lover, a dashing queercore musician who died of AIDS a couple of years ago. By the time I got to England he had been gone six months so I never got to meet him, but I and Alastair became close. The first visit was romantic, with lots of snogging, but this time we've decided to be good friends.

Big Mac, however, is another story entirely. Is it my imagination, or is one of his big mitts, after our eighth Guinness or so, starting to linger a little longer than is strictly necessary each time he slaps my thigh to punctuate the punch line of a funny anecdote? Time alone, undoubtedly, will tell. Meanwhile, it's St. Paddy's day, and the Irish bartender, a dodgy rogue named Tony who seems to have taken a shine to me even though I can't understand a word he's saying, is supplying us with a steady flow of Guinness. Unbelievably, Tony, too, seems a bit displeased with our Fergus: when he brings over the next round, he remarks (according to my translators), "When God made crab apples, he made one big crab apple," gesturing towards our Scot compatriot. The poor devil is beginning to get a complex. I suppose it must be a racism thing.

Later we end up at a nearby house club where Big Mac supervises the sound. We sit in the loud, cramped sound room amidst all the flashing equipment as Big Mac bends my ear about this and that. Things are definitely heading in a romantic direction as thigh slapping graduates to crotch grabbing. I just hope Alastair doesn't mind, or actually, maybe I hope he does. If truth be told, I'm probably still a little bit in love with him.

A couple of nights later, Alastair and I make an appearance at the White Bear at Kennington Oval, a somewhat slightly less Irish pub that is more youth-oriented, where left wing students and even a few punks hang out. It's quiz night: one of the competing team's name for the occasion is "Frank Bruno's Sperm Count," a snide reference to the Brit challenger who, having succumbed to a roundhouse right from Iron Mike Tyson minutes into the match the night before, has become somewhat of a national joke. Ignoring such trivialities in a quiet corner, we are soon joined by a couple of Alastair's mates: Martin, of Therapy?, who is dating Skin, the singer from Skunk Anansie; and Chainsaw, one of the editors of *Purr* magazine which has just published Richard Kern's deliriously trashy postfeminist photo book, *New York Girls*, with which they are having censorship problems in the U.K. I know how terribly stuffy they are about things like that in Angleterre; it amazes me that my movies are quite popular there in spite of the fact that they insist on cutting out all the naughty bits, leaving, je presume, only the credits and a couple of swish-pans for people to scratch their heads over.

After eleven Guinesses we go over to Chainsaw's place, conveniently located directly across from the pub, where he proceeds to show us Polaroids of him and his ex-wife, Stinky Pink, engaged in the oral tradition. A case of too much information, but soon Chain changes the subject, rambling conclusively about some troubles he's been having with an ex-close friend and soon to be former partner in Purr who has allegedly been attempting a hostile take-over, not to mention stealing ideas and taking all the credit. I'm riveted; it's comforting to know that such goings-on are not the exclusive domain of queens. Chainsaw is a lovely man. You would recognize him immediately by his habitual black Stetson and general midnight attire, his Manson-like facial hair (Charlie, not Shirley), and his sparkling eyes—which could also be construed, I suppose, as Mansonesque, if you didn't know him. He also happens to be one of the wittiest people I've had the pleasure of meeting (when I can understand him).

When I tell him about an artist friend of mine who has huge murals of skinheads on the walls of his studios, he says, "What's Muriel doing on his wall?" (That's not meant to be a prime example of his wit; I just thought it was funny.) In fact, he's one of those people who makes me laugh practically non-stop. He's into R. Kern, Harry Crews, Lydia Lunch, Hank Rollins, Boyd Rice—you know, Americana. He is also way into Drew Barrymore, so I promise to send him a remaindered copy of *Little Girl Lost,* as it is unavailable in his land. Later on my visit I will go to the

Brixton Academy with Alastair and Chain to see Garbage because "Stupid Girl", as interpreted by Shirley Manson, has become my London anthem on this trip for some reason, probably because I get turned on by songs wherein girls are mean to other girls. Sorry, that's just the way they built me.

What am I doing in London, anyway? Oh yeah, I'm on the first European *Hustler White* tour. We've already been to Germany and Ireland, so I suppose I'll have to tell you about that too, just so nobody feels left out. Well, let me finish off London first, for Christ's sake. One night I and Alastair go to the second anniversary party of a certain high profile gay restaurant slash club run by someone who has the same first name as his pop-star boyfriend. I'm not being coy, it's just that I'm not supposed to mention that said pop-star has recently had some cosmetic alteration. Although I don't know why I'm bothering to be discreet; both the restaurateur and the pop-star asked me, separately, mind you—have I had plastic surgery since the last time they saw me, darling, you're looking so young. One of those back-handed compliments—peach put down, as it were. Joey Arias, who is a big fan of yours truly, and whom, you may recall, I first met at a Leather Daddy breakfast at the swimming pool of the Chateau Marmont where she kept leaping out from behind palm fronds exclaiming *"Congo"*, performs his Billie Holliday routine and, considering how much I hate drag queens lately, I find it surprisingly good. He really does sound but exactly like the late legend. The rest of his act consists mostly of some coercive snogging with nervous audience members. There's Paul Burston, the *Time Out* scribe who was my host last time I visited London. I guess my theory about befriending journalists doesn't always work (you know I was only kidding anyway), since he forgot to mention me in his latest book—an unfortunate oversight, I'm sure—even though he writes extensively in it about the *New Queer Cinema*, of which I am ostensibly one of the pioneers.

Furthermore, in his *Time Out* piece on *Hustler White* he will reduce me to one rather mundane quote, while the rest of the vaguely sycophantic piece will be hopelessly devoted to Tony Ward—whose butt everyone, particularly gay journalists, seems to be more than willing to kiss just because Madonna once planted her own tree there. Don't get me wrong, it's an impressive butt—why, you could break up an old chifforobe with it—but let's keep things in perspective, shall we? I mean, I realize that I'm merely a low-budget, independent pornographic film-making faggot unworthy of mainstream consideration; so what if I did co-produce, co-direct, co-write, co-fucking grip and co-star in the picture? Even Tony, who is actually very sweet, encourages me to be more aggressive with the press, but you know, lately I just don't give a fuck. Actually, I guess I need handlers to take care of such things. Or wranglers. Whichever applies.

But I regress, er, digress. Truly, I do like Paul a lot, even though tonight he has that annoying glow that people with new boyfriends have—and, even more annoyingly, his new boyfriend, sitting beside him, seems nice enough. I still like his old boyfriend, William, though—another one of those Englishmen whose wit puts me in a perpetual state of giddiness. I and Alastair, who also loves our William to death, will invite him to my farewell gathering at the Royal Oak in a few weeks.

But getting back to the Arias performance, the only other person I recognize in the audience is that famous English porn star to whom I beat off occasionally, you know the one. He's talking to my adorable little tattooed pop star friend and I kind of want to get introduced, but apparently there has been some kind of egregious history between Alastair and the porn star, so I decide not to. Oh well, he's looking a little haggy, anyway. I was going to say AIDS-y, but I thought better of it. After all, decency forbids...

Most of the time during the day I find myself lolling around Alastair's apartment while he slaves away at his day job making fetish gear. Once, at the end of a visit to LA, Raoul, with whom I used to stay, asked me what my favourite part of the trip was, and I replied that it was hanging around his bungalow alone while he was at work. It was sort of meant as a joke, but actually it really is fun hanging out in other people's homes when they're not there, watching their tv, eating their microwavable lasagna, having sex in their bed... well I only did that once at Raoul's, the sole reason being that he specifically asked me not to and I was mad at him. It's kind of like, instead of hanging out with them, you become them. I know its sounds vaguely sinister, but there you have it. You know I don't do it for the same reasons that my ex live-in stalker used to do it to me, i.e., out of obsession; I do it strictly for anthropological reasons.

Alastair has an extensive video collection, so I get to see that disastrous, rarely broadcast post-"Twin Peaks" David Lynch series "On the Air", which I actually think is kind of funny; the Dennis Potter penned mini-series "Lipstick On Your Collar" with sexy new *It* boy Ewan MacGregor; plus a plethora of movies, two of which I am identifying with like crazy: *The Killing of Sister George* and *Sweet Bird of Youth,* to be exact. Why these two films, you ask? Well, *Sweet Bird of Youth* should be obvious: I'm temporarily between gigs, in a strange town, with a handsome young male companion, and hiding out from the media—just like boozy Geraldine Page. And as for *The Killing of Sister George*, well, that should be obvious too. Like the eponymous character, played by the unparalleled, late Beryl Reid (I also watch *Entertaining Mr. Sloane* and presto, it's a Beryl Reid film festival), I have two personae, one private and one developed strictly for public consumption, but alas the latter is assumed to be the real one and everybody starts to refer to me as such; as well, I once had a much younger boyfriend (Childy) who left me for someone more stable and conventional in an influential media position (Coral Browne); and I often sit alone in empty studios, mooing forlornly. Call it

The Killing of Sister Bruce. Of course, the fact that both movies feature aging alcoholic actresses played by aging alcoholic actresses desperately attempting to hang on to their dignity and their audience has nothing to do with it, nothing at all.

Friday night, and it's Vauxhall Tavern and I. The infamous venue is within crawling distance of Bonnington Square, where Alastair lives, so we venture over to club Duckie to meet some friends, including Mark Simpson, the humpy British journalist who contributes to publications such as *Details*—whose masthead, by the way, is lousy with fags, which is probably why they won't touch me with a ten foot polo mallet. In fact, when Brucie, my old-school New York publicist, calls them to enquire if

they would like to sponsor the *Hustler White* party, he is hung up on. Click. Mark, who can hardly be blamed for that, is a fairy trapped in a rugby player's body; Joe Don Baker channelling Truman Capote. Awfully dear man, albeit universally feared for his tendency to speak his mind at the drop of a chapeau. His arms are like tree trunks, for Christ's sake. I'd do him, but he's only into the army now. On his arm at Duckie is none other than intellectual drag wunderkind Glennda O., in town promoting herself—something I would know nothing about, I'm sure. I and she are the most enthusiastic contributors to Mark's latest book, entitled, all too appropriately, *Anti-Gay*. ("Auntie-Gay" may have been more to the point for all concerned, but never mind.)

I am propped up next to Glennda, who is a rare example of good drag, and the two of us are confronted with a classic example of bad drag on stage, some lantern-jawed hulk in a party frock, shrieking unconvincingly about how much she likes girls, and other politically correct platitudes. Sorry, buddy, if you liked girls you wouldn't be parading around in that ugly dress, you tacky faggot. A prime example of why Glennda Orgasm, the right wing drag queen, is throwing in the false eyelashes. You heard right, Glennda is turning in her size twelve pumps. We're even going to produce a special final episode of her show, "Glennda and Friends," in which we burn our wigs and bras once and for all, denouncing this dangerous trend. Of course, it will all be from a feminist perspective. Yes, kids, feminism is back and better than ever. It turns out drag is misogynist after all. Who knew?

Another example of bad—nay, evil—drag confronts us later at the entrance to one of the numerous heinous gay clubs in London: Love Muscle at the Fridge in Brixton, to which Ms. O. has dragged me on the off-chance she might get laid. (Oh, it's all so easy for her: aside from being statuesque and having an effortlessly hard body, she once posed naked in *Inches* under the heading "Home of the Whopper," if you know what I mean.) Holding court in the ticket booth, clutching an imaginary velvet rope, is one of the most grotesque cross-dressing spectacles I have ever seen (Lady Bunny notwithstanding): a wall-eyed harpie wearing what looks like a wasp's nest on the top of her oblong head, clearly drunk.

When Glennda, who also has a cocktail or twelve under her Gucci belt, slurs, sister to sister, a request for a modest reduction of the exorbitant entrance fee, Medusa pulls us into focus and bellows, "I'm not in the mood." Glennda, famous for such door scenes–remind me to tell you about the time she tried to throw some weight around to get us into an Anna Sui party, as we stood meekly in front of a muscle-bound doorman in the pouring rain under our "Shit, it's raining," umbrellas, like a couple of wet Chihuahuas–resorts to the always humiliating and ineffectual plan B: she exclaims "Don't you know who this is?" and pulls me like a fawn into the headlights, "This is Bruce LaBruce!" "I'm calling security," the gargoyle gurgles, picking up the telephone with one of her withered claws, as I turn to stone. We pay full price, plus a penalty. Honestly, it makes me sad to be gay. I hate drag queens. (Oh not you, Glennda.) The drag phenomenon is out of control–there's a female impersonator on every street corner in New York. Bums and blind men with pencils in tin cups are doing drag. It's got to stop.

Anyway, a few nights later it's Glennda O's retrospective at the Institute of Contemporary Art where *Hustler White* is booked for six solid weeks in the summer. Apparently the Queen Mum herself, whose bedroom overlooks the tawdry ICA, got wind somehow of Glennda's show (probably one of her gay foot servants) and requested a private screening, so there's a hint of scandal in the air. Glennda is giving herself the star treatment, and why not, it's her retrospective–which, incidentally, includes me out, an unfortunate oversight, I'm sure. (It's not her fault, she didn't program the damn thing. After all, she didn't deliberately drain the gas tank herself.) I take it like a man, not even complaining when I get stuck with the bill for the pre-show dinner to which she has invited all her London acquaintances. To be fair, she pays me back later in the currency of cocktails.

Which reminds me, did you know there is a new drag café in New York, a la the Hard Rock Café, where they serve you drinks named after famous drag queens? (It makes perfect sense. After all, they're almost single-handedly keeping the liquor companies in business.) If you order a Glennda Orgasm, you will be presented with a deadly concoction; a conspiracy involving vodka, Bailey's, and Kahlua–also known as a mud slide. Another one of those backhanded compliments for Glennda. Dear Glennda. She deserves all the accolades she can get. After all, she's only thirty and has now gone international. At least that's what the headline screamed on the *New York Post*'s Page Six, a direct quote from super drag hag Camille Paglia, our solemn leader whom we worship and adore. Camille, after all, is The Way.

Before I let Glennda off the hook, let me relate one more little incident which may shed some light on our subject. One day she is keen on going shopping with me, having read a blurb in the *London Times* "Style" section about an exiting new boutique at Marble Arch where one can purchase Prada knock-offs for but a few guineas. As it turns out, it was a satirical piece commenting on the new fashion trend of high-profile designers copying cheap polyester work clothes, but the irony was lost on Glennda. After searching in vain a while for the tiny shoppe, we realize that we have been directed to a working class uniform store.

Undaunted, in we march in our sunglasses–which we are wearing despite the fact that London is perpetually overcast and thus people are openly laughing at us on the street–and our resort wear, and browse through the merch like Polly

Mellon and Bernadine Morris at Harrods. "Do you have this McDonald's uniform in turquoise?" enquires Bruce, fingering the fabric. Glennda: "Is this welding smock vicuna?" The people behind the counter are sniggering, and eventually we slink, red-faced, out of the magasin.

That about does it for London. I spend the rest of the time trying to avoid my young Stockholm stalker (don't ask)– my British distributor having generously furnished her with my number, while withholding it from an old friend trying to get in touch with me. I do get frustrated with small distributors, but beggars can't be etceteras. I'm also way over promoting this goddamn movie already.

Lately–purely out of boredom you understand–I've

taken to blatantly contradicting whatever my collaborator says, just for kicks. In one inconsequential gay radio interview said collaborator goes on about how he wants to put sex back in the movies (um, precisely what have I been doing for the past five years?); I say sex is passé, I've lost interest in it altogether. He talks enthusiastically about hustlers and such; boredom is in style, I say, I read it in last month's American *Vogue* (which is absolutely de facto true). Believe me, I'm trying to be professional and mature, I really am. I'm trying to muster up as much civility as I possibly can, but I can only just barely manage it, and then only during press obligations. Said collaborator asks me afterwards if I want to go to some art exhibit with him, I guess as one last gesture towards reconciliation, but I demur, feigning an appointment–and not without guilt, I might add.

As for interviews in general, one can talk about oneself only for so long before one becomes irretrievably self-loathing. At least, that's what happens to me.

Wait a minute. I almost forgot about the premier English showing of *Hustler White* at the National Film Theatre, the raison d'etre of my London excursion in the first place. I'm already over the movie, the star, my collaborator, and myself, so naturally I'm thrilled.

During the screening, as I sit alone in the bar nursing a Negroni, my thoughts naturally drift, as they often do on such occasions, to self-inflicted gun shot wounds. In saunters the late Tony Ward, who has missed yet another introduction of the film, God bless him. He is devil-may-care handsome in his designer duds, as per ushe, and has the general demeanor of someone who just possibly may have woken up last night in a room full of naked asses. Glassy-eyed, he tells me a fascinating story about something or other, then five minutes later, in that charming way he has, tells me the exact same story again. Hang on, Sloopy. Like they say in the movies, "I'll have two of whatever he's having." When our movie is over, we field questions from the audience and afterwards I even sign a few autographs. Three, to be exact. Two of them are elderly queens clutching framed photographs of yours truly and my naked ass which, believe it or not, makes me blush a profondo rosso as I put my brand name on them. One of them, bless his English heart, is disappointed that I didn't give it up in *Hustler White* as I have so often in the past. "Make sure you suck a few cocks in the next one," he admonishes. It's déjà vu all over again as I turn plaid with embarrassment, a scene literally right out of *Super 8 1/2* which was, in turn, inspired by a real-life incident at a London screening of *No Skin Off My Ass* five years ago. This time it remains whimsical; later, in Copenhagen, when someone in the audience yells out "I missed your cock," it'll have gotten a little stale, although I will generously furnish the culprit with the name of my hotel.

All my London friends have come to the reception, including Chainsaw in his Stetson, a beaming Big Mac, and, of course, our Alistair. Two sixteen-year-old girls–one the cousin of one of my British distributors–approach and inform me urgently, like a couple of Hayley Mills, that they think I am both sexier and better looking than Tony Ward. I restrain myself from falling to my knees and kissing their oxblood Doc Martens.

The party moves to Popstarz, the trendy Britpop club, where either Boy George or a very life-like hologram thereof is holding court at the upstairs bar. One of my handlers drags me over for introductions, and he is friendly and gracious, but I have no desire to compete with the small throng of people who are vying for his attention, and who have obviously mistaken him for Liam Gallagher, there's no other explanation. I'm preoccupied with Big Mac anyway, with whom I've been surreptitiously snogging, on and off all evening. I spy him across the crowded room wearing Irish handcuffs, which of course means holding a glass of beer in each hand, one of which he shoves into my hand when I approach him, along with his tongue down my throat. Swish-pan to frottage and foreplay on the top of a deserted double-decker bus; swish-pan to sweaty sex in Big Mac's modest flat; slow dissolve to one of the top ten hangovers ever. In fact, it may end up breaking the top three.

It was that cheap red wine and warm Canadian beer courtesy of the dyke cultural attaché of the Canadian Embassy (homosexuals have a stranglehold on these cushy positions) that did it–that and the even cheaper red wine supplied by Big Mac, not to mention the champagne and Charlie. Big Mac, whose house had just been searched the previous week by paramilitary, machine-gun-toting police–something about the combination of a lethal local bombing and Big Mac's mysterious INFL roommate–is a saint, staying in bed with me and holding my head all afternoon except for his trips to the chemist for tabs and to the bog for painkillers for us both. He informs me that his day job is deciding who will stay confined in the nut house and who won't–essentially determining who is crazy and who isn't. It's somehow comforting to know that I've just been shagged by someone who knows the difference.

Even though the traffic is unbearable and it's noisy, damp, and crowded–albeit stylish–I'm going to miss London. After three weeks of sleeping in the same bed with Alastair, we've gotten really attached. It always happens that way for me. Although it's been two years, Alastair is still trying to cope, understandably, with the loss of his lover of seven years. We talk about it a lot, but there's really nothing a friend can do in such circumstances except listen. He'll be okay; he has to be. He's one of those people who doesn't have a mean thing to say about anybody. You have to drag it out of him. He's got a great heart. I love his heart.

You Can Tell A Lot About a People By How They Design Their Toilets

On the flight back to Canada I pick skeptically at my British beef, which is still served by British Airways at that point–presumably to instill confidence in the product–as the mad cow disease debate rages. I was going to request the seafood, but I figured that it could kill me right away–at least mad cow disease, which makes you froth and foam at the mouth like you're in a David Cronenberg movie, takes ten years to incubate. Anyway, I still have my heart set on the melanoma.

There are few in-flight movies I won't watch, but as this one is *The Scarlet Letter*, I am left with no choice but to put down the headphones and drift off into a reverie about Berlin, where *Hustler White* played at the International Film Festival before London. I like Berliners, I don't care what anyone says. Sure they may seem cold, dour, suspicious, and aloof at first. Even at second or third. But you can warm them up eventually if you rub hard enough. True, they are arrogant and severe, but when they get to know you their generosity and warmth may surprise you. Okay, most of them don't have any discernible sense of humour, but the ones that do are very droll and dry and deadpan—my favourite style of mirth. Maybe I like Germans in general because I have some of the old Aryan blood in me myself. My mother's maiden name was—well I'm certainly not going to tell you my mother's maiden name, and no, it wasn't Braun, either, you bastard.

I'm staying with my Tuntenhaus friends again—Basti, Louis, and Arne—who share a large flat with two shiatsu masseurs, one of whom generously offers me a massage free gratis, which gives me a cold. They're all very hearty with huge, healthy appetites, tearing off big chunks of heavy bread with their bare hands and guzzling down tall glasses of sickly sweet beer. Drugs abound in the subcultural soup of Berlin—E, C, H, K—LMNOP—and yet their Aryan bodies seem impervious to the deleterious side effects. I'm feeling very genetically challenged, like Don Knotts at a Mr. Universe contest.

The film festival is all right, as film festivals go: three sold-out screenings, with some booing after the first one, but nothing to get excited about. Some of the journalists who interview me and Tony and Raoul are pretty cool, as journalists go—like Manfred from Munich who writes for a hip music magazine called *Spex*, a more intellectual *Spin*. He's very stylish and demure and sophisticated and, of course, gay. Much later he will interview Kenneth Anger and ask the notoriously litigious avant-gardist about me and my character in *Hustler White,* Jürgen Anger (no relation); the resultant steam of expletives cannot be repeated in mixed company.

I and Manfred really hit it off, but I don't think he's so taken by Raoul, because when I receive the mag in the mail later, I notice he's been cropped out of all the pictures. The thing that Raoul has to learn is that if you come off as being too eager to be interviewed, too willing to pontificate about yourself, journalists think you have too much time on your hands and lose interest. You have to be a little blasé, creating the vague impression that although you should be off doing something really very important, you suppose you must somehow make the time to share your impressions with the plebeians. Never, ever, ask a journalist if he wants to interview you or would like to spend more time with you. Whenever Raoul does this, I know that once again he will be relegated to the dreaded parentheses.

As for Jürgen, my co-producer, I must say that I am a tad perturbed. While virtually every other movie has its promotional posters plastered all over the city, *Hustler White* has but exactly two, one of which is soon stolen by an ardent fan—or Fanny Ardant, as they say in France. Not to mention that my mug does not appear on said poster, or, it seems, in any of the promotional material, despite the fact that I am the co-star of the damn movie. Jürgen, who is always most diligent in his attempt at keeping my ego—once described as a large airborne zeppelin—in check, seems to take some kind of perverse pleasure in informing me that the journalistas are not interested in talking to me, that they want Tony Ward. In time, I will learn that it is not only the purpose of stars to sell movies, but also a convenient way to take the heat off the director—a blessing in disguise, as it were. At this early stage, however, it just pisses me off. Fortunately, I never seem to stay mad at Jürgen for very long. After all, he did give me my first break, the story of which I will save for a dreary, rainy, suicide-making day.

I seem to have already forgotten much of Berlin—owing to the booze and dope, I suspect. I do almost rekindle a romance with Rheinholt, my Bavarian crush of a few years back; we spend a romantic night kissing and holding hands, staggering drunkenly arm in arm through parks and over bridges, but we don't have sex again, largely due to the existence of his actor boyfriend, whom I like a lot. One night I accompany Tony Ward and his host Andreas—a famous make-up artist—to S.O., a gay club in Kreutzburg. Tony is hip-hop-city with his wool cap and wraparound shades—tres cool, although I think I still like him best when he's doing his *Star 80*-Paul Snider-as-interpreted-by-Eric Roberts impression. I mean, what could be sexier than that? As a favour, Basti entices I and Tony into the handicapped washroom to do speed.

173

Incidentally, why is it that in Germany the toilets are made so that you have a great steaming pile to examine, undiluted by water, before flushing? You can really tell a lot about a people by the way they design their toilets. Anyhow, when I leave at six in the morning with my trick—a Belgian chef with big hands and balls (a recurring motif, n'est-ce pas?)—Tony is still dancing, fresh as a debauched daisy. There's something refreshing about Tony's public persona and his world class gigolo routine—he can still get away with, when at an expensive restaurant, brazenly tucking his napkin into his collar like a baby's bib. He even makes infantilism sexy.

I also recall dinner engagements with the likes of James Carman—the expatriate American *Hustler White* d.p. extraordinaire—recently back from Brazil (gypsy feet!) whose collaboration with Lars Von Trier has, alas, recently fallen through—and my Helsinki pal, Mika, still drunk, with his little red cell phone and perpetually passed out schoolteacher girlfriend. And then there is an interesting night spent with a v. famous ex-patriate Canadian artist known for his epic paintings of skinheads, whom I'll call Alexander the Great to protect him, because I'm going to talk about all sorts of drugs and debauchery and I wouldn't want to get him in trouble by using his real name. (It's the same principle, some kind of hypocritical oath, which occludes me from even mentioning my all-night coke binges with ... Buddy Cole.)

I first meet Alexander the Great at a party for the film festival. We know who each other are, of course, but remain a little aloof, checking each other out à la distance, as is the custom between Canadian artistes whose first intercontinental succès d'estime involves the blatant, somewhat questionable fetishization of Nazi skinheads. Actually, we've been dancing around each other for quite some time. I notice him eyeing me as I chat with Wolf, the cute, and charming German porn star who declined to be in *Hustler White* but says he now, having seen it, rather regrets it.

(Next time, I say, kind of wanting to put the moves on him, but I have a feeling he's a major bottom, considering the trick he pulled with the billiard balls at the behest of butch babe Zak Spears in that awful Tom of Finland video. Not that I never put the moves on bottoms. I guess I'm just insecure.) Finally, Alexander the Great lets his guard down and invites me (and Raoul) to his studio to look at his etchings. He picks us up at Jürgen's after a meeting which had degenerated into a hideous little scene between me and you-know-who, so the mood is a little strained, but I'm sure Alexander the Great didn't get to where he is without witnessing a few major fights, or minor murders for that matter. He is, after all, personally acquainted with Andrew Crispo.

At his studio A the G—who, strangely, has a certain Dick Avedon quality about him—pulls out his series of large paintings, one by one, as I (and Raoul) ooh and ahh. I tell him that the heroic, Germanic skinhead figures should be used on Deutchmarks. He presents us each with a present: two in a series of twenty specially commissioned Russian wooden folk dolls—the ones that contain a doll within a doll within a doll, except instead of a peasant woman, this is a Nazi skinhead, and when you get to the smallest one it's a pierced penis. Oh that Alexander the Great. He's such a camp. I stick around to get a load of the rich art collector who's scheduled to drop in—a clone-y, intellectual surgeon from Stuttgart. He's interested in an over-sized skinhead triptych that hung for ages at E-berg, the world famous rave club. A the G explains to the potential trick—I mean buyer—that he's in the process of trying to remove the nicotine stains, but I kind of like it the way it is.

A few nights later, A the G, who is notoriously big with the gifts, treats me to dinner at a restaurant straight out of *Veronika Voss*, then to drinks at a hustler bar called Tabasco—so named, I assume, to describe the thirteen and fourteen year old Turkish rent boys lounging around smoking cigarellos. With his shaved head and piercing eyes, Alexander the Great looks great in his brown shirt and black tie—very the S.A. as depicted in Luchino Visconti's production of *The Damned*. All he needs is a black arm band to complete the tromp-l'oeil effect.

As we discuss the possibility of collaborating on a dirty movie in the future, I can't help but speculate about my host's sexual history, which must be on a par with mine. I do know that he once placed a personal ad in *J.D.s*, requesting to be the bootslave of a band of skinheads, willing to relocate, but I could never figure out if it was serious or not. His current shaved-head boyfriend seems awfully cute and mean, but you know I can never sort out the tops from the bottoms. Anyway, later we do heroin and watch ancient reruns of substandard American sitcoms. If there's one reason I could never live in Germany, it would have to be television.

Alexander the Great will turn up in my so-called life again soon, but first, to go on about myself, after Berlin there are screenings arranged in Hamburg and Hot Dog—er, Frankfurt—in order to make some much needed bill. Although I've been to chilly Hamburg some several times now, it never seems to register. Something about a club called Purgatory owned by a Canadian... I can never remember. Frankfurt is a cosmopolitan, friendly little city which I'd love to terrorize sometime, avid Baeder-Meinhoff fan that I am, but there isn't enough time in the day. There is one brief excursion arranged by our debonair dyke host to a dingy leather bar called Der Stahl, located in an old musty cellar, where I get picked up by a young buck with a cold who seems to be having some problems maintaining a stiffy. We drive around for a ridiculously long time looking for my rather severe two-star hotel, fumbling with each other in his domestically manufactured car—which is textbook foreplay—but when we finally get into bed, it's a bit of a lemon letdown. Plus—p.s.—he has a disturbing penis.

Guinness: Good For the Nails and Whites of the Eyes

Frankfurt Airport, to Heathrow, to City Airport in Docklands—where an IRA bomb exploded very recently—to catch a flight to Dublin for its International Film Festival. It's one of those small jets that you still get to stroll out to and climb the stairs to board, then descend to the tarmac like Anita Ekberg in *La Dolce Vita* or Jayne Mansfield, my patron saint, in *Will Success Spoil Rock Hunter?* Or even Sharon Stone in *Casino*. The first land-

mark I see once I reach the four star (for a change) Berkeley Court Hotel, is a hologram of Van Morrison sitting at the lobby bar having a pint of Guinness—either a hologram or a Madame Tussaud's wax museum piece, I can't decide. Either way, he's pickled. He's kind of starting to look like that actor from *Rosemary's Baby* whom I saw at the French Market in West Hollywood recently, you know, the one in the Castevet's apartment at the end with the pointy nose and the receding hairline. Who knew she was a queen? The male equivalent of Patsy Kelly.

Our faithful guide and coordinator of hospitality is one Allan Devine. A handsome, dashing young actor full of the proverbial Blarney, he has actually played the Dane recently. He's a full-on rake with a lovely, zaftig girlfriend whom I just can't believe he doesn't cheat on like mad. The Irish—and Allan is about as Irish as you can get—are constantly taking the piss. You get the distinct impression that there is some conspiracy going on that you're not privy to, some joke at your expense, a pretext of magnanimity which veils a slight mistrust and contempt for outsiders. It's very *The Wicker Man,* I have to say, even though that's Scotland. It must be even worse in Northern Ireland, with the IRA and the INFL, where there is so much infighting between factions as well, and where certain cells even kill their own members, double-agents and all. It's all over the papers.

Allan, who is so good looking I don't care whether he's taking the piss out of me or not, whisks us off to dinner at Bono's brother's restaurant, where we are wined and dined by the straight head of the festival—who has bravely, if inexplicably, programmed all my movies over the years—and a fascinating gay couple—one, the apparent mastermind of the festival, the power behind the throne—and the other, his longtime companion; a prominent television news anchorman. Oddly, it is the straight head and Allan who, during our screening, take us to The George, the only gay bar in town.

They're very suspicious at the door, putting us through the third degree before allowing us in: identify yourselves, where were you earlier this evening, why do you want to come here? Apparently, anti-gay violence is one of the more popular national sports. In fact, Todd Haynes, the director of *Safe*, soon won't be: only a week later as a guest of this same festival he will be queer-bashed after leaving this very bar—by George, as it were. Although I have a feeling it may have more to do with that modified shag he's been sporting of late. Oh well, serves him right for what he did to

Karen. (You know I'm only kidding—I and Todd go way back. He used to order *J.D.s,* and once sent me a tape of rare Karen Carpenter bootlegs which I still listen to relentlessly, I mean religiously.) Once safely inside, Allan takes it in stride; he's too handsome not to have snogged with another guy at least once in his life.

The festival head is a bit nervous, but tries gamely not to show it. So we start in on the Guinness, Allan buying me another when the previous one is only half-empty because, as you know, it takes a while to pour a proper pint of Guinness. He informs me, like so many Irishmen before him, that Guinness is good for the nails and the whites of the eyes, high in calcium—a meal in itself. It could be pee for all I care, as long as Allan's buying and I get to gaze into those deep green eyes. When we return to the theatre for the Q and A, we are almost trampled to death by the audience trying to escape the theatre. I wonder if that means they liked it?

Besides another excursion to what Allan assures us is a gay disco, and which, to our amusement, is filled with nothing but straight couples, we really only have time to do press. There is a photo shoot in the posh penthouse of our hotel, where Tom and Nicole stayed for three months during the shooting of *Far and Away The Worst Movie We've Ever Made.* The photog puts me (and Raoul) in white bathrobes and makes us sit in one of the bathrooms—I in the empty Jacuzzi, bored behind sunglasses. The media thing is really starting to annoy me, even on this small scale. It all seems so pointless. I'm tired of the power relations, the insipid questions, the even more insipid answers. Why can't I be more like Johnny Rotten on the Tomorrow Show with Tom Snyder; belligerent and snotty, yet intelligent, scathing, and brilliant. I haven't learned wholly to embrace being hated, but must strive to. Meanwhile, I pose neutrally, lost in thought.

The photo shoot ostensibly done, I pad barefoot over to the other end of the expansive suite to change back into my civvies. Imagine my surprise when, upon my return, I discover Raoul coming on like Verushka, posing dramatically for the shutterbug, himself making like David Bailey as interpreted by David Hemmings in Michelangelo Antonioni's production of *Blow-Up.* Gee, a few months ago Raoul hated having his picture taken. I guess quasi-fame does change you.

My distaste for the media only increases when we are next chaperoned to a television studio to appear on a zany, nationally-broadcast chat show hosted by a chap who obviously listened to too much Devo in the eighties. We are forced to sit on a sofa, on camera, while the freak-show booked in ahead of us does his routine: an overweight fellow pushing forty, in a unitard, performing a combination of modern dance and tai chi to the accompaniment of "California Dreamin'" as interpreted by the Mamas and the Papas. The host and his female consort are obviously playing a little game of "get the foreign guests," doubled over as they are off-camera, but we refuse to be psyched, merely applauding politely and saying how much we appreciate interpretive dance—like Sandy Dennis in *Who's Afraid of Virginia Woolf.* After this incident, my alienation from the media will only increase; for the first time I'm not so obsessed with collecting my clippings (press, darling, not toenail, although lately it seems to amount to the same thing), or interested in reading my reviews (well, at least not the bad ones).

Back in Toronto après London I have a message from Mrs. in LA, to whom I give a bell pronto. It's good to hear her voice; I miss LA. He says they're going up to San Francisco for Wigstock West, which seems really unnecessary. I hate drag queens. They're cultural imperialists. He says our dear friend Fred Maddox Fred has died, rather suddenly, of AIDS. He says they're dropping like flies again. Makes me wonder when my number will come up. He also tells me that while he was holding a drink in each hand at a bar recently, St'Eve came up to him and asked if one of them was for me. I tell Mrs. he had been wearing Irish handcuffs. I miss LA, but I can't afford to go back right now. New York will have to do.

178

I don't know what I'm doing in New York, I really don't. Murdering time again. The pretext of my sojourn is to hang out with Alexander the Great—who's in town hunting for a new studio—to see just how feasible a collaboration with him would really be. I also know that I've been on the road for so long I feel like David Jannsen. You see, when I sing "You'd Be So Nice To Come Home To," I'm singing it to myself. So

The Big Poison Apple

Alexander the Great has this brainy idea to take I and a couple of his closest friends on a helicopter ride of Manhattan ($80.00 a piece, which A the G covers, natch). I meet him at the heliport on East Thirty-fourth along with his dealer (of art, mon chère) and a remarkable queen of the Andre Leon Talley school of coloured queendom.

(Remind me sometime to tell you the story I once read in the *New Yorker* about Miss Leon Talley—the black fashion consultant flambé— at a group photo shoot for the cultural elite. Andre was being his usual gadabout self—making bold fashion decrees, flitting from one dowager to another—and holding up the proceedings in the process. Finally, when the frustrated photog asked if he could get the show on the road, Maxime de la Falaise (or was it Inès de la Fressange, I always get those two mixed up, don't you?) made the pronouncement, and I'm paraphrasing slightly here: "We could, if the nigger dandy would sit down and be quiet." The room fell into a horrified silence, until a single, stage-y laugh rang out to rescue the moment—that of Miss Leon Talley herself. The tension broken, everyone began to laugh, and no one laughed harder than Andre. I don't know why I love that terrifying story so much, but remind me to tell it to you sometime.)

Anyway, who knew that a helicopter ride of Manhattan could be so boring? The only emotion—if envy is an emotion—that it inspires in me is, um, envy. To see all those shimmering blue rooftop swimming pools and penthouse gardens only serves to remind me that in New York there is a whole celestial existence that us commoners are denied access to. I suppose it doesn't help that I am currently flat broke as per ushe. Meanwhile, the helicopter is crammed, it's lousy with the most annoying tourists of all: the Germans. I may love them in their own country, but outside of it they think they own the world with their expensive video equipment and their bossy, après moi le deluge behaviour. Somebody ought to tell them that *The Final Solution* never made it to Broadway, that, in fact, it bombed in New Haven.

Where am I going with this? Oh yeah, afterwards we go to Chelsea for late afternoon cocktails. Alexander the Great's dealer and—you're not even remotely going to allow me to refer to him as the Nigger Dandy, are you—and his other delightful friend tell stories about A the G eating caviar off a boy's belly in Budapest, then sticking foie gras up his ass and sucking it out. "Foie gras already tastes like it's been sucked out of somebody's ass," quip I. Alexander the Great is so glamorous. For instance, did you know that he got drummed right out of a major Canadian city for sexual confinement of a minor, leaving headlines such as "Artist Holds Captive Audience" in his wake? So, he's returning to the Americas after a ten year exile in Berlin. I just can't keep up. Especially the drugs. I mean, the heroin was fine, it just made me feel relaxed and talk like Lou Rawls. But when we get into the Christine, it's just too much for a light-weight like me. We go to all the requisite crystal clubs—LURE, the Roxy, Twylo—but as a Capricorn I find I spend most of my hard drug experiences fighting the effects: trying to maintain, to present the illusion that I'm not fucked up. And crystal doesn't make me horny either, so what's the point? I'm not sure whether or not A the G and I will be able to collaborate.

I mean, I love the guy, but we're so different: he's an A-list fag, I'm a B-movie hag; he comes from a wealthy background, I come from and often remain below the poverty line; his drug use seems so natural and assured, I couldn't work up a decent heroin habit if my life depended on it—I mean, it's practically like having a full time job, which I'm really allergic to. Here's the difference between us in a nutshell: in the helicopter I say, "Hey, wouldn't it be neat if we crashed into the Empire State Building?" and A the G replies, "I'd rather die of a drug overdose." I guess we do have one thing in common—our Mount Rushmore-size egos—but I'm not so sure that would be conducive to a good working relationship. Who knows? Time alone, undoubtedly, will tell.

The remainder of my time in the Big Poison Apple is spent, of course, with our old friend Ms. Orgasm, with whom's resumé, by now, you should be all too familiar. It's refreshing to be with a fellow faggot who has more in common with Newt Gingrich than Candace, who rails against late term abortion and means it. Neither of us care particularly for gay rights legislation or gay marriage, although, personally, I do believe quite strongly in gay divorce. (In fact, I think uxoricide should be legal amongst homosexuals, but that's another story.)

We mostly just freak around, sometimes at Hunter's place—he has every Joan Crawford movie ever made on video, not to mention her address book—or around Glenn's shoebox, where we watch *The Owl and the Pussycat,* featuring Barbra at her peak, over and over again. Glenn and I are both temporarily financially embar-

179

rassed to a mind-boggling degree, so one night we find ourselves walking all the way from his apartment on Third Street between B and C, to Fifty-third between lst and 2nd, to have cocktails and perhaps a free meal courtesy of Jay Blotcher—the current head of media for AMFAR—and octogenarian Miles White—the celebrated costume designer of *Oklahoma* and *Carousel*, friend of Andy, Tallulah, and Tru.

We ask Miles his opinion of *I Shot Andy Warhol,* and he says he didn't much care for it, pointing out astutely that Valerie was a nutcase and should be regarded as a criminal, not a feminist heroine. I think the real crime is how wrong the movie got the Factory, and how the critics are eating it up. Really, Mary Harron, who was around, should know better. I have been told by some rather reliable sources that my

movies are so much closer to the spirit of the Factory without really trying, if I do say so myself, and I do. Don't they understand it even yet? Apparently only the *San Francisco Guardian*, who said in a review of *I Got It Wrong* that it was better than an Oliver Stone biopic but not as "stylish" as *Super 8 1/2,* got it right. Thank-you, at least, for working with me, and not against me.

We're at an upscale alternative to the defunct and sorely missed old school hustler bar, Rounds, and beside us is unfolding the upsetting spectacle of an eighty-year-old man trying to pick up a fifty-year-old hustler. Both clearly drunk. When they get up to leave—tipping over several unfinished drinks—Miles, still sharp as a tack in his over-sized Swifty Lazaar glasses quips, "That man is going to be murdered tonight."

Unfortunately, our broad hints to be invited for dinner in the downstairs dining-room fall flat, so Glennda and I have no choice but to walk all the way back downtown, stopping at various newsstands to check if they have the new *Esquire* in order to steal coupons from it for a free Arch Deluxe at McD's that they've been advertising. It's all very the-beginning-of-*Victor/Victoria*: the two of us gay bums pressing our noses up against the windows of expensive restaurants like Julie Andrews—who, incidentally, has just snubbed all of Broadway with her Tony nomination refusal; the headlines of the *New York Post* stands we pass scream "Tony Balone," "You Can Take This Tony And Shove It," and, my personal favourite, "Mary Poppins Hoppin' Mad." Unsuccessful in our coupon quest, and with our dogs barking, we settle on the Odessa Café, the cheapest in the East Vill. Is this any way for faggots only thirty and already gone international to live?

The next day I scare up some currency grâce a Jürgen, via Western Union. We celebrate by having an expensive lunch, my treat, at the Coffee Shop on Union Square where all the coathangers hang. Glenn and I have been dressing tres gay all week, with our tight pants and little t's, so when we prance into the cunty café, the hostess looks us up and down like the trash we undoubtedly are. Glenn is sporting a VH-1 Fashion Chanel t-shirt or something, which, being so fashion-forward in a fashion restaurant, where even the waitresses are not unsuccessful models, is probably a non-non. Ignoring the rolling eyes of the hostess, we sashay over to one of two empty booths at the very front of the café, declaring it ours.

Minutes later, who should stroll into the joint but one-third of the Trinity, Christy Turlington herself, accompanied by the v. famous runway model Gail Elliott, the two of whom automatically slide into the adjacent booth like Melba toast into a fat four-slice toaster. Apparently we have unwittingly sat in the supermodel section—probably Turly's favourite table, even—which further explains, if not excuses, the hostility of the hostess. Turly and her consort are tall and angular and freakish, alien beings in tight Gucci shirts eating vegetarian burgers and iced tea. Turly sits with her back to le tout restaurant the entire time, her boney appendages wrapped in a plain brown cardigan. I love models. They're so unhealthy looking. I don't care if Kate Moss and Jody Kidd do look like concentration camp victims, I think they're sexy. In fact, that's why they're sexy. It's the current standard of beauty. Accept it. And, p.s., I'm officially tired of Stella Tennant bashing.

The day I am scheduled to leave New York, I check my messages only to discover that my friend Pepper has had to put down Spike, her pug of fourteen-odd years. Having lived with the pair of them on and off over the years, and knowing how attached Pepper was to her little charge, I feel compelled to do something. I can still see the little creature dragging herself across the room after the stroke which paralyzed her two hind legs, yapping bravely. Even though I'm late for my flight, I find myself dragging my own two hind legs half way across Manhattan island in the rain, sans umbrella, to buy Pepper the soundtrack of *The Trouble With Angels*—one of her favourite movies—which I saw for an exorbitant price at Footlight Records the other day. It's really hard for me to do things like that without feeling self-congratulatory, although as Barbra Streisand proves in *The Owl and the Pussycat*, self-congratulatoriness needn't be an altogether unattractive quality. By the way, in case you're wondering what ever happened to my sweet pit bull, Cookie, remind me to tell you sometime about the tragic scuba diving accident. I told her to spit in the mask first.

Pretentiousness is Definitely a Career Option

Next stop: Denmark. Copenhagen, to be exact.

I'm back in a hotel, which suits me fine; believe me, if I could afford to, I'd be living in one full time. It's an expensive city—cigarettes are eight US dollars—and there's nothing on television, which is killing me. The bathrooms are one big shower with a drain in the middle, a toilet, and a sink. Danish furniture, I'm happy to report, is modern, as advertised. Denmark has a reputation for sex-change operations, pornography, and sexual liberation, but according to the local gentry, this is not attributable to liberalism, permissiveness, or progressive ideals—as one might expect—but to corruption and apathy. It figures.

The Danes themselves are a rather stunning people: well-dressed, statuesque, big tits, good posture, somewhat aloof, and a bit on the vague side of seems totally Tadzio: distant, haughty, chilly, all too aware of his beauty, and unattainable–making him all the more desirable. I don't stand a chance.

Fortunately, there are other diversions, namely, a couple of female strippers from New York of whom I am immediately enamoured in a different way–there's Viva (not to be confused with Viva!), a short, dark Ecuadorean beauty who used to be in the punk band Thrust and is an alumnus of Billy's Topless where my friend Glory Hole Domination works, and Kelly Webb, a.k.a. the Ass-assin, a cute redhead soon to be a cover girl for *Big Ass* magazine, even though hers seems just right to me–both of whom currently work at Babydoll. Actch, Viva Kneivel (that's her last name) once did an S & M act with a close friend of mine at the Vault where I once free-based with the coat-check guy, but I think I already told you that story. They're both diminutive and cheerful and large breasted and they dress in short, tight little outfits with g-strings sticking out all over the place and they look like streetwalkers in the very best sense of the word at all times. They have just come from Budapest where they performed with my old feminist nemesis Penny Arcade, the ex-Warholite–who once informed me menacingly that I was acting like a man (how presumptuous of me)–accompanied by a couple of film-makers with whom they've made some videos that are showing at the festival. The film-makers are Super-8 Stanley a.k.a. Little Annie, ex-girlfriend of Christeen and Arlene a.k.a. Daddy, ex-girlfriend of ex-girlfriend of Christeen. (In the twisted lesbian world, there are only two degrees of separation, usually situated on either end of a double-headed dildo.)

Little Annie, who swaggers and struts like a young buck who has just talked a girl into giving up her virginity, is famous for making a super-8 movie in which she shaves her pussy and reapplies the hair to her puss (her chinny-chin-chin, i.e.) with spirit gum to form a beard. Daddy, whom, appropriately, the girls seem to find a tad overbearing, is apparently an ex-model turned photog, or something. Anyway, we end up hanging around a lot together, as Americans and Canadians at foreign film festivals sometimes do, eating the free meals in the commissary, getting drunk on vodka at gay bars, and even seeing the sights–something I rarely bother to do when travelling, or otherwise.

After one particularly heavy night of partying, I and the four horsewomen of the apocalypse decide to go on a boat ride along the canals like

things, I have to say. The first Danish boy I get to see up close is the one who works in the office of the film festival we're attending with *Hustler White*, and he wrecks me. He saunters into the reception area barefoot in jeans and a t-shirt, glancing at me casually as he crosses to his desk and continues his work. He is in his early twenties, a strapping six foot three inches tall with enormous hands and feet (size eleven), broad shoulders, a square jaw, wide nose, dimples, and shortly-cropped blond hair with a widow's peak–Tom of Finland redux, i.e. When I'm introduced to him–his name is Carsten, of course–I notice he has huge thumbnails, which really turns me on. The gene pool is deep here, it's true, but somehow he

BLAB
BLAB
BLAB!!

ANONYMOUS BOY '94

THIS ISSUE IS DEDICATED TO BRUCE LABRUCE.

good tourists. It's one of those long vessels with seats like a bus and a bored guide speaking into a microphone at the front in four languages. We all head automatically for the back of the boat, as is the habit of strippers and pornographers, hiding our bloodshot eyes behind dark glasses, trying unsuccessfully to be chipper and enthusiastic.

The rocking motion of the glorified bus soon puts us all in a half-conscious state, and when I open my eyes, I notice that Viva and Kelly have passed out cold in their short shorts, their legs splayed open and revealing what one might expect to see upon inadvertently stumbling into a gynecological examination. Neither has it escaped the notice of our fellow tourists, many of whom have suddenly lost interest in the history of

Copenhagen in favour of the wide-open beaver in the back, their heads twisted around as they peer down the aisle at the stripper spectacle. A few even take some souvenir snap-shots. I would have taken some myself, but I haven't really had a decent camera since that cool Ricoh I lost when I got rolled by a trick in San Francisco.

Copenhagen faggots, or Copenhags, run the gamut from v. assimilated, liberal bourgeoisie types who get legally married with all the fringe benefits but become apolitical and dull in the process, to wild, wanton sexual hedonists who do louche Eurotrash drag like Helmut Berger in *The Damned*—one of the few examples of cross-dressing I find acceptable and, yes, even sexually stimulating. Carsten, for example, sews all his own costumes for the Miss World contest, which he organized this year. Normally that would turn me right off, but when you look like Tom Berenger did in drag in *Looking For Mr. Goodbar,* you can do anything you like, even hit me.

Carsten shares an apartment pedagogically with Knud, the most famous living gay Danish film-maker—a bald, middle-aged homosexual with a twinkle in his eye who looks but exactly like Donald Pleasance circa *Cul-De-Sac*—in the red light district where kiddie porn is casually displayed like lollipops in the window of a candy store. Knud makes me laugh all the time, whether he is righteously defending Leni Riefenstahl (later I would hook him up with Glennda Orgasm, who is also a Riefenstahl devotee of the first order, in New York) or talking with gravity about his experiences living with headhunters in Borneo for four months.

The list of remaining Danes I encounter reads like the cast of a not altogether successful cinematic Agatha Christie adaptation: Cor (or Softcore, as I and the strippers come to call him), a sweet, straight masochist who lives in an enormous old apartment with a rich film history professor and a punk rock chick; Bynke, a stern mistress film-maker, tall and striking, formerly married to Dave, a bisexual ex-patriate American film journalist with a sacred heart tattooed on his chest—he interviewed me for an avant-garde film magazine called *Rage* (Dave also tends bar at the trendy techno lounge Stereobar). I even meet the Crown Prince of Denmark, believe it or not. He attends the festival to see a Danish film called *New York Undercover,* which will later nepotistically win the big prizes, and hangs out at the reception for it.

184

Viva and Kelly the Ass-assin have got him cornered *Prince and the Showgirl* style, flirting up a storm, so I brazenly introduce myself and join the conversation. The handsome prince, who is looking very trim after his compulsory military service, I must say, claims he has visited Score in New York, the strip bar where Demi Moore did most of her vertical research for Striptease. I invite him to see *Hustler White* and excuse myself, leaving the girls to the spotlight, particularly since it seems he is heterosexual and therefore of no use to me; later I discover that it is widely believed he is in fact gay, making him the most eligible bachelor this side of Kevin Spacey, and that I blew my chance to marry into royalty.

It makes perfect sense—all that blue-blood inbreeding is bound to cause genetic mutations. His little brother is the straight one, having recently married a girl from Hong Kong, much to the chagrin of the surprisingly large number of Danish racists. The cast is rounded out by the likes of a by-the-numbers New York avant-garde film-maker who is touring with a very square S & M movie that everybody hates, not because it is extreme, but because it is silly. She is well meaning and earnest, in a nihilistic kind of way—with her black clothing and shades worn perpetually indoors, her black bangs and serious art talk—very much the Beth B. school of pretentiousness: v. condescending without necessarily meaning to be. I kind of like her act, though. I mean, pretentiousness is definitely a career option.

Her movie stars poor little Maria Beatty, the messy masochist whom Glennda and I once witnessed sniffing around on all fours at the Sprinkle Salon in New York as we cowered together, practically holding hands in the corner as we often do under such unsavoury circumstances. Meanwhile Glory Hole Domination was squirming around on the bed with Annie Sprinkle, who was taking her latest model dildo (patent pending) on a test ride for all to see. The thing about Annie Sprinkle is, she's like a three year old who enters a room full of adults rubbing her vagina and no one has the good sense to tell her to knock it off. Did I say that?

I spend most of the Danish festival mooning over the unattainable beauty of Carsten until one day, Fate intervenes, in the form of Danish disorganization. I and Raoul get unceremoniously booted out of our hotel two days earlier than planned, leaving us without shelter, so I get the bright idea to ask Knud if I, singular, can spend the rest of my visit with him and, coincidentally, Carsten. Later I find out that Raoul has followed suit, even though there are only two beds and no couches in the cluttered flat and I have arranged for my own mattress to be borrowed. That night Knud and I watch a bunch of his movies on video while killing off a couple of bottles of red wine, then head over to Stereobar where a festival party is happening.

When we arrive, the soirée is already in full swing, the strippers dressed to the tits as per ushe, Raoul whispering furtively to Dave, and beautiful Carsten sitting regally in the corner, shooting me a crafty look as I enter with his mentor. After enough martinis to float Fire Island, Carsten gets the brainy idea for all of us to head over to a gay karaoke bar. I'm really getting amorous, but I don't want to make the same mistake made by the Groovy Ghoulie—an avant-garde film-maker friend of mine from Berlin who, until his departure yesterday, had been putting his none-too-subtle moves on Carsten non-stop all week with no success. When we enter the karaoke bar, a little middle-aged man in a funny suit–who looks like the owner but isn't–is dancing drunkenly with an invisible partner. Already on automatic pilot, I try to foxtrot with him like boozy Maureen Stapleton at the wedding reception in Woody Allen's production of *Interiors*, but he isn't having any of it, giving me, in fact, the finger, before waltzing away. Somebody cruel signs up me and Viva and Kelly the Ass-assin for karaoke. My first choice is "Saturday Night's All Right For Fighting," but they goof and give us "Car Wash" and "Big Spender" instead. Unfortunately, Softcore has his trusty camera in hand to record the event for posterity–or, in the case of Kelly the Ass-assin, posteriority.

Before our turn at the mike, a group of very sober Danish drunks start to sing an earnest rendition of "Let It Be." Super-8, Viva, Kelly and I, who have by now deleted the bar of its entire supply of dry

vermouth, begin to drown them out with our own rousing chorus of "Let Me Pee." "There will be a toilet, let me pee," we sing as loudly as we can, our arms around one another like drunken alley cats in some goddamn Warner Brothers cartoon. The serious Danes are clearly not amused, but we are well past the point of caring even about the prospect of being crucified by an angry Danish mob. Martinis no longer feasible since there is no dry vermouth, we move on to the sweet, mixed with whiskey–an ad hoc Manhattan, if you will, and you will. Back at our table Knud is making a pronouncement: it seems that Dave, whom everyone says is interested in me but he's not my type, is in the process of being made by Raoul, and Knud is stating none too subtly for all to hear that Dave gets very emotionally attached to his tricks and begins to exhibit stalkeresque behaviour because it happened to Carsten after Carsten participated in a threegie with Dave only as a means to having sex with the third party in whom he was primarily interested. Dave, who doesn't like Knud's films, continues being made anyway.

Finally our names are announced for the big number and up we get; the girls, however, are clearly not schooled in the karaoke sciences, and keep forgetting to read the lyrics on the screen, so I have to keep screaming at them, "Read! Read!" like a demented first grade teacher. I start in on a very blue, punk version of "Big Spender," throwing in all sorts of curse words and karate kicks as Softcore snaps away. God only knows where those photos will turn up. Our effort is summarily booed by the Copenhags, but I don't care, buoyed as I am by some several gallons of poorly constructed Manhattans. By this point we have very nearly cleared the bar. I make a beeline for Carsten, and at some point I guess I make some comment about how I would sleep on the street with the junkies and the prostitutes before sharing a slim mattress with Raoul–which is rather sad because we have shared more than one bed together in the past. When Carsten tells me conspiratorially that I can sleep in his bed, I shout a silent hallelujah to myself, Noel Coward-style.

Back at his place I slip surreptitiously into his bed because I have a feeling Knud-the-Father may be slightly miffed about it. I do a tour of the world on Carsten. The sex is very tender and rough and nice and the whole thing ends with me making him injaculate for the first time, then coming again outside only moments later. Of course I'm instantly in love, and miserable that we will only have one more night together. The next morning when we

LaBruce, the award-winning director, at the zenith of his career. Photo by Mom.

emerge from the boudoir, Knud takes it all in stride. Noticing the hickies on our respective necks, he says, in that way he has, "Cannibalizing each other, I see." Later he takes me aside and whispers, "You know, if it was foreskin you were after, you should have tried mine. It is much bigger and juicier than Carsten's." Knud kills me, he really does.

After the lacklustre awards ceremony the following night (I still haven't won one fucking award), I and Carsten walk back to his flat through the red-light district. Watching the junkies openly punch holes into their bruised arms, we hold hands romantically without raising any eyebrows, as one can in Copenhagen. I find out more about the boy: he has an evil stepfather, has lived in London and Israel, was a boy scout, once married a girl impetuously out of platonic love as I almost once did, and is an expert scuba diver and underwater photographer like Leni Riefenstahl. We have one final night together and then I have to rip myself away from him, possibly forever. Such is my life.

The Fjord Was Really Pretty

The next day on the plane to Oslo, Raoul, sitting, thankfully, across the aisle, is bugging me. Just because I managed to have a little affair with arguably the hottest lad in Copenhagen—a sweet, sensitive guy whom everyone, including the New York strippers, was hot for, truly beyond the valley of Tom of Finland—and just because Raoul ended up with a guy who, while very nice, I had no interest in sleeping with although people kept informing me he wanted me—just because of that, he has to make some deprecating comment about Carsten, the dreamboat, being cold and aloof. Carsten, that

angelic kid. True, he may have a bit of the hauteur about him, but when you're that beautiful, you're allowed.

It's just like when I finally had sex with St'Eve in LA after everyone else coveted him, and Raoul, who had come on to him as well as half the cast and crew and was rejected, felt he had to denigrate him to me, calling him a superficial asshole. So what if St'Eve did turn out to be spelled with an apostrophe? Raoul claims to have changed, but he hasn't. I feel like Joe Pesci in *Casino*, observing the schmuck from a distance, griping and complaining as he preens and kisses ass.

And if he doesn't stop playing with his heavy metal hair I swear I'm going to pull it out by the roots, so help me God. I try to concentrate on something else, like seeing if there's any stewardesses worth gaping at, but no such luck. Although the cult of youth and beauty has gotten a bit out of hand, I wish they hadn't lowered the standards for stew-

187

ardesses, both female and fag, quite so very much. There's nothing to look at anymore on a plane, no Jacquie Bissetts or Karen Blacks, not even a Patient Zero. It's kind of depressing.

Oslo is way up north in the middle of nowhere, surrounded by endless square miles of coniferous forests, with a suicide rate commensurate to its latitude, I have no doubt, no doubt at all, so I should feel right at home. It is so far north, in fact, that at this time of year there are only four hours of night, which is definitely not my idea of a good time.

Our genial host, Halvard, whom I first met in Berlin, is Max Von Sydow redux with a bit of Herman Munster thrown in for good measure, which doesn't mean I don't find him attractive because I do. I think he may be interested in me, but I have a non-

compliance policy with film festival programmers. He is a sweetheart, though, one of those lonely homosexuals, not unlike myself, who longs desperately for his better half, feeling unattractive in a cruel gay world where beauty is prized a bit too highly.

He is also a wild man, appearing as he does in a punk band called, somewhat unfortunately, Genitalia. His two fellow members, whose odd Norwegian names I can't even begin to retain, are also freakishly tall, though skinnier than Halvard, and equally sweet. Their band of choice: Marilyn Manson. Drug of choice: speed. Film-maker of choice: moi. We also share an appreciation of Veruca Salt, the Make-Up, and fascist pin-up Boyd Rice, a compilation tape of which they make for me, and to which I am now listening on a plane to Milan, a cruel gay world where beauty is prized a bit too highly.

Oslo was beautiful but dumb, full of Vikings—tall, masculine men and tall, large-breasted blond women. Scandinavian cities are v. urbane and cosmopolitan, but they're not above their petty jealousies and rivalries. For example, as I understand it everyone hates the Swedes, the Danes don't particularly like the Norwegians, although the Norwegians like the Danes, the Swedes don't like anybody, and as for the Finns, no one cares. The aboriginals are from Iceland and, like the Native Indians in North America, susceptible to the decimation of fire water.

About 450 people came to the screening of *Hustler White* and, surprisingly, casualties were minimal—only a couple of dykes walked out, plus one salty sailor who almost fainted at the razor blade scene. Strangely enough, said sailor later came on to me at a gay bar, but when I responded, he got cold feet. I guess he was afraid I'd carve him up. Just as well—I noticed he had a lot of hair coming out of his ears. At the same bar, Christian, whom we met at an art exhibit held in a public toilet, discovered that one could call anywhere in the world for free from the old-fashioned red phone booth in the corner, so we did. Thanks to new technology, my telephone now has all the memory, so the only numbers I could recall were those of Glennda and Mrs., with whom I generally stay when I am in New York and Los Angeles, respectively, and whose numbers from time to time virtually become my own.

Otherwise, Oslo was brief and fairly uneventful. Raoul was up to his old tricks, like bringing his portfolio to a dinner party, which I thought was vastly inappropriate, but we won't go into that. The

Fjord or whatever the fuck it's called was really pretty, with this old twelfth century castle overlooking it under windswept clouds, all very dramatic, the way I like it.

Oh yeah, one last thing, not that it matters. Scandinavians seem to have this thing about kidnapping and mutilating statues. In Copenhagen, the famous Little Mermaid statue has been decapitated twice, the head having to be replaced, and at this amazing statuary park in Oslo they keep stealing this famous statue of a ranting baby, but the perps, fearing retribution, always leave it abandoned at the side of the road on the outskirts of town. I'm not sure exactly what it means. Maybe it has something to do with those famous Norwegian death rockers or those killer Swedish bikers or something. Americans aren't the only maniacs in the world, you know.

On the Verge of Being Spiritual

Having been told over the years by oh, so many Italians–albeit of the non-Milanese variety–that Milan is an ugly industrial city, I was shocked to discover that it was absolutely charming, not to mention breathtaking, crammed full of beautiful cathedrals and smart boutiques. As Fashion Week was quickly approaching, the whole town was crawling, it was lousy with male models. You would always see them, for some arcane reason unknown to the average man, in gaggles of four, with the tallest, most gorgeous and established model appointed the leader and consulting the map, leading them in circles or directly into walls: one of the most satisfying ironies of the Universe is that when great beauty is created in the stew of life, the brains are left on the back burner, burning. Wandering around the city I felt myself inexorably drawn into each cavernous cathedral where locals on their knees confessed face to face with priests in surprisingly wide open confession booths, as part of a daily ritual I began to find strangely compelling. One day I found myself in a dark, cool, and eerie cathedral, completely alone except for a young woman playing Bach on the organ, and a very muscular Jesus looking down at me longingly. It was almost spiritual, on the verge of being spiritual.

In the Ariston, our elegantly appointed yet environmentally friendly hotel–something which could only be pulled off successfully in a city like Milan–Raoul is right across the hall, and Glenn or Glennda, who is, thankfully, also here for the Fag Film Fest, is in a room directly behind his. Also on the same floor is Barry Shills, the director of the movie *Wigstock*, and Alexis Arquette, the actor-inexplicably-turned-drag queen. As soon as Glenn arrives we're on the horn with each other kibitzing in hushed tones about our fellow hotel dwellers. "Wait a minute, let me turn on the bidet," I say, sitting on the toilet with the phone, "So as nobody can hear me talking about them through the walls."

Soon we are gathered by the handsome head of the festival, Gianpaolo, or Jumpy, as he is known, a truly amazing fellow: tall, talkative, and twenty-nine. A typically temperamental and passionate Italian, he will have talked himself Brenda Vacarro by the end of the festival, liter-

189

ally losing his voice by berating and cajoling the Milanese audiences, as if arguing with a vendor at a local market. He will chastise them for not supporting the festival, for being unresponsive.

One night at a leatherish bar, whose owners had been reluctant to place ads in the festival catalogue until it proved to be a big success, I observed him getting into a heated argument that ended up out on the street. His butch assurance comes, I'm convinced, from the compulsive military service young Italian men are forced to complete; Jumpy drove big army trucks and had numerous affairs with straight, sex-starved boys who were no doubt smitten by his big bovine eyes. The gay movement, which is just taking hold in Italy, is really kind of exhilarating, I have to say:

brash, political, naive. *Hustler White*, in its own modest way, causes quite the sensation; in fact someone—I believe it's Fabio, the Prada shoe designer I met—said that the screening was like Milan's Stonewall, that it had that big an impact, although I didn't exactly see anyone hurling any cobblestones at the cabinari or anything.

James, Jumpy's longtime companion, an ex-patriate Texan living in Milan for six years now, is an excellent tour guide, especially when he goes into gossip mode about their own little Italian version of *The Boys in the Band*, with Valerio and Claudio in the Larry and Hank roles. Valerio is right out of a Pasolini movie and Claudio, with his masculine, swarthy face and moist, feminine eyes, is an Italian Ben Kingsley. Apparently there has been moto drama amongst the principals—usual fag-type stuff, with a lot of throwing of objets and not speaking to each other for long periods of time and such. It's kind of reassuring to know that a fag is a fag is a fag, the world over.

The highlight of the Milan experience was a little spectacle cooked up by I and Jumpy, just for kicks. Apparently, whilst drunk one night, I came up with the scathingly brilliant idea to pull a hoax on the festival—to pretend that we were hooked up overseas on the Internet, live from LA, with Tony Ward, who couldn't make it in person. Tony, the featured model, along with Evangelista, of a recent Dolce & Gabbana campaign, and a long-time runway model, is very popular in Milan, so we didn't want to disappoint anyone or anything.

Jumpy, taking me all too seriously, blew it up into a big production number—as fags are wont to do—in which I and Raoul would talk to Tony on the movie screen in front of five hundred people, except it wouldn't be Tony on screen, but a model shown only from the neck down, and it wouldn't be his voice, but that of my dear friend Glenn Belverio (who is half Italian), and both body and voice would be hidden away along with a computer technician in a closet not twenty feet from where we would be standing in front of the audience.

Owing to technical difficulties, the hoax got off to a shaky start: Glenn, as the voice of Tony, was directed to start speaking, but for some reason his voice didn't come out over the speakers and you could hear it coming out of the closet. The technician managed to iron out the bugs before anyone got wise, though, and the phony intercontinental conversation with our star seemed ready to commence. The pixillated body of the Tony Ward stand-in came up gloriously on screen, the body double in question being a very humpy go-go boy from the previous evening's outing, with the most defined six-pack I have ever appreciated. Glenn informed me later that he was stuck in such close proximity to the young lad in the closet that he started to involuntarily drool, *Mad* magazine-style, onto the mike. More technical glitches ensued, so Jumpy informed me that I had to kill five minutes.

Have you ever tried to kill five minutes in front of five hundred people? That means you are responsible for wasting 2500 minutes of people's lives. That's like forty hours. It's just too much responsibility. To make matters worse, the night before, my introduction to *Hustler White* didn't go over very big, not that I cared. My big opening joke, "Gee, I didn't even know there were any gay people in Italy," was strictly lead balloonsville, as was my comment, "This movie is Vatican-approved." So anyway, we killed the time. I actually got a laugh, when asked of Tony's sexual preference, by responding that he was a convertible. No one understood my "ba dum bump tshhh's", the old Borscht Belt high hat imitation designed to punctuate a particularly cornball joke. They probably thought I had a speech impediment. Finally, it was all systems go. Glenn, who used a voice somewhere between Ed Norton and Rocky Balboa, improvised beautifully.

When we asked "Tony" why he wouldn't let us see his face, he said that he had had a chemical peel that day, and as to the matter of his missing tattoos, he said that he had also been to the laser therapy centre. In real life, there had been talk of the actual Tony Ward appearing in a new Catherine Deneuve movie, so when we asked our ersatz Tony what new movies he had in the works, he replied that he was considering a thriller with "Catherine Denoovey," which he thought was called *Murder de Jour*–either that or *The Slaughter of Cherbourg*. No one in the audience, of course, laughed at these shameless in-jokes but I, for one, was literally doubled over. Then it got really far-fetched. "Tony," God bless him, said next that the only reason he made *Hustler White* in the first place was so that he could make out with Bruce LaBruce, to which I modestly responded that I paid him to say that.

When asked his opinion of *Frisk*, the movie based on a Dennis Cooper novel, that the audience was about to watch, Glenn as Tony ad-libbed, "Is that a movie about a cat?" which really wrecked me, and then added, "Oh, is that a Dennis Hopper movie? I loved him in *Blue Velvet*." The jokes were so esoteric and untranslatable that five hundred Italians sat non-plussed, watching me giggle uncontrollably in front of them. Unbelievably, as it turned out, everyone fell for it, even the people who worked for the festival–they really believed we had had a live, intercontinental conversation with our supermodel, who was actually probably in rehab somewhere at the time. Jumpy thinks it was because they all wanted to believe it was Tony Ward, and that it was some kind of mass hypnosis or something. It frightened me.

The only other exciting things that happened in Milan were, one: having fashion designer Marina Spadafora as a celebrity translator for a television interview, and two: getting really drunk and jumping up and down on the vinyl furniture to the *Mission Impossible* theme at the closing night party. Glennda performed a killer Donatella Versace drag routine at said party, and Alexis Arquette did a disturbing strip number to "Macho Man", starting out in full drag and ending up completely nude, which haunts me still. Alexis also fell flat on his ass while reading Glennda, which pleased her to no end. The media in Milan attempted to set the two of them up as arch rivals or something, but they ended up getting along okay for drag queens.

As I checked out of the Ariston at six in the morning to catch an early flight, dead drunk—something I promised myself I would never do again—Alexis was just dragging himself into the lobby, one high heel missing, and a bolt of fabric trailing behind

his half-naked self. Two drunken, internationally famous faggots passing in the wee small hours of the Milanese morning. How exceedingly trivial. But as long as we're dealing in trivia, did you know that in Milan, a tenaciously Catholic city, nuns are considered bad luck and when confronted in public with the presence of a nun, a young Milanese man will grab his balls to ward off the evil effects? Balls, in fact, are big in Milan; for example, the likeness of a bull is embedded in the piazza by the Duomo, and if you step on its balls, it's supposed to bring you good luck. There's something incredibly sexy about these superstitions, but let's not analyze it too closely, otherwise it might cease to be so.

Upon leaving Milan, I can't help but be reminded of the lyrics from an old Bing Crosby movie: "Thanks for the champagne/Kindly pour me on that plane," an all too frequently appropriate ad line for my various world tours.

From "Alcoholism" to "Problem Drinking"

Back in Toronto, I decide that what I desperately need is a little domesticity, to get off the booze, and to check out this brand new fad I've been hearing so much about called "health". Fortunately, to that end, I'm currently living with a member of the new generation of homosexuals: a fiscal conservative in a monogamous relationship who was, in fact, not so long ago the leader of the Progressive Conservative Youth Party of the Greater Hamilton area—as opposed to some perpetually zoned out, murderous club kid à la Michael Alig, with the corpse of a poor drug dealer stashed in the closet beneath a layer of feather boas and faux fur. If I want drama, I'll watch PBS. So I join the west-end YMCA—the straight one, i.e.—start to work out regularly again, and try to get drunk only once a week, so as to downgrade my "alcoholism" to "problem drinking". I spend quiet afternoons shopping with Grief and her baby, Dexterity, pretending, if only for a few hours, not to be gay. It's so rewarding.

192

Of course I'm still compelled to make the occasional foray to M'sieur le baths for a little extra curricular sexual adventurism. Although I rarely bother in this context to make the acquaintance of those gentlemen with whom I am engaging in the most intimate act imaginable between two or more human beings, there are a few noteworthy exceptions. Take, for instance, Gaetan, the twenty-one-year-old French Canadian kid with a cold (what is it always with the colds?)—a budding little patient zero with a rather unfortunate tattoo that reads "Yes, I am," in French under the rainbow freedom rings. (In all fairness, I didn't check it out until after the dirty deed was done, otherwise I might have had second thoughts.) In the dark he seems young; later, when I see him in the showers, he looks all of twelve years old.

Normally, I don't go for jailbait, but I figure it's as good a time as any to practice my paedophilia. I'm sure it must be an acquired taste, like rattlesnake. Like everybody, he has a sad story to tell. His father was a gay priest who acquired a lover from the secular world, eventually left the priesthood, and currently has a new boyfriend the same age as his son. Gaetan, himself, who was raised by his mère, fathered twins (a boy and a girl) at the age of seventeen, but isn't allowed to see them because he's gay, which really tears him up. Kids. Or, more to the point, French Canadian kids.

After we do it two or three times—all during which he chews a big wad of blue bubblegum—I'm convinced he's a hustler; but when I ask him, he gets all offended, as if it weren't meant as a compliment. I try to conceal my disappointment. The next day I find myself picking little blue sticky traces of Bubblicious off me all day.

The Sodom and Gomorrah Festivals

Hustler White, that marvelous movie I'm beginning to wish I'd never made, is to be released theatrically in the autumn, but before that there are the Sodom and Gomorrah festivals to contend with. San Francisco is utterly unmemorable, at least by me. I vaguely recall—mostly because it's staring me in the face as I speak—drunkenly getting a tattoo in a nightclub, a little blue-black dot on my inner arm—heroin chic, you see—and spending an abnormal amount of time in the usual Jacuzzi, but that's about it. Fortunately, I come down with a case of hysterical influenza the day before Pride, so I get to spend the whole weekend shivering

193

share some quality time in the ladies room before the screening, where she has to undress completely in order to pee. Tony has charmingly invited his mother to the show in that ingenuous way he has, although somehow I never get within a hundred mile radius of her.

So we're introducing the movie in front of the full house of 1500, and Raoul is giving his usual spiel, which if I hear one more time I'm going to strangle him with his own hair ("I've been photographing hustlers on the Boulevard for six years...") and at one point, speaking of the hustling phenomenon, he turns to me to ask what word he's searching for to describe it. "Boring?" I

under a Navajo blanket in front of the tv, drinking those citric cold medications which are routinely used in the manufacturing of methamphetamine.

Mr. Ward and his girlfriend Dede attend the Castro premiere whacked out on something or other. Oh well, that's life in the big city. Dede, as usual, looks about as glamorous as you can without getting arrested, in her Suzie Wong dress with tight black corset overtop and her punk tattoos which, in my opinion, few straight women can pull off like she does. We

194

offer generously. I play up our alleged feud for the crowd, unplayfully shoving him away from the microphone when it's my turn to talk. Nothing quite like a severed alliance to keep the public entertained.

Otherwise, I just hang out with my young San Francisco pals: Brooke, Donal, and Marky Mark Ewert, the latter of whom is now a full-blown hustler, so to speak. Cute, bald, little Mark, *Japanese poster for "Hustler White", evidently.*

former plaything of the gay literary trinity—Ginsberg, Burroughs, and Cooper—is sweet and smart and very talented. I know, I know I once called him the Pia Zadora of queercore, but I know he knows I meant it strictly in the most favourable way.

"Do you think Chloe Sevigny is a methadrone actress?" I ask Mrs. Glass one afternoon upon seeing the *Kids* wunderkind on the cover of some Japanese magazine on a newsstand in Larchemont Village. Yes, I'm back in my spiritual homeland, Los Angeles, Ca., and I couldn't be more enthralled, or less demonstrative about it.

Japanese poster for Super 8 1/2, clearly.

I and the Mrs. (that's Mrs. Glass, not Mrs. AIDS. Mr.andMrs.Athey has taken to calling the over-hyped disease "the Mrs. AIDS" in LA, but by the time it filters cross country to Glennda Orgasm in New York, it has become known simply as "the Mrs."—as in, if you have AIDS, "The Mrs. and I will be over for dinner at eight; make sure you set an extra place at the table." Confused? Good)—like I was saying, I and the Mrs. are just tooling around town in, ironically, Raoul's white Cougar with the black top—it's the very one Tony steals in *Hustler White,* and which Raoul has had to sell owing to the fact that he didn't believe me when I told him about a million times that this movie we've made isn't about to make us millionaires so he'd better not give up his day job.

Now every time Mrs. G. runs into him, he says, "Mrs. Glass, I gave you a r-e-e-eally good d-e-e-eal," in that sinister Weirdly Gruesome deadpan of his, which begins to get a tad irritating. Perhaps I'm being too hard on Raoul, and it's a cinch that our travelling together on our little tour, as it were, has aggravated the sitch, but believe it or not, I'm actually holding back a lot of vital information. In fact, I'm being a model of restraint. True, there are two sides to every story, but in this case, both are mine. I do, however, get a bit misty-eyed when I recall the good times: like how hard Raoul laughed when nobody could hit the piñata at his birthday party; or how much fun we had when we visited the Holocaust Museum together (I thought I'd bust a gut when he asked one of the employees there how we could be sure real gas wouldn't come out of the shower heads); or having high tea with the Dainty Satanist on Rodeo Drive. But that, as they say, was then, and this is now.

It doesn't help matters much when, at lunch one afternoon at the French Market in WeHo with Jeffrey, Mrs. G. and Miss Davis, the latter asks me if I would like an invitation to, in effect, my own party. Said invite reads "Rick Castro and Vaginal Davis invite you to the *Hustler White* Party at the Spotlight," is accompanied by a picture of Tony, and neither my name nor my likeness is

anywhere to be seen within a thousand mile radius. As Jeffrey and Mrs. G. discreetly exchange raised eyebrows, I graciously accept the invitation, enquiring politely—if ironically—if I might invite a few friends. Miss Davis magnanimously encourages me to do so, her obliviousness to this disastrous breach of social protocol either aggressively deliberate or blissfully ignorant, you can never quite tell with this blacktress.

Dear Miss Davis. Who knew they still grew that way? She is soon to have a show at the prestigious Milch Gallery in London—an installation consisting of a precise recreation of her apartment when she lived at Sunset and Fairfax, the very first location I stayed at for my Hollywood debut. The roach motel in question, a tiny little one room affair with closet-sized kitchen and bathroom, was decorated in Early Filth—a mattress on the floor and a large disco ball the primary furnishings. Her gowns and wigs were all stuffed into plastic bags and hung on nails on the wall; the stove, never turned on, heaped with magazines and papers; the bathtub, covered in a thick black scum, unusable. Her bed was surrounded with *Night of the Lepus*-sized dust bunnies and various half-filled bottles and mason jars, some of which contained her own pee—although the toilet was only ten feet away (two steps for Miss Davis), she would piss into the nearby containers in the middle of the night and forget to empty them for days on end. I felt right at home; it reminded me of my own crummy dive at Queen and Parliament in the eighties.

Miss Davis was to inhabit her installation around the clock, and I fully intended to fly to London to sleep over in it with her, but I just heard that it got cancelled because the gay male curator who commissioned it fell in love with a female member of Mr.andMrs.Athey's entourage when he performed in London, then followed her to LA and married her. Maybe we should all find a good woman and settle down. Which reminds me of a story I recently heard about Jerry Lewis, wherein he was once at a bar with his new wife SanDee, a.k.a. Sam, and they happened to run into Dean Martin, to whom he introduced his blushing bride as "my new wife, Sam," to which the soused singer replied, "I always knew you'd end up with a fag." I love that story.

Mrs. Glass has made up a manger for me, as he refers to it, in his mid-Wilshire apartment, and I couldn't be more comfortable. He's the only woman I know with whom I could indulge in a Marisa Mell film festival—like we do one night by watching a double bill of *Danger: Diabolik* and *Mahogany*—largely because he's the only woman I know who knows who the hell Marisa Mell is.

While my host is at work, I spend the afternoons watching the aftermath of the TWA Flight 800 disaster on television while eating every last one of his frozen dinners save for the one he requested me not to. When I hear the name Jed Johnson amongst the litany of victims, I begin to become very disturbed. Imagine surviving Andy Warhol, only to die in a plane crash—which, of course, to add insult to injury, was the subject of one of his most famous early paintings. Jed Johnson (who had a twin brother named Jay) was, of course, Andy's boyfriend, whatever that might have entailed—he had worked his way up from assisting Paul Morrisey on *Flesh*, to directing *Bad*, after which he gave up the film biz to start his own interior design business. He had, in fact, been on his way to gay Paris with his assistant to purchase antiques.

I mean, you can understand why crazy Freddie Herko did a grand jeté out of the window of a high-rise, ditto Andrea "Whips" Feldman, or the drug-related deaths of an Edie Sedgewick or an Eric Emerson, or even the demise of Halston or Jon Gould, Andy's other "boyfriend," from the Mrs. AIDS, but to have survived all the drugs and madness and disease and disco only to perish in an unexplained air disaster is simply too creepy.

I just hope Andy and Jed are reunited somewhere in faggot heaven. It's almost too much when, several months later, the famous model Agnieszka Kotlavska, who was booked on the doomed jetliner but missed her flight, was stabbed to death in Warsaw. I guess when your number is up, your number really is up.

The screening of *HW* at the Director's Guild is, of course, sold out, but that doesn't stop Herb Ritts from strong-arming his way in with his little boyfriend. This means I can't get my editor Rider's two teenage sisters in even though I promised them tickets, so they're really disappointed and I'm peeved.

There are other second string members of the velvet mafia present—Greg Gorman, Matthew Rolston, Theirry Mugler, who is, of course, accompanied by our own little porn star Kevin Kramer as they have been having a rather low-profile triste—but as you know, celebrity in and of itself does not impress me. At the after-party at the Spotlight—the infamous hustler bar on Selma Avenue—to which, you may recall, I had so graciously been invited, there are more celebrities: Scott Thompson and Bellini, Tony and Dede, cute little Wilson Cruz from *My So-Called Life*—to whom I gush I loved him in *Nixon*—the faggot from the first year of "The Real World" whose boyfriend was talk show host Charles Perez, etc.

Apparently, I spent a good part of the party back to back at the bar with Joe Dallesandro without even knowing he was there, and, of course, no one deigned to introduce me, as usual. One really needs handlers to take care of that sort of thing. Oh well, I never know what to say to famous people anyway.

Besides avoiding those parts of town in which fleas are currently said to be carrying the bubonic plague, the rest of my stay in LA is spent in the pure pursuit of sexual gratification. One night, for example, I end up going home with Duke, a by-the-numbers Daddy bear. I mean,

this guy could be the poster bear. Not only does Duke chew tobacco ("Red Man" brand, with a picture of an American Indian on it) which, while driving me home in his four wheel drive vehicle, he spits into a 7-11 cup that sits by the stick shift, but he also has a full beard down into which it dribbles as his deep, booming voice recites his history. He's originally from Kansas City, where he returned to farm for five years after leaving semi-pro baseball in Austin due to an injury. His father is a gay Republican and an artist slash cartoonist like Duke, who has been married for fifty years but has not had sex with his wife in forty.

I'm not sure whether or not Duke is a Republican: he has a "The Religious Right Is Neither" bumper sticker, side by side with one extoling the NRA. He is best known, apparently, for the cartoons he draws on bar napkins: gay folk art. When we reach his Glendale home, outside of which hangs a huge rainbow flag, we are greeted by his two hounds, Blue and Thunder. The interior of the house is a disconcerting mix of butch and femme—guns and wood panelling on one wall, a framed print of Avedon's photograph of Nastassja Kinski with the snake on another. Yes, we have sex, and his dick, predictably, is beer can thick. A few nights later I make a date with Beau, a gay porn star who once generously allowed me to blow him, which suited me fine since I can get into non-reciprocal sex. After doing Silverlake, Beau escorts I and Mrs. G to Rage (which I've never been to before for good reason), the famously unappetizing WeHo bar where Madonna once showed up with an entourage—clearly lost. It's the only explanation.

Beau tells me the story of his older brother—a taller, more muscular version of himself who went into the marines, got into drugs, freaked out on acid, decked an officer, got dishonorably discharged, and now thinks he's a general. Beau recently saw him walking down the street in Venice with his big beer belly hanging out, barking orders at startled passers-by while taking big bites out of a whole cabbage as if it were an apple. Beau also tells me about his younger brother, who got hooked on crystal and got into a fight with Beau, who knocked him through a wall at his parents house before they shipped him off to rehab in Santa Fe.

Beau is currently quasi-stalking his pregnant girlfriend; she kicked him out of the house when he insisted on going to the premiere of *HW*, in which he has a bit part, because she wants him to stop being a gay porn star and is threatening to tell his parents about his career if he doesn't. I discover the next day that after he left I and Mrs. G at Rage he went over to her place where, after he questioned his paternity of her unborn child, she decked him and then called the cops, who tried to arrest her but Beau wouldn't press charges. That's what I like about America—you're always only one degree away from an episode of "Cops." Unfortunately, Beau was too preoccupied this time to notice me trying to seduce him, but that's okay, I still like him. How could you not like somebody who says things like, "Nice day for a suicide," and means it?

The next day I have lunch with my friend Sam Schadd, porn directo slash producer extraordinaire who produced *Uncut* starring John Wayne Bobbitt, who, by the bi, Sam informs me, is about to star in a gay porn flick. Sam has great stories to tell about making adult movies in the seventies and eighties, before the advent of video made everything so terribly cheap, literally and metaphorically. For example, he danced at the infamous gay strip joint, the Ramrod, in New York in the eighties (owned, incidentally, by a married lady whose husband owned the Gaiety, a rival strip club—a swinging couple if ever there was one) on the same bill with Robert LaTourneaux, the original Cowboy from *Boys in the Band* who was subsequently claimed by the Mrs. (I refer, of course, to AIDS, not the owner of the Ramrod.)

Apparently, the demure Mister LaTourneaux did a modest burlesque routine whilst singing "Let Me Entertain You," stripping down to a codpiece, coming on like Gypsy Rose Lee. Sam was also friends with porn legend Casey Donavon, who starred in such classics as *Boys in the Sand*, and who also, sadly, had a fatal date with the same married lady. Sam, who has starred in countless porno movies himself under the brand name Gino Colbert, is so generous that he once blew five guys in a Jeff Stryker video as a favour, for free.

(I recently met Mr. Stryker, on the patio at Ryan Block's birthday party. He was short and leathery and sexy, in a seedy kind of way, and spoke very movingly about the frightening prospect of having to inform his five year old son someday about how Daddy made his millions. Porn director Chi Chi LaRue, his arch-rival, was also present, holed up in the kitchen; the two legends refused to appear together in the same room.)

Incidentally, an up-and-coming film-maker, whose next movie is to be produced by my dear friend Gus Van Sant, (name-dropping? What do you suggest I drop, pronouns?) recently worked on *Black and Blue*, the Sam Schadd-produced directorial debut of sexy porn star Ryan Block, who also appeared in *HW*. Working under the pseudonym Gordon Bleu, the up-and-comer acted as a grip—whatever that may have entailed—and shot the glory-hole scene. *Black and Blue* features adult video star Blue Blake having sex with a cast of black men—a scene right out of *Hustler White*. I offer this as yet another example of the incestuous nature of my little twilight world, sexually speaking. Homosexuals. Aren't you glad we only comprise one percent of the population?

By the way, did I mention the august panel upon which I was asked to sit during the LA faggot film festival, made up of such gay Hollywood players as Barry Sandler, screenwriter of the classic Raquel Welch vehicle *Kansas City Bomber* featuring Jodie Foster as her daughter, and the underrated, not to mention pre-

scient (remember Harry Hamlin's cancer slash AIDS scare) *Making Love* and Don Ruse, who penned the screenplays of *Single White Female, Boys on the Side*, and the disastrous Hollywood remake of *Diabolique*? The topic: what in the wide, wide world of sports is a gay movie anyway? I, of course, was cast in the role of maverick outsider although, ironically, my views tended to be ostensibly more conservative than those of the old school industry faggots with whom I shared the platform.

When it was my turn to pontificate, I began with my obligatory case for the closet, arguing that not only have there been scads of great Hollywood films created by closeted homosexuals, but also that these masterpieces may well owe their greatness to the trauma and turmoil engendered by their makers being forced to live their lives under such dramatic, tortured circumstances. That went over big. Never one to rest on my laurels, I fearlessly extended my argument to the secular world, stating baldly that for some people coming out of the closet is clearly not the coolest of moves, that certain of us are better suited to a double-life of clandestine relationships and gay intrigue—a point of view which to this queerer-than-thou audience, was tantamount to treason.

Before there was time for an ad hoc lynching committee to be organized, I forged ahead with a defense of the representation of homosexuality in Hollywood cinema, positing that it has in the past and, in fact, continues to be, exemplary in this regard, if you disregard the meddling of those insipid GLAAD queers. For is it not the function of art not only to convey homosexuality with all its contradictions and ambiguities intact—sarcomas and all, as it were—but also, particularly in the case of a popular art form, to reflect the zeitgeist, the dominant perception of homosexuality at a particular historical moment, something at which Hollywood excels? And as for the emerging gay cinema, Hollywood or otherwise, it must be purged of ideology.

As Gertrude Stein once said, "Literature is not commentary, Hemingway," and, likewise, neither should pink pictures be enlisted as some bland prescription for the advocacy of a monolith-ic, sanitized, and emasculated gay identity. I'm not sure I said it quite so eloquently or loquaciously at the time, but that's what I meant. The point is (I continued), and I'm only going to say this once, these queers who are responsible for such atrocities as *Jeffrey* (if only it had been about Mr. Dahmer), *To Wong Foo, Thanks For Nothing, Priscilla, Queen of Whatever,* and their ilk are about as accurate in representing the homosexual experience as was the portrayal of Jews in Nazi propaganda films, except the Jews came off better.

The scary thing is, those movies (the gay ones, that is, not the fascist ones, although I realize how difficult it is to distinguish between the two) are actually pretty precise in their representa-tion of the direction of the new gay movement, the embourgeo-isment of homosexuality, as one New York magazine scribe recently described it.

The sad thing is that previously marginalized and subversive stereotypes like the fop and the drag queen have been recruited in the service of the New Gay Reich to propagate such ideals as sexu-al normalcy, "It Takes A Village" community and family values, and bland, superficial New Age empowerment—platitudes which make the slogans and sound-bites of eighties AIDS activism seem like wise Maoist homilies by comparison.

That's all I have to say (I said, coming on now like Louis Farakhan), except that what gives us power is precisely that we are an invisible minority, that we are ubiquitous, that we can infiltrate and control from within. Assimilation destroys what we are: spies in the house of love! (At least, that's what I wanted to say.)

For the most part, the queers in the audience listened politely to what I had on my mind, but it became abundantly clear that what they really wanted was for some tacky movie to come down the pike which would not only encapsulate the common gay experi-ence, but also become a box-office bonanza to boot. I sincerely hated to wreck their party, but I had to point out the minor detail that there is no common gay experience. Jim Bakker's experience of homosexuality is not the same as Jeffrey Dahmer's. (Actually, maybe that's not the best example, consider-ing the prison angle, but you know what I mean.) Nor is a shared, unifying experience necessarily desirable. Homosexuality used to be about the accep-tance of non-conformist behaviour, of sexual indi-vidualism, about being the vanguard, not the follower.

Besides (I actually did say this), let's not forget that homosexuals only con-stitute about one per cent of the population—you heard right, one per cent. That ten per cent figure people bandy about much too liberally is actually based on the *Kinsey Report* from the sixties which claimed that statistically one out of ten people has

201

had at least one homosexual experience, hardly qualifying him as a certified, card-carrying cake boy. No, with numbers like that, *Jeffrey* is not about to replace *Jurassic Park* on the list of all-time box office champions although, as I've argued elsewhere, the latter is essentially a movie about lesbian separatism.

Suddenly, the straight (as he was almost too quick to point out) Scott Silver—another panelist, and director of *johns*, the other current feature about hustlers on Santa Monica Boulevard, shot roughly on the same locations as *Hustler White* at about twenty times the budget, and starring, appropriately, our old shoplifting pal, Lukas Haas—interjected that he definitely wants to see such a gay blockbuster in the future, but then again, he would. He doesn't have to be gay.

Anyway, and in conclusion, the thing about gay cinema is, as Glennda so astutely pointed out to me recently, the most exciting homosexual characters in that pot-boiler *The Cellulite Closet* (in fact the only ones with a pulse) were far and away those two mincing, marauding, limp-wristed hitch-hiking thieves whom Barry Newman picks up on the highway in *The Vanishing Point*, the ones who ineffectually try to rob him at gunpoint before he unceremoniously boots them out of the car. Not only did they have style, but they were clearly the most entertaining thing in the picture. And remember, after all, like the song says, homosexual is criminal.

I Guess It's the Beginning of the End

All right, there is one more event I want to cover for this disgusting little book and then I'll shut up for a change. At the end of August it's back to New York on a press junket for the theatrical release of *HW*, and not a minute too soon. I really want it to be all over with, it's starting to get on my nerves. I've been on the horn all week in Toronto with my New York publicist, Bruce Lynn, whom you may recall from previous musings. Ironically, Strand Releasing, my American distributor, offered to set me up with a more prestigious publicity firm this time around, but I declined, requesting Bruce instead. He may be a character straight out of Larry Kramer's *Faggots*, but he gets the job done.

Besides, the high class publicist they suggested is terrified of me: at Sundance this year he was supposed to be representing my movie but he never even deigned to introduce himself to me. Cradling the receiver under my chin so that I might varnish my nails lavender, I listen to Bruce rant and rave about this and that. "Give me a few seconds to pour a cuppa coffee down my gut," he says in that delightful way he has about him. "Brucie," as he calls me, "Are you there? This movie of yours is going to go right through the wahoosie. The response at the press screenings has been euphoric, Brucie. And as for the ones who don't like it, a zucka ma vey." That last phrase, he fills me in, means "who the fuck cares," in Yiddish, the second language of old school queens. "I want you to come over to my place around six-ish to meet a few people," he continues. "It's an orgy. I'm kidding." Bruce gets sentimental for a moment: "This is our third movie together, Brucie. I've been with you since your infancy," he croaks. "It feels like childbirth."

Actually, Bruce is kind of growing on me, in a fungoid kind of way. Before he hangs up on me he promises there will be "beaucoup men" at the party he's arranging at the Roxy. I know that's his way of showing just how much he cares.

When I arrive in New York, Bruce shows me the invitation to the party, designed in his usual good taste: a beefcake photo of Tony under the bold caption "Come See Madonna's Ex Get Porked," followed by way too many exclamation marks. He informs me that certain members of the press are reluctant to give *Hustler White* any publicity. *Details*, for example—as I've already mentioned—hung up on him at the mere mention of the movie, even though its Conde Nasty masthead is about as faggoty as you can get, including the executive editor, who interviewed me for almost an hour on the phone a couple of months ago. They'll do a story on straight patricidal flipper people or violent and demented straight porn stars, but they won't touch a gay romantic comedy about hustlers. Therein, je suppose, lies the essential flaw of my homosexual invisibility argument: unhappily, I've never really subscribed to my own advice.

Oh, well. A zucka ma vey. Now he's got me saying it. As for *Interview*, Bruce informs me that Graham Fuller despised it. Despised it, mind you. I'm not surprised. After he grumbled what I can only assume was some sort of salutation when I was introduced to him at Sundance a couple of years ago, he proceeded to look exceedingly annoyed that I had been allowed access into his field of vision. Oh well. *Interview* sucks ever since they dropped the "Andy Warhol's" anyway, Benjamin Lui and Paige Powell notwithstanding. Or has my exclusion merely made me a tad bitter? You decide. In general, for some inexplicable reason, while our Los Angeles notices will be uniformly excellent, our New York press will be less than stellar—literally, in fact, in the case of the *New York Post* which, for my second film in a row, will award me the coveted "Zero Stars". Even the usually reliable *Village Voice*, which has raved about my other flicks, gives *HW* a luke-warm review. It might have something to do with the fact that it is covered this time by a stupid, stupid queer who takes umbrage with the representation of the hustler as what he perceives as heterosexual.

Obviously he knows nothing about hustler psychology. First of all, if hustlers call themselves straight or refuse to be pinned down on the subject of their sexuality, it is usually because they are either in denial about their homosexuality or they are truly bisexual but are not comfortable with the gay aspect, and who can blame them? That's one of the reasons they become hustlers in the first place—it allows them to express their homosexual impulses in a 'legitimized' context; i.e., they're only doing it for the money. Second of all, many hustlers try to father as much progeny as they can, precisely in order to prove their virility and sexual potency, to prove that they are not fags even though they may well be. Thirdly, just because in *HW* the protagonist is represented as having fathered a child and having had a girlfriend in the past, it does not mean that he isn't gay. The fact that at the end of the movie he has one of the longest screen kisses in history, gay or straight, with a man of his

203

own gender and skips off hand and hand with him into the sunset, might give one the vague impression that he could, indeed, be gay, but I don't want to read anything into my own movie. The silly faggot who wrote that review really needs to get a clue. (Hey, I rhymed.) I suppose he also doesn't like straight gay porn stars.

What a loser. But not as big a loser as Boy George, who reviewed *HW* for his weekly column in the *London Daily Mirror*. It seems Mr. George, who was all over Tony Ward like a cheap sari at the party for *HW* at Popstarz, finally got around to seeing the movie at the ICA, but stormed out of it half way through, mumbling something about it being a cornhole movie. I guess Hare Krishnas don't believe in cornholing, and well, now that John Moss is nothing more than a memory... George said in his

review that it was just an excuse for Tony to show off his tattoos and piercings, that it was sad pornography dressed up as art. Hey, isn't that what they used to say about his act? The worm, apparently, has turned. Cheer up, Sister George. I hear they're casting for a new Clarabelle Cow. Moo. The rest of the London Dailies slaughter *Hustler White*; one, the *Daily Telegraph*, after proclaiming that the film has no artistic merit, is poorly acted, badly scripted, and abysmally produced, that it calls into question the entire certification process in England, and that the ICA, a government subsidized institution, should be ashamed for programming it, suggested that the film-makers should seek psychiatric help. The kids liked it though. It got great notices in the *Face, iD*, and *Blah Blah Blah*—the European MTV magazine. Kids like cornholing. It's hip.

Back in New York, I show up for an interview at Bruce's spacious Chelsea apartment only three quarters of an hour late and lo and behold, there is Raoul, having arrived early, no doubt, to give his side of the story. By the time the interviewer gets to me, he's out of tape, but that's okay. It's only a gay magazine. Bruce surreptitiously arranges a meeting later that evening with some gay bar rag that wants me to interview Tony exclusively, which apparently drives Raoul almost to distraction.

Fortunately, as we now only speak to each other in interview situations, I don't have to deal personally with his sour persimmons of wrath—that's the publicist's job now. I start the interview with a barrage of questions about Madonna, just to be different from all the other gay journalists in the world. Apparently, Tony showed her the movie and she liked it. She also said that she could tell by looking at me that I'm a real egomaniac, and she also called me a twerp, God bless her. She did say that she thought the sex scenes were a little harsh and, in fact, she had previously turned us down for financing claiming that she could not be associated with pornography. This coming from a woman who was photographed in her book *Sex* being raped by two men and loving it; participating in a gay sadomasochistic orgy; and having a rather unsavoury relationship with a pooch, not to mention two plucked chicken S & M lesbians and a partridge in a pear tree.

But you know, actually, she's right. I'm definitely on the other side of that line you're not supposed to cross. The cornhole line.

The only other interview that sticks in my mind like a bad dream is a cable access thing with an aged leatherman in a threadbare leather diaper which barely conceals his alarmingly low hanging balls, who keeps thrusting the sticky microphone in my face as if it were a dildo and I were interested. When he says that he hears Tony is refusing to do gay press, I quip, "Can you blame him?" which stops him in his tracks. He asks me what kind of sex I'm into. I reply that I'm really into procreative sex (ever heard of it?), that I like to hang out with my straight friends and their babies and maybe will have a kid of my own some day. He can only process this information by insinuating that I must be into procreative sex as some kind of extreme queer perversion. I'm forced to remind him that penis fits vagina.

The rest of my oh, so valuable time is spent, of course, with Glenn and his pussy posse. The gag-du-moment is: attempting to work a joke about partial-birth-abortion into every conversation, inspired by a recent editorial by James Wolcott in the *New Yorker*, which proclaimed that it is impossible to make a joke on this touchy subject. By the end of the week we're up to partial-birth-abortion joke #147. I'm not talking about subtle, tasteful jokes either: my New York friends are very much into the single entendre. For example, I and Glenn and Hunter–who works for trendy jeweller Robert Lee Morris–decide one night to visit a famous stylist friend of ours who has hit a bad patch and is currently paying the bills by tending bar at a black club in the no man's land of West Thirty-Third Street and Eleventh Avenue.

At first, when the stoned queen at the door can't find our names on the guest list and forces us back out on the street, it seems like things might escalate into a low rent version of *Bonfire of the Vanities*. However, just before we get mugged, the bouncer informs us that our names have been miraculously located, and we are whisked into the cutting edge epicentre of black street-style. After surveying the crowd, which looks like the thousand bastard children of the *House of Xtravaganza*, Hunter makes the astute observation that it is but exactly Bill Clinton's worst nightmare: everyone present is on welfare, pregnant, and HIV+. This inspires Glenn, who is watching the kids dirty dance so low in the hips that they are all practically grinding their groins into the dance floor, to make a crack about the partial-birth-abortion macarena, which opens the floodgates for partial-birth-abortion jokes.

Meanwhile, our friend behind the bar, who is making his bartending debut, is surreptitiously slipping me his mistakes–poorly constructed Mai Tai's, swampy Cape Cods–which is getting me characteristically drunk. Our next stop is that oh, so gay punk club called Squeezebox which, not that I want any recognition, I probably at least partially inspired, if you want to get historical about it. As it happens,

it is crammed full of Uber-Eves like Coffee Awful, who circle and circle subcultural icons the likes of I and Glenn like sharks.

Which reminds me, who should I run into but our old friend Fergus, who has recently relocated here from London. Fergus is taking Manhattan by storm, having immediately bagged as his boyfriend none other than The Troubador of Avenue Something or Other–A or C or P, I can't remember which– some impoverished East Village musician who's making it big and now living in a luxurious Fifth Avenue apartment. To my New York posse, said musician is known as Schlock, short for Schlockhead, so named for the Ankh tattooed on his forehead or neck or something, I can't remember which. I suppose I'll have to elucidate further.

When Jacqueline Sussann came out with *The Love Machine*, her follow up to *Valley of Dolls*– literally the biggest selling book of all time next to the Bible–she used as part of her ubiquitous marketing campaign an ancient Egyptian symbol called the Ankh. This led jaded journalists to refer to said symbol as the ancient Egyptian symbol for schlock, hence our nickname for Fergus' new Margo. Maybe now you can begin to understand the sick inner workings of the homosexual mind. I try to strike up a conversation with Schlock, who is really cute and has a great physique, but he is one of those boomerang people who no matter what you say to them always bring the conversation back to themselves. He is also a faux-naif, so it's kind of ironic that he's with Fergus, the most cynical boy under thirty I have ever met.

Anyway, Squeezebox is kind of fun, I suppose. One of my stripper friends that I met in Copenhagen, Viva Kneivel, is dancing on the bar, and I have a long conversation with sweet Howie Pyro from D Generation. There are the usual celebrity suspects like Meisel or Amber or whoever, the requisite modelizers, and an aging rock star with his date who seems a tad young. In fact, I think she may be a partial-birth-abortion. But it's way too lousy with drag queens for my taste. When one of them passes by holding a sign promoting Jacquie Beat, I and Glennda grab it, throw it on the floor, and trample it, saying "We don't like LA drag queens. In fact, we don't like drag queens period." Before they bring on the tar and feathers, we book.

All that is left to talk about is the promotional party for *Hustler White* at the Crystal Palace, but there's really nothing to talk about. There are more Manhattan Cable tv interviews, more Eves, more partial-birth-abortion jokes. Glenn has dutifully accompanied me, despite the fact that he may or may not have come down with a case of amoebas. Earlier, at dinner, I had to remind him to make sure he ordered enough food because he may be eating for ten billion. I'm not worried about him, though. He's always been an excellent host. There's glamorous Kembrah Phahler from the hot band The Voluptuous Horror of Karen Black, which apparently was the inspiration for Marilyn Manson; here's Michael Musto, who scurries away from me nervously, like the White Rabbit, and whom I see a few nights later at a screening of what is generally conceded as the worst movie ever made, *Skidoo!* starring Carol Channing and an acid-dropping Jackie Gleason.

One disturbing thing happens to me at the party that I hesitate to mention. At one point a couple of queens approach me because I'm wearing an expensive bespoke-tailored navy-blue pin-striped sixties-style suit—and thereby look like somebody who knows what's going on and ask me if I know where they might locate Bruce LaBruce. After I inform them that they're looking at him, one of them shrieks and says that he is Bruce LaBruce, i.e., that he has come to this party dressed as his idol, me. Of course he got it all wrong, but I'm simultaneously flattered and frightened. The same thing will happen at the Toronto Film Festival in a couple of weeks. I guess it's the beginning of the end.

Apologies of a Sort

That's it from the campy LaBruce, as I was dubbed recently in some glitzy magazine. Some of the names have been half-heartedly altered to create the impression of protecting the innocent, and to prevent the guilty from receiving too much undeserved publicity. Please bear in mind that the lion's share of the material in this book was originally written for *Exclaim*, a non-gay alternative music publication with a decidedly youthful readership, hence the overdetermined homosexual references and general faggotiness of it all. Get them when they're young, I always say. Remember the immortal words of your local chapter of the League Against Homosexuals: queers don't produce, they seduce. Most of the pieces were also written feverishly the night before deadline, which may have contributed to the off-hand, stream-of-consciousness style; process oriented kind of guy that I am, I've decided to preserve this quality, no matter how cringe-worthy it may be. Future travels, including spiritual pilgrimages with my movies to the home towns of some of my gay role models–i.e., Jeffrey Dahmer's Milwaukee, Andy Warhol's Pittsburgh–will be documented in the next volume of the diary of the reluctant pornographer, in case you're interested.

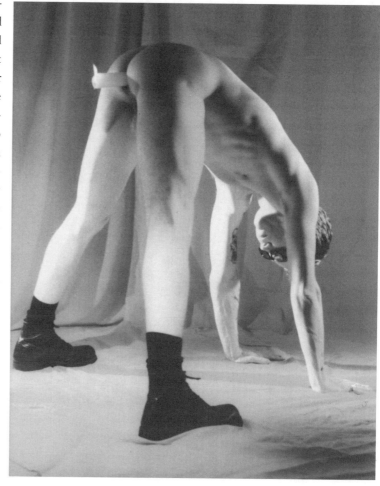

The End. Photo of Bruce LaBruce by Richard Kern.